Social Anthropology in Eastern India

SOCIAL ANTHROPOLOGY IN EASTERN INDIA

Edited by

SACHCHIDANANDA
VINAY KUMAR SRIVASTAVA

SERIALS PUBLICATIONS
NEW DELHI (INDIA)

Edition: 2009

ISBN: 978-81-8387-250-8

Published by
SERIALS PUBLICATIONS
4830/24, Prahlad Street, Ansari Road
Darya Ganj, New Delhi-110002 (India)
Phone : 23245225. Fax : 91-11-23272135
E-mail: serials@sify.com

CONTENTS

PREFACE

Sometime back the Indian Association of Social Science Institutions (IASSI) set up regional chapters to broad base its activities. One such chapter was set up in Patna a couple of years back. It was decided to organize a workshop on anthropological studies in eastern India. The theme of the workshop was the State of Art in Social Anthropology in Eastern India. The exercise was to make a critical review of anthropological studies in the states of Chhattisgarh, Jharkhand, Orissa, and West Bengal. The issues to be discussed were distributed to each author to facilitate comparability. Experienced scholars were identified from each state to contribute papers. Some of these scholars came together for a seminar on this theme in Patna in March 2007. The papers were presented at length in two days and they resolved to revise them in the light of discussions in a short time. On account of their academic engagements and other pressing demands on their time, all the papers reached the editors' desk only by the end of the year. At about this time, the editors felt that the volume would be enriched by a brief review of the contributions and thoughts of some celebrated anthropologists who inspired and influenced social anthropological studies in the region. This accounts for papers on the work of Sarat Chandra Roy, Verrier Elwin, Nirmal Kumar Bose, and Shyama Charan Dube.

This volume is a result of collective efforts of a number of scholars. I am deeply obliged to all the contributors for sharing their valuable time for the preparation of the papers amidst all the multifarious activities in which our senior academics are engaged. I am especially indebted to my co-editor, Professor Vinay Kumar Srivastava, who has been involved in this project from its inception.

He has gone through every line in the book, making changes wherever necessary. He has also penned the Introduction as well as the first chapter of the book. Professor R.P. Sinha, Secretary and former Professor of Sociology, A.N. Sinha Institute, and Dr. S.P. Jaiswal, Joint Secretary of the Patna Chapter of the IASSI, have rendered valuable help in keeping a tab on correspondence with the contributors.

The volume could not have been conceived without the encouragement and active help of Professor A.K. Dasgupta, the Member-Secretary of the IASSI. He sanctioned a handsome grant for the entire project. I am highly grateful to Shri S.K. Jha of the Serials Publications, New Delhi, for seeing the book through the press in a short time.

Sachchidananda

INTRODUCTION

This book comprises papers presented in a seminar on 'Anthropology in Eastern India' that took place in Patna in March 2007. In addition, it also has a paper that Surajit Sinha wrote on Nirmal Kumar Bose, for we thought it was one of the best introductions and assessments of Bose's anthropology. Eastern India led the country in starting the first anthropology department in Calcutta in 1921, and today, it is one of the important centres of research and teaching. Following it came into existence the other departments of anthropology in different parts of the country, and they respectively attended to the study of communities in their immediate regions, as well as the state, besides those in other parts of the country and the world. Anthropology is truly comparative, studying both the local and the global, using the methodology of first-hand research.

Although anthropology studies all types of societies in time and space, its foremost commitment has been to tribal peoples, since no other subject devotes itself to their study. It was left to anthropologists to provide an understanding of the working of the societies of tribespersons and the issues of their integration with the outside world. It is unsurprising, therefore, that the department of anthropology at Bilaspur (Chhattisgarh) has added the phrase 'tribal development' to its name. Other departments specifically mention in their agenda their specialization in tribal studies.

In this volume, S.N. Chaudhary gives an account of the trends of studies in agrarian and tribal studies with reference to the state of Chhattisgarh, which came into existence on 1 November 2000. It may be noted here that anthropology is taught in only one university of Chhattisgarh, i.e. Ravi Shankar University at Raipur. Madhya Pradesh has an anthropology department at Dr. Hari Singh Gour University, Sagar. Teaching for a master's degree in social anthropology was also started at Barakatullah University, Bhopal, but after continuing for a couple of years, it was wound up.

Tribesmen account for 32.5 per cent of the total population of Chhattisgarh, with some of its districts (such as Sarguja, Raigarh, and Bastar) having more than fifty per cent of these people. Reviewing agrarian studies, Chaudhary shows that one of the prime problems of tribals and *dalit*s is of land alienation, which takes place through debt-bondage. Since 1980, there have been protests, but the practice has continued unabated.

Chhattisgarh is highly vulnerable to out-migration. Uncertainty of agriculture, rampant indebtedness, unemployment, and alienation of land have been the major factors. Added to these, industrialization has caused an irreparable damage to forest resources, and thus, people dependent upon them are constrained to look for alternatives, which are also meagre. Chaudhary also highlights the 'strong arm tactics of the landlords', who usurp the land of tribals and *dalit*s. Only with the intervention of police are the legitimate owners able to get their land back.

From his survey of the anthropological publications, Chaudhary concludes that in contemporary anthropology, the monographic study of a community is no more the dominant trend. Studies of inter-disciplinary nature have replaced it. Approaches from political economy have greatly affected tribal and agrarian studies. The techniques and methods generally used for data collection are interview schedules, case studies, and group discussion. Chaudhary also notes that in Indian anthropology, the tradition of long and intensive fieldwork, by which anthropology as a discipline is identified, has woefully declined. Unless we revitalize it, anthropological researches are destined to remain bereft of the impact they are expected to produce.

Sekh Rahim Mondal offers an appraisal of anthropological researches in north Bengal. He says that non-professional scholars started anthropological and sociological studies in north Bengal, followed by the work that the Cultural Research Institute, the Anthropological Survey of India, and the Indian Statistical Institute undertook. In addition, researchers located outside north Bengal in other universities conducted their studies here. In 1976, the department of sociology and social anthropology was established in North Bengal University. It was bifurcated in 2001 in separate departments of sociology and anthropology. The University of North Bengal also has the Centre for Himalayan Studies, which also carries out the anthropological work.

Both traditional and modern societies have been studied, but due to ethnic, social, and cultural diversities, and the extent of change taking place in north Bengal, a large number of areas have remained unstudied. Mondal submits that since a variety of social and cultural practices are disappearing, and a set of new ones is emerging in north Bengal, our first task is to document and analyse them. Also, we need this knowledge for planning policies for this region.

Earlier, the studies were conducted with a structural-functional perspective, but in recent years, Mondal points out, subaltern, post-modern, and reflective approaches have come into existence. In terms of methods also, these cross-cultural studies make use of focus group discussions, interview schedules, and key-respondent interviews. Survey research with a macro-social view has also become quite common. Those concerned with development work rely on the methodological cluster of Rapid Rural Appraisal (RRA), Participatory Rural Appraisal (PRA), and Participatory Learning and Action (PLA). Like Chaudhary, Mondal also notices a decline in lengthy field studies, with more and more people depending upon the Internet and secondary sources for their data.

One of the important centres of anthropological research and teaching is at Ranchi University, with which have been associated eminent scholars like Sachchidananda, L.P. Vidyarthi, A.B. Saran, K.N. Sahay, and V.S. Upadhyaya. Vijoy S. Sahay, in his contribution to anthropological researches in Jharkhand, says that Rai Bahadur Sarat Chandra Roy, the founder of the famous journal, *Man in India*, dominated Indian anthropology for over three decades and a half. Although his approach was monographic, quite like that of his counterparts in colonial administration, to him goes the credit of initiating anthropological researches in India.

Sahay summarizes the contributions of the scholars associated with the Ranchi School of Anthropology. Vidyarthi, a doctorate from Chicago, emphasized the 'Indian-ness of social sciences', contributing to a battery of concepts (such as the 'sacred complex', 'man-nature-spirit complex') for the analysis of Indian society. Founding the Ranchi department of anthropology, Sachchidananda's work has covered a myriad of areas in sociology and social anthropology, adopting a dynamic approach. Both quantitative and qualitative approaches have been brought together in A.B. Saran's study of murder and suicide among the Munda and Oraon.

Identifying four phases in the evolution of anthropological studies in Jharkhand, Sahay discusses the contribution that anthropologists with the tribal background have made. Here, he notices that the writings of many of these anthropologists are 'prejudiced' against the non-tribespersons. He also shows that in these auto-ethnographic writings, history is distorted and facts manipulated to lend credence to the 'glorious past' of one's own tribal community. Sahay rightly asserts that anthropology is not an instrument of political agenda or 'glorification campaign'; it is an objective and scientific understanding of social processes and formations.

Another centre of anthropological research and teaching is at Calcutta University. Besides this, West Bengal also has the departments of anthropology at Vidyasagar University and Visva-Bharati University. Buddhadeb Chaudhuri's paper is devoted to the trends of social anthropological study and research in Bengal. Although tribal ethnography has been a hallmark of anthropology, several anthropologists (such as Nirmal Kumar Bose, Surajit Sinha) have contributed to the understanding of tribal societies in relation to the Hindu civilization. Bose's famous article titled 'The Hindu Method of Tribal Absorption' is still read with profit.

Chaudhuri's review shows that anthropologists in Bengal made a notable contribution to urban studies. Bose worked on the city of Calcutta, publishing an article in *Scientific Americana*. Anthropologists following him studied the changes that followed in a community after its migration to an urban location. These writings showed that people continued to maintain their identity even after their migration to towns and cities. There have also been studies of poverty-stricken people, the slum and pavement dwellers, and beggars.

Noticing the changes that have surfaced in the perspectives of social sciences, Chaudhuri says that we are more concerned with economics (i.e., 'economics with wealth') than with people; we wish to maximise income rather than improve upon the quality of life of people. Anthropology, by contrast, has always been concerned with the lifestyles and thoughts of people, their quality of life, happiness and satisfaction. Because of this, it has attended to areas that have been ignored in other social sciences. Here, Chaudhuri draws attention to the important areas of anthropological research, viz. environment, development, and forest; indigenous knowledge and wisdom; and human rights.

The two articles that follow Chaudhuri's paper are concerned with Orissa. N.K. Das meticulously traces the emergence and development of social anthropology, and S.M. Patnaik writes about the NGOs working for tribal development in Orissa.

It is well known that Orissa is a 'meeting place' of the cultures of Indo-Aryans, Dravidians, and Mundas, and provides one of the best places to conduct the studies of cultural syncretism. Das begins his review of anthropological works on Orissa, observing that we cannot ignore the contributions that historians, archaeologists, political scientists, and linguists have made. British officers (such as E.L. Samuel, J.P. Frye, and J.A. May) wrote first-hand monographs on Orissa communities. S.C. Roy wrote a monograph on the Bhuiyan; Verrier Elwin wrote on the Juang, Bonda, and Saora. But it was not only tribal studies, writes Das, that attracted the scholars, but also the relations between castes and tribes, as was exemplified in the work of F.G. Bailey. In his own study in western Orissa, Das showed a fusion of the processes of sanskritization and tribalization, and how they have brought out a change in society.

That Orissa did not have a viable Kshtriya *varna* has also been reconsidered by Das. There have been indigenous ruling lineages in Orissa, quite like the peasant warrior castes, viz. the 'wielders of the sword', the Khandayat, who emerged in medieval India. Das shows that Karan-Kayastha emerged as state functionaries and the masters of the classical texts.

Towards the last section of his paper, Das discusses the issues of development and social change to which anthropologists have paid a specific attention. The review of development planning and investment over decades in different regions shows a higher human resource development in five districts. Along with the work that university based anthropologists have done, Das also reviews critically the work that several research organizations (such as the Anthropological Survey of India) have carried out on Orissa.

That the NGOs have assumed a great significance and importance in development is the theme of Patnaik's article. Based on an ethnographic work carried out from 1995 to 2001, Patnaik examines the organizational set up and work culture of non-governmental agencies and their impact on tribal societies. An important issue taken up here is the distinction between voluntary association, non-governmental organization, and people's organization.

After discussing the main concepts, Patnaik gives a sketch of the tribes in Orissa, which constitute almost one-fourth of the state's population. More than fifty percent of its tribal population is found in the districts of Koraput, Sundergarh, Mayurbhanj, Nowrangpur, Malkangiri, and Rayagad. Like tribal societies in India, in Orissa also, there are tribes which lead a relatively isolated life, and at the other pole are those that are indistinguishable from agricultural communities. On the whole, the condition of the tribes is far from being satisfactory; because of crude technology, unproductive holdings, land alienation, indebtedness, and lack of irrigation, the productivity is low and people perennially face economic hardships.

The NGO movement began as a reaction to bureaucratic red-tapism and corruption. It started with the conviction that the democratic process and decentralization can help involve local people in decision-making. Paradoxically, Patnaik finds that the NGOs under study have become so large that to manage them a bureaucratic apparatus is required. An evaluation of the fifteen NGOs that Patnaik takes up shows that they have succeeded in winning over the support of people than has been the case with the state. It points towards the significance of the NGOs in carrying out the programmes of tribal development.

2

Following the six articles dealing with the growth of different aspects of anthropology in eastern India, are five papers on anthropologists who have made unforgettable contribution to the development of anthropology in India in general and eastern India in particular.

On the 'father of Indian ethnology', as J.H. Hutton called Sarat Chandra Roy, is Sachchidananda's article. Born in 1871, Roy earned a degree in law from Calcutta's Ripon College. As a legal professional, in connection with commission from the courts of law, Roy used to visit the interior areas of Chotanagpur that the tribal communities inhabited. Such visits rendered him an opportunity to observe tribal life closely, their sufferings, episodes of exploitation and oppression, and their fortitude to withstand injustices in life; this planted in him the seeds of anthropology. Whatever he had observed among the Mundas resulted in his first monograph (of 1912) titled *The Munda and Their Country*, which captivated the attention of Sir Edward Gait, who granted him financial assistance to work with the Oraons.

Although Roy began as an empiricist, the first lesson we all learn as anthropologists, he was equally committed to Indological researches, thus bringing together the 'field view' and the 'book view' of society. Thus, when he became the General Secretary of the Bihar and Orissa Research Society, he included anthropology and folklore as its two aims. He also lent solid support to applied anthropology, and used its basic principles to solve tribal problems.

In his studies of caste, Roy made an abundant and appropriate use of the Indological texts, such as the *Purana*, *Dharmashastra*, *Samhita*, and *Grihasutra*. His studies of caste also aimed to show that anthropology was just not a study of bizarre and exotic customs and practices of tribal communities; it was also concerned with a study of 'familiar institutions' (such as the caste system). This shows Roy's comparative approach to delineate the scope of anthropology in India, covering under its ambit all types of human societies and cultures. Further, Roy also subscribed to evolutionism. He believed that the primitive society exhibits the 'ground plan' on which complex structures are built up. This would explain Roy's interest in the theories of the origin of caste.

Surajit Sinha and Sukant K. Chaudhury, in their respective chapters, highlight different aspects of the work of Nirmal Kumar Bose. While Sinha gives a synoptic view of Bose's total contribution to anthropology and allied sciences, Chaudhury is chiefly concerned with the 'civilizational approach'.

Sinha begins with listing the anthropologists and other thinkers whom Bose considered as his *gurus*. Among them were Franz Boas,

Alfred L. Kroeber, Sigmund Freud, Karl Marx, Bronislaw Malinowski, and a host of scholars concerned with diffusionism and anarchism. Gandhi, for Bose, was an anarchist. Along side, Bose was an avid reader of novels and short stories. He had also read closely the classical religious and philosophical texts, including a lot of Buddhist literature. Then, Bose also attributed his learning to the social movements in which he had participated; for instance, whilst in his teens, he participated in a relief operation in Bankura district. Even when he had no inkling of the disciplines of anthropology and sociology, he conducted a survey of the economic conditions of a large number of famine-stricken families. At a young age of twenty, Bose, in association with two others, organized the repatriation of indentured Indian labourers from Fiji. Like in the first case, here also he conducted a rigorous study of the social background of four hundred and fifty families. In the same spirit, when he was engaged in a Gandhian village reconstruction programme, he kept a detailed note of people's responses and their adaptation to the changes. Bose was committed to the idea that the theory emerges from action, and in turn, guides it.

Like Roy, Bose was also interested in the study of different sections of Indian society. Both castes and tribes received his attention. As Chaudhury shows in his paper, he was far from considering tribal communities as isolated entities, like 'windowless monads'. Bose intended to carry out a piece of intensive fieldwork among the Juangs of Orissa, beginning with a short spell of stay with them in 1928, from which resulted three papers on the themes of marriage and kinship, and associations. Then, his dream of a lengthy fieldwork was shattered as he was asked to leave the state of Keonjhar under a police order.

Although Bose could never return to the Juang for fieldwork, his brief stay with them gave him sufficient insight into how tribes pursuing a 'primitive production technology' (such as slash-and-burn cultivation, hunting and food gathering) were being absorbed into the multi-community (or multi-caste) villages based on agriculture and craft. This led him to consider the idea of two types of social organization, differing in terms of their respective modes of production – the tribe and the caste. The superior technology of caste attracted the tribals to take up an occupation and become a part of the multi-community social reality. The processes of accretion and integration work hand-in-hand, leading tribals to be a part of the Indian civilization.

Bose knew, Chaudhury tells us, that societies differ in terms of their interaction with the outside world, thus the impact of civilization upon them differs; this would explain why some tribes are more Hinduized than the others. In other words, Bose made a noteworthy contribution to tribe-caste continuum. He showed that in some contexts, tribes and castes merged to such an extent that it was difficult to distinguish one from the other. It was also the experience of census enumerators and officials at the beginning of the twentieth century. Bose's dynamic approach to the study of Indian society was carried forward by Surajit Sinha, with the result that under the rubric of 'civilizational approach', the names of both these scholars from Bengal are kept.

The next paper is on Verrier Elwin's anthropology by Sachchidananda. Born on 29 August 1902, Elwin graduated in 1924 from Oxford in literature. In 1927, he left for India along with four of his colleagues to work with the Christ Seva Sangh, a missionary organization, located at Poona. Elwin wrote that he "did not want to be a 'missionary' in the ordinary sense of the term, but [he] was greatly interested in the monastic life." In January, 1928, he met Mohandas Karamchand Gandhi at the Sabarmati Ashram, and this event, writes Sachchidananda, profoundly changed his life.

Elwin was looking for a community of people to work with, to help it through schools and hospitals, when a Congressman, Jamnalal Bajaj, suggested that he spent time with the Gond of central India. This was the commencement of Elwin's anthropological career, resulting in two dozen books on tribal societies of India settled in different parts. Elwin also collected the folk literature (songs, riddles, myths, stories) of tribespersons and published it extensively.

For conducting anthropological studies, Elwin thought, we need people with a humanist background. We have to understand human feelings, sentiments, and meanings, and also, think in terms of bringing about changes in human condition. From the outset, Elwin was attracted to A.C. Haddon's dedication to the practical application of anthropology. Haddon's anthropology was rightfully called 'philanthropology'. One of the chapters in Elwin's 1964 book titled *The Tribal World of Verrier Elwin* was called 'Philanthropology', and a book of his selected writings that Nari Rustomji edited in 1989 bore the title *Verrier Elwin, Philanthropologist*. For Elwin, 'The essence of anthropology is love. Without it, nothing is fertile, nothing is true.' He did not see, writes Sachchidananda, any contradiction between opting for a scientific approach to the study of people and an 'intense affectionate interest in them', in 'desiring their progress and welfare and in regarding them as human beings rather than as laboratory specimens.'

The last paper in this book is on S.C. Dube. Written by Yogesh Atal, it records an overall sketch of the work that Dube did in a variety of fields. After obtaining a doctoral degree for the study of the Kamar, a tribal community, he moved to Lucknow, where he taught anthropology courses. He then moved to Osmania University in Hyderabad, where the teaching of anthropology within the department of sociology had started with the involvement of Christoph von Fürer-Haimendorf.

Dube's movement from Lucknow to Hyderabad also marked his transition from anthropology to sociology and from tribal to village studies. There, he organized an inter-disciplinary team to study an Indian village called Shamirpet in the Telangana region. Later, he carried out another piece of team research, popularly known as the Cornell-India Project, in the villages of Rankhandi and Jhaberan in western Uttar Pradesh. In 1957, Dube joined the University of Saugar (in Madhya Pradesh) as its first professor of anthropology.

One of Dube's well-known works is on the Kamar, which was originally published in 1951, but has recently been reprinted. Dube's interest in tribal communities started crystallizing when he came in contact with the two communities of Chhattisgarh (namely Kamar and Bhunjia). These tribespersons had been periodically approaching his father with petitions or in connection with court cases that he was hearing. Later, he conducted an intensive fieldwork with the Kamar. The strength of his anthropology lay in the approach he proposed for tribal welfare. He did not lend support to the policy of isolating tribes from the wider world so that they could preserve their pristine culture. He was also opposed to the thesis of assimilating tribes with the Hindu civilization. He favoured an approach where tribes would maintain their identity and be the proud builders of their country. Dube was the architect of this approach, for which, Atal thinks, he would be remembered forever.

3

The first article in this volume is on the future of anthropology. Written by Srivastava, it provides a general view of the state of anthropology in India, reflecting upon the process of its marginalization. In the U.K. and the U.S.A., not only does social-cultural anthropology enjoy a respectable status, but also, is considered to be more adventurous, insightful, and intellectually stimulating than the other social science subjects and humanities. It is common to come across students of professional courses (such as engineering, medicine, law, architecture, management) taking a semester off to read anthropology. Anthropological perceptions are believed to trigger theoretical developments in other disciplines; for instance, Lewis H. Morgan's evolutionary scheme inspired Karl Marx and F. Engels to a large extent to look into the origin and development of human society from the state of 'primitive communism'. Several approaches (like functionalism, structuralism, symbolic interactionism), which found an honourable place in other disciplines, had their origin and initial development in anthropology. Moreover, anthropology has time and again challenged the understanding of society and culture from the vantage point of the west, thus bringing in the perspective on reality from the so-called 'primitive' societies.

Nevertheless, in spite of these credits in favour of anthropology, it has not really caught up in India. Taught in not more than forty universities, usually by a slender staff and with a poor infrastructure, anthropology is also not a popular subject with students. It is invariably opted as a last option, when a student is unable to get admission in a coveted course. Not much is being done, Srivastava writes in his paper, to popularise anthropology as a subject of great potentiality and future. The crises emerging against this backdrop compel professional and university anthropologists to search for the 'market value' of their discipline rather than impressing upon the unparalleled contribution it has made to the understanding human life and behaviour in a comparative perspective. Thus, as it has happened, anthropology is reduced to 'forensic science', and its role in crime detection is highlighted, or is equated with 'DNA studies'; the spokespersons of anthropology adopt these stratagems to attract public attention and also to claim that their subject is a science *qua* science.

The greatest strength of anthropology lies in following the idea that the 'proper study of mankind' comprises in studying human beings as 'biological-cum-genetic beings' and as 'socio-cultural beings'. It is the only subject among the 'ecology of subjects' that has a bio-cultural and bio-behavioural perspective. This, however, does not imply that every research in anthropology has to be bio-cultural or bio-behavioural. What it implies is that the student of anthropology knows the dynamics of biogenetic and socio-cultural aspects, and the fact that human living is constantly impinged upon by both of them. And, if the subject under exploration – for example, the issues of health and illness, population variability, adaptation to the environment, human growth and development, culture-bound syndromes, disaster management, rehabilitation – requires a consideration of both the biological and socio-cultural aspects, the anthropologist is most suitably placed to carry out its study. This, in our opinion, is the meaning of 'holism' in anthropology (or, when we say, 'anthropology is a holistic science').

Several writers in this volume note an abysmal decline in the tradition and quality of fieldwork in India. Fieldwork, it is well known, is the soul of anthropology. Our data come from a long, sustained observation of a group of people living in their natural habitat. It is essential to inculcate the importance of fieldwork among the young research students, advising them to spend not less than one year with the people of their study *in situ* so that they understand their social life in its roundness. Even when the researcher intends to study his own community, he is expected to internalise the principle of 'de-familiarization' (i.e., making the familiar look strange), and then study it from distance. Intensive field studies not only help in a re-examination of theories, but also in the evolution of new theoretical perspectives and tools of research. An ethnographic location, which hitherto has not been studied, needs to be given an utmost priority. A conscientious following of the fundamental principles of anthropology is imperative for making it full of impact and acquire a place of honour among other sciences and humanities.

1

THE FUTURE OF ANTHROPOLOGY

Vinay Kumar Srivastava

This paper submits that practical concerns have overtaken the theoretical in contemporary anthropology, especially in India. A perilous consequence of this trend is that instead of illuminating the functioning and dynamics of society and culture in particular and general terms, it confines itself to the question of policy prescription. By directing their energies to the 'issues of usefulness', anthropologists have come to think that the future survival of anthropology is incumbent upon its immediate market value. The future of anthropology can be enhanced, instead, by giving primacy to an interpretive understanding of societies and cultures, thereby making comments on existing policies for development and social justice more perceptive and relevant.

The future of their discipline, or one of its offshoots, has seriously concerned the anthropologists. Several seminars and workshops have been held under the aegis of 'retrospect and prospect' or the 'relevance of anthropology', where thoughts of the possible futures of our subject have figured. One of the topics of addresses and discussions in the centenary meeting of the Royal Anthropological Institute of Great Britain and Ireland (RAI), the proceedings of which appeared in *Man* in 1944, was 'The Future of Anthropology'.[1] Murray Leaf's *Frontiers of Anthropology*, a book of 1974, carried a chapter in the end, on the 'anthropology of 2000' (pp. 311-24). The statement – 'Anthropology has a notorious past, dismal present, and uncertain future'–broadly summarises our collective anxiety about the integrity of our discipline and its survival [Srivastava 1986]. In other words, regardless of the time and the progress of anthropology, its professionals have often pondered over its future.

Questions of the future begin zooming large when a culturally-constructed time period is to be replaced by another. One may imagine how bold and big this question would be when a century is to be replaced. In the 1990s, many contributions have appeared on the future of anthropology; some important ones are by Hart (1990), Kahn (1990), Sponsel (1990), Firth (1992), Grimshaw and Hart (1993), and Giddens (1996). None of these writers ever hints that anthropology is devoid of a future. That we are contemplating the future itself strikes a chord of optimism: there is a future *of*, *for*, and *in* anthropology. But, where does it lie? In theory or policy prescriptions, or in a better, evolving relationship between the two? In making the discipline frontierless, unbounded, or in a precise delineation of its aims? What is our vision of future for which anthropology should be made to work? [Hart 1990: 14; Firth 1992: 208].

Why does the question of their discipline's future worry anthropologists? To my knowledge, such a question is generally not raised in other subjects.[2] Is the crisis in anthropology, wherein storms the debate about its future, imaginary? Is it simply a panic button so that the quality of research improves with continued introspection? In a strongly-worded article, Keith Hart (1990: 14) says that British anthropologists are 'overspecialised, fragmented, alienated from the society in which the majority of people live,' and they lack 'any vision of [their] own or humanity's future'. This has also been the conclusion of many observers of national anthropologies [Pathy 1981; Gerholm and Hannerz 1982; Hastrup 1987; Mahajan and Srivastava 1978].

Today, anthropology discovers itself in a multicultural world of reflexivity which 'demands new forms of inventiveness and subtlety' [Clifford 1986: 23]. We are skeptical of and wish to enquire into 'all grounds of authority, assumption, or convention' [Fischer 1986: 194].[3] Knowledge-producers in the contemporary world are not just academic professionals. Journalists, media persons, tele producers, film makers, and even bureaucrats, are concerned with all those social issues on which we anthropologists claimed intellectual monopoly some years ago. A programme, for instance, on the Yanomamo Indians made and telecast by Discovery Channel, is not only worth thousands of words, but reaches millions of cross-cultural viewers [refer Giddens 1996: 121]. Today, anthropology finds itself in the midst of myriad theoretical perspectives, the contest between them is not like the blood-feud which characterized the relation between the descent and the alliance theorists in British anthropology. Contesting paradigms co-exist today with exemplary tolerance of another's vantage point. These are the times of postmodernity, post-structuralism, post-colonialism, post-savage, post-positivism; or as Geertz (1998:69) says, of 'post-everything'. Anthropology faces a set of new challenges in this world.

Against the background of the contemporary practice, this paper outlines the conditions which will affect the future of anthropology. Not offered here are the tasks for the twenty-first century. Unless adequate steps are taken, the already existent crises of ecosystem, resources, society and culture are bound to escalate with the passage of time, and the anthropological researches will be expected to understand the genesis of these crises and suggest remedies. The practising anthropologists are hopeful about the contribution their discipline can make to ameliorate human condition. Marketability of anthropological skills (especially fieldwork) has been recognized by development and welfare organizations, but the full potentiality of the subject is yet to be tapped.

So far, a study of the impact of anthropology on its learners has not been carried out, but I learnt from my students that anthropology brought about a marked difference in their orientation to life.[4] They developed a higher degree of sensitivity to other human beings and their problems, besides trying to understand the 'other' (a fellow being, a community, a group) in holistic terms. Some Indian bureaucrats, who read anthropology as one of the subjects for the civil services examination, told me about the profound impact that anthropology made on them. In their actual workings, they have become comparative, analytical, field-oriented, and contextual. Now they understand human predicaments in a better perspective.[5] Yet, anthropology is not the first subject-priority of a college student who casts his eyes on courses which promise him a lucrative profession.[6]

At the outset, I submit that the future of anthropology will depend upon its conception that we hold and reproduce didactically. If its vision is of a discipline without frontiers, then we have already started ringing its death knell. Further, anthropology's future is conditioned by the sound analytical and theroretical perspectives that we are able to generate. We cannot sustain it by an array of policy suggestions, the long list of pleas, viz. 'what should be done?' A dialectical relationship exists between theoretical conclusions and the areas of application. In it rests the strength of anthropology. We also note with concern the woeful decline in the quality of fieldwork (especially by Indian anthropologists and neophytes) and in the sophistication of analysis.

II

In 1978, six young anthropologists from the University of Delhi, three each from physical and social anthropology, decided to launch a journal with their pooled resources titled *Spectra of Anthropological Progress*. Its acronym SAP acquired popularity in academic circles in years to roll. These men were crystal clear about their aim. They did not want to merely add another volume to gather dust on the library shelves. They were deeply concerned with the question of *quo vadis*: whither goeth anthroplogy?[7]

The inaugural issue of SAP (1978: i -iii) carried a brief editorial which spelled out the direction anthropology had taken, its overspecialization, concluding that the specialized research did not quite connect itself with the central aims of anthropology. Twenty years later, Bhattacharya (1999: 24-5) observed that the 'distancing of archaeology from anthropology has now gone to the ultimate. It is a consequence of this that archaeologists are now trying to have their own agenda of ethnology which need not concern itself with cultural themes.' The likelihood of unconnected and ceaseless specializations existed in anthropology, because, to begin with, it dealt with two facts–the biological and the cultural–and each one of them could become the pivot of a separate discipline with its distinct methodology, terminological apparatus, and epistemology. The relation of the observer with the observed is bound to be different in a biological science in contrast to a socio-cultural discipline.[8]

The SAP editors did not denigrate the tendency of overspecialization, seeing it as an index of the progress and development of a subject. However, they advised the specialists to think carefully of their grounding in the parent discipline and relate their specialization to it. Otherwise, the specialist's work would become alien to the anthropological concerns. Moreover, he would be marginalized in other disciplines he intends to venture into. If this differentiation of the discipline is permitted to go unchecked, with no attempt to integrate the new branches with the goal of anthropology, the danger is that the specializations will fall apart. The Spencerian proposition – 'Integration compensates for differentiation of parts' – asserts the truism. Anthropologists should devote themselves to the task of integrating their discipline. Each stream of differentiation must relate to the central aims of anthropology. If we proceed in this manner, a higher differentiation of the discipline will inevitably imply a higher degree of integration.

A discipline should not be allowed to become pigeon-holed, for this would render intense inbreeding, thus lowering its creativity and scholarship and eventually, making it sterile. At the same time, let it not become so porous that, as in our case, almost every biological, sociological, or cultural study of humans could claim a place in anthropology. We already know of health scientists, historians, experts in foreign affairs, journalists, film makers, and many others, who not only call themselves anthropologists, but compete with hard-core anthropologists for scarce funds for research, tenurial positions, chairs of committees, awards, etc.[9] Osmosis is creative; flooding is destructive. We may borrow theories and techniques of analysis from other disciplines to understand our data better or to illuminate our concerns. But the crises, which the SAP editors called the 'identity crises', surface when a specialization of some other subject is placed under the rubric of anthropology by an enthusiast without its relationship with the principal anthropological concerns being properly worked out.

It is not only with respect to physical anthropology that social anthropologists, or vice versa, find it difficult to maintain academic communication and to undertake collaborative research, but within social (or physical) anthropology, a number of branches have emerged which increasingly emphasise their separation. Each of these, what I would call, 'special anthropologies' (such as linguistic anthropology, medical anthropology, ecological anthropology, demographic anthropology, etc.), which acquired prominence in the second half of the twentieth century, interacts with another full-fledged discipline having its own history and preoccupations. Linguistic anthropology, for instance, has an intimate connection with linguistics, in the same way as is the proximity of ethnomusicology to the science of music.

Closeness to other disciplines applies to the main branches of anthropology as well; for example, the British social anthropology is considered closer to French sociology; and cultural anthropology, the American variant, to history and folklore. However, not all the practitioners of social or cultural anthropology assumed that their subject was a branch of humanities or one of the specializations of the arts. Radcliffe-Brown (1948), the chief architect of British social anthropology, ardently believed that his subject was a natural science of society. Similarly, the American neo-evolutionist, Leslie White (1943), considered the natural science of culture as culturology, a term most dear to him. But these analogies between social or cultural anthropology, on the one hand, and natural science, on the other, were based on an assumed isomorphism of methods and techniques. The methodology employed for the study of natural systems was extendible to social systems.[10]

The idea that social or cultural anthropology was a science of society or culture, or both as Kroeber's (1948: 5) collocation socio-cultural anthropology suggested, did not imply its active interaction with biological or natural sciences. None of the campaigners of the scientific status of social or cultural anthropology ever thought of working out its relationship with physical anthropology (or archaeology), or of planning a study in which these branches could be meaningfully integrated. Radcliffe-Brown (1952) and Evans-Pritchard (1951) wrote extensively on the nature of social anthropology and the relation it bore with psychology, history, and sociology, but never chose to examine its kinship with physical anthropology or archaeology.[11]

It may be suggested that the relationship between social and physical anthropology in the British tradition was almost like that of the kinspersons who stood back to back. But, it did not imply any hostility or competition between them. Social and physical anthropology (and also archaeology) were non-interacting disciplines but sharing the same hearth. Social anthropology forged its alliance with sociology and history, whilst physical anthropology (which in Britain is called biological anthropology) shared common concerns with medicine and other biological sciences.[12] Anthropology, therefore, can be conceptualized as a myriad of disciplines having close contact with other independent subjects, rather than amongst themselves.

The pattern established in Britain at the beginning of this century has continued till date. Separate departments of physical, social, and archaeological anthropology exist in British universities, and are placed under the faculty of anthropology. Interaction between these departments is negligible. Each one of them is almost like a *gemeinschaft*. Anthropology for the British is either biological anthropology, or social anthropology, or archaeology. The issue of its integration does not worry them. Nor do they engage themselves with the question of what 'anthropological' part in physical anthropology is homologous to the 'anthropological' quiddity in social anthropology? The British pattern is replicated in many other universities of the world. At the level of the work, the microstudies take precedence over the philosophical discussions about a discipline's total identity, integration, and the boundary-maintaining mechanisms.

The American anthropology began with its division into physical anthropology and ethnology, the latter being further segmented into cultural anthropology, linguistic anthropology, and prehistoric archaeology. Physical anthropology studied bio-genetic facts, while culture in all its manifestations, and in spatio-temporal dimensions, was the key concept in ethnology. Although not clear in the beginning on how biological and cultural facts could be meaningfully integrated in a study, American anthropology nevertheless furthered its holistic conception. The textbook definition (almost like a 'holy litany') that anthropology is the 'study of man in all his aspects in time and space', seems to me an American view. The founders of professional anthropology in America insisted on an integrated anthropology. We are reminded of Franz Boas (1948) for whom fieldwork meant the collection of socio-cultural, archaeological, linguistic, and biological facts of a given people. This was the encyclopaedic approach to anthropology which is amply reflected in American textbooks. Some American scholars have discussed the issue of the integration of anthropology at the level of the syllabuses, teaching and research seminars, and common projects and investigations [Tax 1956; Godelier 1974; Leaf 1974, 1979]. But they were all conscious of the fact that the subject was fast fragmenting. Their concern can be estimated from Eric Wolf's aptly-titled article: 'They divide and subdivide and call it anthropology' (*New York Times*, November 30, 1980).

Because of these divergent specialisations, which are strange bedfellows, anthropology has become a 'dilettante's discipline', including in its scope 'literally anything from lemur feet to shadow plays' [Rabinow 1977:3].[13] In a trenchant criticism of overspecialization, Needham (1970:46) envisaged an 'iridescent metamorphosis' of anthropology. The field might be redistributed among many other disciplines.[14] Many authors have reconciled to the academic disintegration of anthropology and see their works as part of the 'metamorphosis' of which Needham spoke.[15] Anthropology today is a 'group of subjects'.[16]

III

Integration of anthropology has the following facets: first, certain aspects of human existence can be fully comprehended when equal attention is given to its biological and socio-cultural dimensions. Some 'special anthropologies' lie at the confluence of biological and socio-cultural anthropology; for example, ecological anthropology, demographic anthropology, medical anthropology, and the anthropology of development. Other anthropologies are preeminently biological, but use several socio-cultural factors and indices; anthropology of growth and physiological anthropology may be cited as examples. Even in highly technical fields such as foetal anthropology, one cannot ignore the political economy of health and various declarations of the international organizations (like UNICEF) [Chandra 1990].

In those specializations which are at the interface, a restriction of analysis to either fact (biological or socio-cultural) is bound to be myopic. Medical anthropologists know full well that if illness is cultural, disease is a pathological concept. Pain is both a culturally-constructed reality and also, biologically inscribed on the body. The first lesson a student learns is that medical anthropology is a bio-cultural discipline. We analyse the medical system as a biological system and as a sociocultural system, which we further break down, following the systemic approach, into social system and cultural system. In the integration of the three subsystems of the medical system can one locate the spirit of medical anthropology [Foster and Anderson 1978; for a similar argument on Indian material, see Joshi and Mahajan 1990, Bhasin and Srivastava 1991].

A similar argument can be adduced for demographic and ecological anthropologies. Some of us may be skeptical of the place I have given to the anthropology of development, for this specialization is dominated by social anthropologists. Those who think that development has nothing to do with physical anthropology are mistaken because the issue of the biological survival of people is of utmost importance. We have a significant literature on the diseases caused by development, and how the health of the natives was jeopardized as a consequence of the measures the planners and development specialists thought were ameliorative [Kunitz 1994]. For depopulating tribes, the health-related programmes score priority over those dealing with cultural matters. Development is a bio-cultural phenomenon, and for the future survival of anthropology, this notion is crucial.

Besides this, another way to integrate anthropology is to generate a paradigm which can explain both the biological and cultural facts. In one such attempt, Mahajan and Srivastava (1978) examined the possibility of using dialectical materialism to integrate anthropology. Jan Wind suggested the use of cybernetics for a similar purpose (personal communication, December 12, 1978). Neo-Darwinian philosophical traditions could also be explored [Ashley Montagu 1960, 1981]. Forde (1948) argued that ecology can unite physical with social anthropology. Howsoever promising these theoretical insights are, they have not become popular in our subject. Whatever integration is visible, it is at the level of studies which require a knowledge of both physical and socio-cultural anthropology.

IV

One of the consequences of the American encyclopaedic approach is that anthropology has gradually become more and more porous and spongy, offering a respectable place to people from varied disciplines, but losing its identity in the process.[17] What has really been detrimental to its progress is the oft-repeated statement, pronounced with boastfulness and pomposity, that it is a subject without frontiers, without boundaries. The protagonists of this view present a catalogue of different anthropologies and show several empty shelves to the academic world where more and more specializations could be placed.[18] We may beam with satisfaction on seeing a huge list of anthropologies, but in this process we have eroded the concerns of the discipline. The future of anthropology depends upon these pivotal concerns, and not on the unwieldy list of its specializations.

Often, a question like 'what is anthropological' in economic anthropology', or in 'medical anthropology', is asked. We want to know the distinctions between collateral disciplines or interests — for instance, between political science, political sociology, political philosophy, and political anthropology. Engaging debates ensue on whether the study of economic systems of tribes and peasants be termed 'economic anthropology' or 'anthropological economics'. Such taxonomic debates are in other specializations as well. Some scholars believe that if we opt for titles such as 'anthropological economics', or 'anthropology of development', or 'ethnolinguistics', then we emphasise in them the anthropological content more than that of the other discipline with which they interact.

Whether or not we accept the suggestion about a proper nomenclature of the discipline or its branch, there is no doubt that such borderline or inter-disciplinary enterprises are required to interact with other disciplines. The student of 'anthropological economics' or 'economic anthropology' needs to acquire an arduous competence in economic theory and techniques of analysis. In a similar vein, an anthropologist of transcultural psychiatry is expected to be familiar with western psychiatry, its modes of treatment, and its concept of man. In such disciplines, the anthropologist has to do an extra labour to gain competence in another subject. Dalton remarked that 'economic anthropologists' suffer from 'nervious inferiority' while corresponding their ideas with hardcore economists who tend to look down upon their counterparts in anthropology [Dalton 1971: 30]. Similar observations can be culled from the practitioners of other borderline anthropologies who have to interact regularly with other closely allied subjects. One would like to read a detailed account of the professional experiences of a medical or physiological anthropologist working in a hospital or medical college, and trying to justify his place amidst those who might consider such positions as sheer appendages, easily dispensable.[19]

Needham (1970: 40) called an anthropologist's encounter with the other discipline(s) 'awkward'. It is bound to generate 'nervous inferiority' in him unless he stands on the steady feet of his discipline, is committed to intellectual osmosis, and constantly reminds himself of his goals and purposes. If he is an 'economic anthropologist', he judiciously and critically examines the propositions of economics to determine their suitability in understanding his data. He does not use his data to illuminate or support the economic theory. When his aims are lopsided, his encounter with economics will become 'awkward' rather than fruitful, and he will suffer from 'nervous inferiority' in relation to the economist, rather than becoming a 'coparcener' in the production of alternative perspectives on society.

All this boils down to our own conception of anthropology. If a study of what different anthropologists mean by the subject is conducted, we shall come across highly divergent opinions. For many, anthropology will be what they do: the practice will define the subject and not the other way round. Some will subscribe to the encyclopaedic notion: there is anthropology in everything and everything can be studied anthropologically. Rarely do we ask: What is 'anthropological' in what we do?

V

Problems for an anthropologist's work 'can be found everywhere human beings are in communication' [Firth 1992:211], wherever groups are formed and sustained. The anthropologist's laboratory is the entire mankind; the way in which people structure the reality around them, is what he studies. The human universes are not 'museumified' entities, static, neatly-kept and catalogued. They are perpetually changing. Those orders (and institutions) which men themselves proudly created at one time are rejected by them at another time. Taxonomies are challenged; the catalogues need to be constantly updated. Human beings have tremendous capacity to perfect themselves. This process is however punctuated with crises – with contradictions and conflicts. Change is ceaselessly occurring; it is imperceptible and needs to be constructed. Geertz (1995: 4) writes: 'Change, apparently, is not a parade that can be watched as it passes'.

The anthropologist did (and does) many things with societies and cultures. In the formative era, he studied the origin of institutions, customs, groups and collectivites, and the stages through which they were believed to have passed. Then, he compiled the detailed accounts of the past of these societies by focusing on the 'memory culture' of his respondents. How social institutions had diffused from the centre of their origin, or from one society to another, greatly interested him. In the wake of the repudiation of earlier pseudo-historical approaches and psychological reductionism, and the aimless documentation of cultural traits, came the much celebrated functional approach. With this, anthropology became a synchronic study, of 'here and now'. The criticism of functionalism revived many earlier approaches. The French became interested in the working of the human mind and unraveling its underlying structure. Their contemporaries in America, those who became popular as cognitive anthropologists, intended to study culture by getting into the heads of its bearers. Some French and American scholars applied the Marxian approach to the superstructure of society. Network analysis, transactionalism, modern variants of structuralism, feminism, reflexivity, interpretivism, have been other corrective alternatives.

The aforementioned approaches and their several kindred variations, known by different technical names, barring those which were conjectural, co-exist in contemporary anthropology. But, the most rallying is around the one which is concerned with meaning. Some of its advocates derive their intellectual authority from Weberian sociology and its further development in the hermeneutical tradition. In a nutshell, the contemporary anthropologists do the following. They conduct a lengthy fieldwork with a 'community' of people, far-away or nearer home.[20] During the course of study, they are 'hued' by the 'object' of study.[21] From this experience is born the ethnography.

Anthropology is a 'sceptical study' [Firth 1992:210]. It does not take anything for granted. Whether acknowledged or not, we begin with the Durkheimian rule: 'I do not know a social fact unless I have studied it' [Durkheim 1938]. Our aim is to understand the plexus of meanings people attribute to their thoughts and actions. Alongside, we unravel those meanings and interconnections of institutions of which their creators may be unaware. We keep a distinction between the perspectives and analyses of the actor and the observer.

The anthropologist is an empiricist ('world-observer'), an interpreter ('world-describer'), a comparativist ('world-comparer'), and a futurist ('world-imaginer'), whose cosmic ambition is to know about the human society as a whole.[22] His aim is pre-eminently academic: to interpret and explain. It is not to delve in the charters of policy prescriptions.[23] Today, especially in India, many anthropologists are solely concerned with the issues of policy, churning out the agendas of action; or criticizing the governments for not having done anything for the communities, and suggesting measures that are known to all (such as, roads should be laid down, electricity should be provided, seeds should be freely distributed to people, schools should be opened up, etc.). Perhaps they feel that in this market-oriented world they have to be utilitarian. They try to prove their Darwinian fitness in the academic world as well as in the market-society by formulating hypothetical programmes for the betterment of human beings. Their comments on policies, lists of pleas, designs of action, scarcely rise above the commonplace.[24]

None of the scholars concerned with the future of anthropology has argued against action anthropology, putting knowledge to real and concrete use.[25] Giddens (1996:126) writes: "Anthropology must be ready to contest unjust systems of domination, along the way seeking to decide what 'injustice' actually is, and be prepared to bring potentially controversial issues to light". For Hart (1990: 14): "Anthropology is 'for' making a better, more democratic world for everyone". To achieve this, we should be 'politically' and 'morally' engaged with social problems. Our vision of future is of greater freedom and equality of human beings, both as a right and policy, and anthropology must work towards their achievement. Inspiration for applied work, Hart thinks, can be drawn from Leach's lectures published as *A Runaway World*? where he argued that anthropology can be used for resolving crises of the contemporary world. He also suggested that we should try to spread the anthropological vision amongst the mass audience.

Sponsel (1990) argues for greater involvement of anthropologists with the people they study. Grimshaw and Hart (1993: 44) say that the 'resolution to anthropology's dilemma' requires new 'patterns of social engagement'. For Ingold (1994: xviii), anthropology is a 'science of engagement'. The 'subjects' of our research are not 'objects'; they are fellow beings. One of our duties is to take overt action to defend human rights. Cultural relativism is simply a 'frame of mind', a methodological tool. It does not imply, or should not be confused with, ethical relativism. The topic of universal human values and basic needs has become central to contemporary anthropology [Hatch 1983; Scupin and DeCorse 1995]. None should starve, none should be inflicted with physical or psychic torture, none should be stripped of basic human rights and needs, are some examples of universal values. The anthropologist should render his firm commitment to them in academic as well as practical terms. Firth's summary expresses it well: "[The] anthropologists must have a social awareness, a social conscience, some degree of commitment to the people among whom they work. Locally, an anthropologist can sometimes defend the peoples' interests against bureaucratic ignorance, the rapacity of salesmen or the arrogance of developers" [Firth 1992: 219]. The role of anthropology in exposing various myths which perpetrate inequality in society is well acclaimed. And, famously known is its contribution in planning and executing development.

The applied role will definitely condition anthropology's future, but the list of suggestions, policy prescriptions, must entail from a rigorously conducted study in which the focus is on understanding. Theoretical and applied researches are two sides of the same coin: 'knowledge for practice' and 'practice for knowledge' are intimately connected [Srivastava 1990: 316]. Before peoples' interests are defended, we should acquire a thorough knowledge of the conditions which breed rapacious salespersons or arrogant developers. Understanding and interpretation are placed before action, advocacy, and activism. A good anthropology is one which yields sound, detailed, and convincing knowledge of a society; and from this follows a culturally-rooted, endogenous, and holistic plan of development.

The social responsibility of the anthropologist has increased manifold presently. It is bound to enlarge further. Anthropology began in the mid-ninetieth century as the evolutionary study of the entire human society. As it grew in time and space, especially with the addition of ethnology sections in museums, it progressively became a mode of producing knowledge of the 'exotic other', the 'primitive society'. By the time the term 'social anthropology' was invented for the Liverpool Chair founded in 1908 for James Frazer, the 'intellectual object' of anthropology – the savage, the pre-literate, the simple, the non-western – had fully been found. Gough (1968: 403) writes: 'most of our field work was carried out in societies that had been conquered by our own government'. The we-they distinction, or the distinction of the self and the other, was the pith of the anthropological work: '...anthropological knowledge came to be a map of difference, of alterity' [Das 1995: 3]. That the 'they' was qualitatively different from the 'we' constituted the discourse. Anthropologists wrote what they thought was right, proper, and just, on and about the primitives, who were mute, who did not answer back [Giddens 1996: 121-2; Geertz 1998:72]. The monographs thus produced were for the literate, white, western public.

Overtime, as a result of culture contact with modern societies, the primitives have been de-primitivised. No more are they 'they' in pristine terms, but are gradually assimilated with the 'we' [Geertz 1998]. As globalisation progresses apace, the difference between the 'we' and the 'they' narrows down tremendously. The erstwhile primitives now read and write; question the inquisitive ethnographer on the purpose of his study, and wish to share the results of his enquiries; read monographs to discover their past moorings and also detect grave errors made by the anthropologist in understanding their culture. The staunchest critics of ethnographic writings on a society are now its 'literate' people. They answer back and interrogate their ethnographers.[26] The latter have to be cautious about the veracity of ethnographic details they collect. Furthermore, the 'natives' now study their own societies where they enmesh their experiences of being a native with an objective project. Native anthropology, or autoethnography, as it is designated, brings with it its own commitments and values [Srivastava 1995b]. Anthropology is now produced in a different set of social conditions. It has to be far more reflective and humanistic.

This changed scenario does not suggest that we become 'subjective' in our approach. Rather, we have to combine the requirements of a dispassionate study with an unflinching commitment to universal human values and right. Our methodology adheres to the principle of objectivity, whilst our 'practical anthropology' (to borrow Malinowski's term) does not compromise on the agenda of human welfare; it is value-loaded.[27] It is wrong to assume that if we 'side' with particular arguments regarding human condition, then we tend to lose our objectivity. To recall Cresswell (1968:411-2): 'A physicist can fulfil his sense of social responsibility by speaking out, for instance, against the use that politicians and the military make of the atom bomb he has made possible, without affecting the laws describing the behaviour of atoms and molecules'. In a similar way, we endeavour to understand human society as objectively as possible, but speak out against all those social contexts where human rights are abrogated, where values of equality are suppressed, where injustice prevails.

The people whom we study, wherever they live, are no longer hidden, forgotten, lost, or cloistered.[28] No more is the tribal society 'isolated', a 'complete society', an 'anthropological whole'. Not only the national but also the international economic systems affect the micro-societies. The genesis of rural poverty can be traced to the unjust social and economic system of the international order. Ethnicity has become a transnational phenomenon. The future anthropologists will need to study the socio-cultural aspects of international relations [Foster 1984: Wright 1988; Messer 1993; Cole 1995; Srivastava 1995a]. Impact of the fast-changing technology, global consumption patterns (overconsumption of a few co-existing with the underconsumption of many), shifting geo-political configurations, and new forms (and strategies) of domination on human communities all over the world, are the areas of priority. The relation of the local with the global will be central to future anthropology [Moore 1996].

Although defined as the study of the entire human society, anthropology has predominantly dealt with tribals and peasants. Its emphasis in urban studies has been on slums and squatters, shanty satellite towns and migrants, religious communities, and lower-class neighbourhoods. It has not so far conducted detailed field-based studies of elite societies, of people who 'answer back' and reflect on the methods used and conclusions reached. The effect of functionalism, or any other method which searched for fixed categories, has been so overwhelming that we did not contribute much to the understanding of social turbulence. For the future survival of anthropology, it is imperative that we study societies in distress, in hunger, in collective pain and war [Das 1995: Nordstrom and Robben 1995]. We should apply anthropological knowledge to understand social issues and apprise the lay public in a de-jargonised language with our findings and suggestions for improvement. I may refer here to Bhattacharya's recent researches (1998) on the history of hunger and starvation. The lesson we learn is that no more is anthropology esoteric, the 'engagement of colonial masters' or the 'sport of kings'.[29]

VI

We have tremendous faith in the analytical ability of anthropology. Even other disciplines have been considerably influenced by anthropological perspectives. The future of our discipline is incumbent upon a better understanding of human society and culture, because from this will logically follow the steps to be undertaken for ameliorating human condition. Whether we are physical or social anthropologists, we view a system (biological, social, or cultural) in a state of dynamic equilibrium. We consider a numbr of factors–intrinsic and extraneous –which condition the working of systems. Biological and cultural factors should be seen as complementary, in a state of 'heuristic synergism' [Srivastava 1990:314]. If we erroneously believe that one fact is 'superior' to the other, or is hermetically sealed, then we are likely to fission the discipline as well the 'tribe' of anthropologists (to borrow the popular words of Max Gluckman). We hear of incessant conflicts between physical and social anthropologists over the allocation of resources, and teaching and research positions in a department. These cleavages reflect the orientations these 'sub-tribes' of anthropology have towards the two great anthropological constructions – the biology and the culture. Some physical anthropologists think that their accomplishments are true to the scientific tradition, whereas their counterparts in social anthropology are simply raconteur, not more than story-tellers. The social anthropologists may regard their work as more important, by claiming that their work begins where science ends. Instead, if we begin with a model of complementariness between different facts that concern us, the tenor of our research will be qualitatively different. We can learn a lot about it from the actual practice of medical anthropologists. The future of anthropology lies in such studies.

Anthropology is principally a field science. This is not to say that anthropologists have depended upon field work for their ideas, but have always referred to the field for a critical scrutiny of their theories and ideas [Fox 1975]. Unfortunately, the quality of fieldwork, especially in Indian anthropology, has become poorer. Our students prefer to study their own societies rather than venturing into ethnographic landscapes where they struggle to learn a new language and pass through the non-assuaging pangs of loneliness. Since they study their own society, they start with the assumption that they know enough, thus overlooking the nuances, the finer points, the underlying currents, the subterranean elements, and the subtleties. It is here that they commit the error.[30] Needless to say, a good anthropology depends a great deal upon the quality of our fieldwork.

To sum up: a future *of* and *for* anthropology lies in constantly struggling to evolve a sophisticated theoretical and methodological apparatus, conducting solid fieldwork, and unswervingly subscribing to the premises of human rights, democratization, welfare, and the development of people of all shades of life.

Notes

1. Four addresses were delivered on the futures of physical anthropology, archaeology, social anthropology, and material culture, respectively by G. M. Morant, V. Gordon Childe, Raymond Firth, and R. U. Sayce. See *Man* 1944, vol. XLIV: 16–24.
2. However, I refer to a piece on the future of British sociology in Payne *et al.* (1981).
3. In these words, Fischer (1986) has paraphrased Jean-Francois Lyotard's concept of the 'postmodern'.

4. For the last few years, I have been collecting data on this topic. At the close of the teaching session (generally mid-March), I make students write in whichever language (Hindi or English) they have adeptness, a short essay on the impact of anthropology on their personal lives and orientations. I have read these essays but so far have not analysed them properly. The observation I make here is based on these write-ups. The students have invariably noted that they became less prejudicial after studying anthropology. In this context I remember Firth [1944: 22], 'Ignorance and prejudice about other peoples, particularly peoples of a different colour, is still widespread, and it is part of our [anthropologists'] job to try and break it down'.

5. Before 1995. anthropology was one of the most popular options for the Indian civil services examination. Its popularty declined after its syllabi in both the papers were frighteningly increased. Many topics were included on which good reading material did not exist. My comments on the revised syllabi appeared in Hindi in *Pratiyogita Samrat*, January 1996, 4 (12): 53-4.

6. This observation is not only based on Indian experience. Many western writers have pointed this out. Mayer (1981: vii) noted that when Fürer-Haimendorf decided to read anthropology, it was an 'unconventional choice'. A Delhi anthropologist, Abhimanyu Sharma, was reported (in *The Hindustan Times*, June 26, 1976) to have said that the 'rejected lot' of students joined anthropology. I refuted his observation (*The Hindustan Times*, July 2, 1976). The drop-out rate of students in anthropology department is quite high; these students leave anthropology to seek admission in other coveted courses. The heads of anthropology departments all over the world are engaged in increasing the popularity of the subject among the wider public. See MacClancy and McDonaugh (1996).

7. These six Delhi anthropologists were Surinder Nath, V. C. Channa, S.L. Malik, Anil Mahajan, Lalit Kumar, and myself. Today, four of them are teaching in the Delhi department of anthropology. The other two are employed elsewhere but do the anthropological work. Later, P. C. Joshi, N. K. Chadha, and M. P. Sachdeva were also inducted in the editorial board of SAP. Chadha is a psychologist but is reputed for many works on psychological anthropology. SAP continued its uninterrupted publication till 1991; then its publication was suspended following financial problems.

8. Because of his lengthy stay (often not less than a year or so) with a community, the social anthropologist develops almost quasi-permanent relations with its members. In many cases, he 'adopts' the community of people forever. Empathy, therefore, is an important element of the relationship between the observer and the observed.

This is, however, absent in a physical anthropological work which treats its 'subjects' of study as mere 'objects'. In my opinion, physical anthropologists and archaeologists do not conduct the 'fieldwork' as social anthropologists define this term. Physical anthropologists may collect data from the field or laboratory situation. Archaeologists conduct excavations on sites likely to yield an industry of human artifacts. See Wolcott (1995) for the notion of fieldwork.

9. By 'hard-core' anthropologists, I mean those who have undergone a professional training in anthropology. They are not 'self-taught' anthropologists. Today, sociologists write articles and books which bear the word 'anthropology' in their titles. 'Anthropology' has become a sort of 'discourse' in these writings rather than just remaining a discipline. Refer to works by Das (1995), Thapan (1998).

10. Leslie White (1943) submitted that all sciences dealt with energy and motion. Culture and civilization were also forms of energy: the sciences were therefore unified methodologically. The organismic theorists developed the concept of society by comparing it systematically with that of the organism about which they knew well, courtesy the growth of biology. Organic analogy was a procedure to know the unknown ('society') with the help of the known ('organism'). See Harris (1968).

11. Well known are their conclusions on the status of social anthropology. For Radcliffe-Brown (1952), it was a branch of 'comparative sociology', another name of sociology according to Émile Durkheim. And, it was a kind of historiography for Evans-Pritchard (1951).

12. In his reply to Forde's question regarding the integration of anthropology's branches, Firth (1944:22) said that the four branches (physical anthropology, archaeology, social anthropology, and material culture) 'called for entirely separate disciplines, and that the ties of social anthropology were with sociology, rather than with physical anthropology or archaeology'.

13. Anthropologists are seen as those 'dilettantes who flit from one area to the next' [Kleinman and Copp 1993: 6].

14. I have often heard of a suggestion that physical anthropology should be placed along with zoology, archaeology with ancient history, and social anthropology with sociology; and departments of anthropology should be done away with.

15. For instance, see Clifford (1986) and his joint venture, *Writing Culture*. He writes that 'man' has disintegrated as *telos* for a whole discipline (p. 4).

16. Ingold writes: "...anthropology, as it exists today, is not a single field, but is rather a somewhat contingent and unstable amalgam of

subfields, each encumbered with its own history, theoretical agenda and methodological preoccupations" [Ingold 1994: xiv]. Also see, Moore (1986:1): "Anthropology is no longer a singular discipline, if it ever was, but rather a multiplicity of practices engaged in a wide variety of social contexts".

17. In a recent paper, Sillitoe (1998: 224) notes that agricultural economists, human geographers, and plant pathologists are 'stealing our [anthropologists'] disciplinary clothes'. They themselves conduct the anthropological work required for their study. If I may add, the quality of their anthropological work is inferior which brings bad name to the subject.

18. In his keynote presentation at a seminar (on 'Anthropology in India: Problems and Prospect') in the Department of Anthropology, Punjab University, Chandigarh, from March 6-9, 1986, Indera P. Singh presented a long list of anthropological specializations. An idea of special anthropologies can be gathered from the list of seminar topics prepared for the Xth International Congress of Anthropological and Ethnological Sciences (see *Indian Anthropologist*, Vol. 7, No. 1, 1977, pp. 68-70).

19. Here, we may refer to the following observation from Needham: "The more the anthropologist specializes the more he will be obliged to observe the standard of the discipline that he enters: and if he is to induce the practitioners of that discipline to take serious notice of his knowledge and understanding of ethnographic evidence, he must in his own work earn their professional respect by conforming to the scientific or scholarly criteria which they acknowledge" [Needham 1970: 40].

20. Besides the conventional areas, the 'community' could be of laboratory scientists, homosexuals, psychiatric clients, drug addicts, sex workers, professionals and politicians, etc. Anthropologists have worked on the impact of the new reproductive technology on kinship, family, and gender [Strathern 1990] and on the ethnography of the immune system [Martin 1996]. The 'field' or research is not given; it has to be constructed. Geertz (1995: 106) remarks: '...research sites are not found, they are made'.

21. Geertz (1995:210) describes this in the following words: "You don't exactly penetrate another culture, as the masculinist image would have it. You put yourself in its way and it bodies forth and enmeshes you".

22. Anthropology is as much about 'us' as it is about 'them'– the 'other' culture [Leach 1982].

23. Giddens (1996: 125) writes: 'The practical connotations of anthropology are likely to depend upon a rekindling of the

anthropological imagination than upon a narrowing-down of the subject to limited social policy issues'.

24. See, for instance, Samal (ed.) (1996), a book of six hundered pages.
25. This however is not the opinion of many other anthropologists; see Leach (1982), Béteille (1993). Hugh-Jones writes about Leach, '...throughout his [Leach] life he remained deeply suspicious of the supposed benefits of applied anthropology' [Hugh-Jones 1989: 14]
26. There are many cases where the people are aware of the fact that they were studied anthropologically. For instance, Pul Eliya, the Sri Lankan village, which Leach studied, had a notice at its entrance placed many years after Leach had done his field work there. It read: 'This is the village of the famous anthropological study' [Hugh-Jones 1989: 21].
27. Some anthropologists believe that ethnography is not a fact but only personal opinion, a view which Firth termed 'egoistic or solipsistic anthropology' (1992: 219). For Leach (1987), as well as Hugh-Jones (1989:34), ethnography was fiction; for Geertz (1988) it was a 'literary enterprise'. But this is not the opinion which will help the future social anthropology.
28. But many coffee-table books on tribes may carry these words in their titles, or descriptions of people, in order to increase their sale. See, for instance, a French publication on Indian tribes titled *L' Inde des Tribus Oubliees* (Chene, Paris, 1993). Perhaps the publishers are motivated by the idea that the 'exotic' sells, the 'familiar' does not.
29. I have borrowed the last phrase from Godfrey Lienhardt. Lewis writes: "When Prince Charles began his anthropological study at Cambridge, Godfrey Lienhardt (at an RAI council meeting) quipped that 'anthropology had become the sport of kings'" [Lewis 1998: 567].
30. It is relevant to remember here Béteille's observation: "I have seen many young British and American anthropologists return physically exhausted from the field, looking lean and hungry, like Cassius in the play. My Indian students show less wear and tear during their movements in and out of the field... Indian research scholars stretch field work out longer, doing it in several short spells, but rarely spend as much time in the field as their counterparts from overseas. They also rarely choose to do field work in a region other than the one to which they belong; this enables them to dispense with the trouble of learning a new language, and it allows them to take other shortcuts that in the end detract from the quality of their field work" (1996:234).

References

Ashley-Montagu, M. F. (1960): *Anthropology and Human Nature.* The Merlin Press, London.

——(1981): *Socio-biology Examined.* University Press, Oxford.

Béteille, André (1993): 'Sociology and Anthropology: Their Relationship in One Person's Career', *Contributions to Indian Sociology* (ns), 27(2): 291-304.

——(1996): 'Epilogue: Village Studies in Retrospect', in *Caste, Class and Power: Changing Patterns of Stratification in a Tanjore Village.* Oxford University Press (second edition), Delhi: pp. 231-48.

Bhasin, Veena and V. K. Srivastava (1991): 'Medical Anthropology: A Review' , *Journal of Human Ecology,* 2(1): 1-19.

Bhattacharya, D. K. (1998): 'Onion: The Warning of Nature We missed' (unpublished paper).

——(1999): 'Prehistory in India: An Urgent Need for Change', Presidential Address (January 4, 1999), Anthropology and Archaeology Section, 86th Session of Indian Science Congress Association, Chennai.

Boas, Franz (1948) : *Race, Language and Culture.* Macmillan, New York.

Chandra, N. Satish (1990) : 'Foetal Anthropology, Problems and Prospects', *Indian Anthropologist,* 20(1-2) : 81-98.

Clifford, James (1986) : 'Introduction: Partial Truths', in James Clifford and George Marcus (eds), *Writing Culture: The Poetics and Politics of Ethnography,* Oxford University Press, Delhi: pp. 1-26.

Cole, Johnnetta B. (1995): 'Human Rights and the Rights of Anthropologists', *American Anthropologist,* 97(3) : 44-56.

Cresswell, Robert (1968): 'Comment (Social Responsibilities Symposium)', *Current Anthropology,* 9 (5): 411-2.

Dalton, G. (1971): *Economic Anthropology and Development : Essays in Tribal and Peasant Economics.* Basic Books, New York and London.

Das, Veena (1995): *Critical Events: An Anthropological Perspective on Contemporary India.* Oxford University Press, Delhi.

Durkheim, Émile (1938, original 1895): *The Rules of the Sociological Method.* Free Press, New York.

Evans-Pritchard, E.E. (1951): *Social Anthropology.* Free Press, New York.

Firth, Raymond (1944): 'The Future of Social Anthropology', *Man,* XLIV: 19-22.

——(1992): 'A Future for Social Anthropology?' in Sandra Wallman (ed), *Contemporary Futures: Perspective from Social Anthropology,* Routledge, London and New York, pp 208-24.

Fischer, Michael M. J. (1986): 'Ethnicity and the Postmodern Arts of Memory', in James Clifford and George Marcus (eds), *Writing Culture: The Poetics and Politics of Ethnography,* Oxford University Press, Delhi, pp. 194-233.

Forde, C.D. (1948): 'The Integration of Anthropological Studies', *Journal of Royal Anthropological Institute, 78.*

Foster, G. M. (1984): 'The Role of Anthropology in the Enhancement of Peace and International Understanding', *The Eastern Anthropologist, 39(2): 139-44.*

Foster, G. M. and B. G. Anderson (1978): *Medical Anthropology.* John Wiley and Sons, New York.

Geertz, Clifford (1988): *Works and Lives : The Anthropologist as Author.* Polity Press.

——(1995): *After the Fact: Two Countries, Four Decades, One Anthropologist.* Harvard University Press, Cambridge, Massachusetts.

——(1998) : 'Deep Hanging Out', *The New York Review of Books,* October 22, XLV (16) : 69-72.

Gerholm, Tomas and Ulf Hannerz (1982) : 'Introduction : The Shaping of National Anthropologies', *Ethnos,* 1-2 : 5-35.

Giddens, Anthony (1996): 'The Future of Anthropology', in *The Defence of Sociology : Essays, Interpretations and Rejoinders.* Polity Press, Cambridge.

Godelier, M. (1974): 'Anthropology and Biology: Towards a New Form of Co-operation', *International Social Science Journal,* XXVI (4): 611-35.

Gough, Kathleen (1968): 'New Proposal for Anthropologists', *Current Anthropology,* 9 (5): 403-7.

Grimshaw, Anna and Keith Hart (1993): *Anthropology and the Crisis of Intellectuals,* Prickly Pear Press, Cambridge (pamphlet no 1).

Harris, Marvin (1968) : *The Rise of Anthropological Theory.* Thomas Y. Crowell Company, New York.

Hart, Keith (1990): 'Swimming into the Human Current', *The Times Higher Education Supplement,* (May 18), 13-4.

Hastrup, Kirsten (1987): 'The Reality of Anthropology', *Ethnos,* 52(3-4): 287-300.

Hatch, Elvin (1983): *Culture and Morality: The Relativity of Values in Anthropology,* Columbia University Press, New York.

Hugh-Jones, Stephen (1989): *Edmund Leach, 1910-1989,* King's College, Cambridge (private circulation).

Ingold, Tim (1994): 'General Introduction', in Tim Ingold (ed.) *Companion Encyclopaedia of Anthropology,* Routledge, London and New York, pp. xiii-xxii.

Joshi, P. C. and Anil Mahajan (eds) (1990): *Studies in Medical Anthropology.* Reliance Publishing House, New Delhi.

Kahn, J. S. (1990): 'Towards a History of a Critique of Economism: The Nineteenth-Century German Origin of the Ethnographer's Dilemma', *Man*, 25(2): 30-49.

Kleinman, Sherryl and Marth A. Copp (1993): *Emotions and Fieldwork*. Sage Publications.

Kroeber, A. L. (1948): *Anthropology*. Harcourt Brace, New York.

Kunitz, Stephen J. (1994): 'Disease and the Destruction of Indigenous Populations', in Tim Ingold (ed), *Companion Encyclopaedia of Anthropology*, Routledge, London and New York, pp. 297-325.

Leach, E. R. (1967): *A Runaway World?* A B. B. C. Publication, London.

——(1982): *Social Anthropology*. Oxford University Press, New York.

——(1987): 'Tribal Ethnography: Past, Present, Future', *Cambridge Anthropology*, 11(2): 1-14.

Leaf, Murray J. (1974): *Frontiers of Anthropology, An Introduction to Anthropological Thinking*. D. van Nostrand Company, New York.

——(1979) : *Man, Mind and Science: A History of Anthropology*. Columbia University Press, New York.

Lewis, I. M. (1998): Book Review in *The Journal of the Royal Anthropological Institute (Incorporating Man)*, 4(3):567-8.

MacClancy, Jeremy and Chris McDonaugh (eds) (1996): *Popularising Anthropology*. Routledge, London and New York.

Mahajan, Anil and V. K. Srivastava (1978): 'Social Anthropology Reconsidered : Quest for a Meaningful Social Science of the Third World', presented in the Xth International Congress of Anthropological and Ethnological Sciences, Delhi (abstracted in the Proceedings, No. 1374, Vol. II: 208-9).

Martin, Emily (1996): 'Interpreting Electron Micrographs', in Henrietta L. Moore (ed), *The Future of Anthropological Knowledge*. Routledge, London and New York, pp. 16-36.

Mayer, A. C. (ed) (1981): *Culture and Morality: Essays in Honour of Christoph von Fürer-Haimendorf*. Oxford University Press, Delhi.

Messer, Ellen (1993): 'Anthropology and Human Rights', *Annual Review of Anthropology*, 22: 221-49.

Moore, Henrietta L. (1996): 'The Changing Nature of Anthropological Knowledge: An Introduction', in Henrietta L. Moore (ed), *The Future of Anthropological Knowledge*, Routledge, London and New York, pp. 1-18.

Needham, Rodney (1970): 'The Future of Social Anthropology: Disintegration or Metamorphosis?' in *Anniversary Contributions to Anthropology*, E. J. Brill, Leiden, pp. 34-47.

Nordstrom, Carolyn and Antonius C. G. M. Robben (eds) (1995) : *Fieldwork Under Fire: Contemporary Studies of Violence and Survival.* University of California Press, Berkeley, London.

Pathy, Jaganath (1981): 'Imperialism, Anthropology and the Third World', *Economic and Political Weekly,* April 4, pp. 623-7.

Payne, Geoff, Robert Dingwall, Judy Payne, and Nick Carter (1981) : *Sociology and Social Research.* Routledge and Kegan Paul, London, Boston and Henley.

Rainbow, Paul (1977): *Reflections on Fieldwork in Morocco.* University of California Press, Berkeley.

Radcliffe-Brown, A. R. (1948): *A Natural Science of Society.* Free Press, New York.

——(1952): *Structure and Function in Primitive Society.* Oxford University Press, London.

Samal, Prasanna K. (ed) (1996): *Tribal Development: Options.* Gyanodaya Prakashan, Nainital.

Scupin, Raymond and Christopher R. DeCorse (1995): *Anthropology: A Global Perspective.* Prentice-Hall, New Jersey.

Sillitoe, Paul (1998): 'The Development of Indigenous Knowledge: A New Applied Anthropology', *Current Anthropology,* 39(2):223-52.

Sponsel, L. E. (1990): 'Does Anthropology Have any Future?' *Anthropology Newsletter,* p. 32.

Srivastava, V. K. (1986): 'Culture and Development', *Man in India,* 66(1): 67-80.

——(1990): 'Practice of' and 'Practice in' Anthropology, *The Eastern Anthropologist,* 43(4):301-23.

——(1995a): 'Role of Anthropology in Understanding International Relations', *The Toppers' India.* 2(10):70-1.

——(1995b): 'An Auto-Ethnography of the Tangkhul Nagas', *The Eastern Anthropologist,* 48(2): 185-93.

Srivastava, V. K. and Anil Mahajan (1978): 'Towards a Paradigm of Integrated Anthropology', presented in the symposium, 'Biology and Culture', Xth International Congress of Anthropological and Ethnological Sciences, December 1, 1978, Delhi (Abstracted in the Proceedings, No. 1515, Vol. II, pp. 286-87).

Strathern, Marilyn (1990): 'Enterprise Kinship Consumer Choice and the New Reproductive Technique', *Cambridge Anthropology,* 14(1): 1-12.

Tax, Sol (1956): 'The Integration of Anthropology' in William L. Thomas, Jr. (ed), *Current Anthropology : A Supplement to Anthropology Today.* The University of Chicago Press, Chicago, pp. 313-28.

Thapan, Meenakshi (ed) (1998): *Anthropological Journeys: Reflections on Fieldwork.* Orient Longman, Delhi.

White, Leslie A. (1943): 'Energy and the Evolution of Culture', *American Anthropologist*, 45: 335-56.

Wolcott, Harry F. (1995): *The Art of Fieldwork.* Altamira Press.

Wright, Robin M. (1988): 'Anthropological Presuppositions of Indigenous Advocacy', *Annual Review of Anthropology*, 17: 365-90.

(This paper was presented on 4 January 1999 in the Section of Anthropological and Archaeological Sciences of the 1999 Session of the Indian Science Congress Association. I am grateful to Professor D. K. Bhattacharya, Professor P. K. Seth, Dr. Ananta K. Giri, Professor M. A. Kalam, Dr. S. B. Roy, and Dr. Kumkum Srivastava for their generous comments on this paper. Its revised version was published in the *Economic and Political Weekly [EPW]*, 27 February 1999. It is being reproduced here with the kind permission of the Editor of the *EPW*.)

2

TRENDS OF STUDIES ON AGRARIAN AND TRIBAL ISSUES: The Case of Chhattisgarh

S. N. Chaudhary

The objective of this paper is to examine the changing patterns of studies on tribal issues and agrarian relations with reference to Chhattisgarh. The study deals with the patterns of change in terms of the issues of research methodology adopted and social and academic importance of the study.

Chhattisgarh (with having different explanations of its origin and naming) came into existence on November 1, 2000. There are 16 districts having 96 *tehsils,* 146 Development Blocks and 20,308 inhabited villages. There is no significant gap in sex-ratio in both rural and urban areas of the state. Besides being rich in underground mineral resources, there are dozens of mega industries in the state. 12% of India's forests are in Chhattisgarh and 44% of the state's land is under forests. Identified as one of the richest bio-diversity habitats, the state has the densest forests in the country, rich wildlife, and above all, over 200 NTFPs are found in the state.

Tribes constitute about 32.5% population in the state. Brahmins and Banias are dominant force in the state. In some of the old districts like Surguja, Raigarh and Bastar more than 50% population is of tribals. Gonds, Muria, Bhumja, Baiga, Kamar, Kawars and Halba are major tribes in the state. The central plains of Chhattisgarh are known as the "rice bowl" of central India.

During the last 350 years tribes of the state have witnessed eleven rebellions or revolts.

II

Agrarian Studies

Dunu Roy (2002) has discussed agrarian issues in Chhattisgarh. The author discusses land issues since 1853, when Triennial Settlement was introduced to empower landholders so that they may invest in land and can provide revenue to the administration. Needless to mention that during those days Brahmins were, in particular, the dominant force, and most of the revenue land in Chhattisgarh was either owned or controlled by them. The author has discussed the role of Satnami Movement in challenging the hegemony of the upper castes in the 18th century. The author also discusses the reformative role of Satnami movement. It is interesting to note that the conflict between Brahmins and Satnami movement was seriously taken by the Raj and since the former had good relations with the government, therefore, a number of repressive steps were taken by the Raj against the supporters of Satnami movement, most of whom were Chamar by caste.

The author has also discussed the nature of exploitation faced by the tribals by the King of Ratanpur. Needless to mention that in Ratanpur villages, the British administrators encouraged the growth of trading agents to collect the grains from tribals. Most of these traders were Brahmin and they used the caste factor to gain entry in the village community and entered into the money lending business with very high interest rate. Because of their control on land, money lending business and collection of revenue for British Raj, Brahmins were economically powerful in Chhatisgarh. The famous drought of 1856 broke the backbone of tribal masses and strengthened the backbone of traders.

The author systematically and chronologically discussed the role of tribal *zamindar* of Sona Khan, Narayan Singh, who encouraged tribals for relief from local non-tribal influences and also his arrest and overall failure of his agitation. Roughly after about 120 years of the revolt of Narayan Singh which took place in 1857, Chhattisgarh Mukti Morcha (CMM) was formed and not only it declared Narayan Singh as a liberator but also inspired tribals for social justice through protest (Mukherjee, 1983; Sadgopal and Namra, 1993).

The author observed that land alienation among tribals and dalits of Chhattisgarh had taken place through debts and land mortgage. Hence, there is a high number of bonded labour in Mahanadi valley. The author discusses the protest against this practice since 1980. There is intensive documentation of the role of Janjagriti Kendra (NGO) of Rajpur, Bandhua Mukti Morcha (BMM) and Peoples' Union for Civil Liberties (PUCL), which jointly freed about 10,000 bonded labors within ten years. Origin and functioning of Chhattisgarh Grameen Sharamik Sangh as an antithesis of exploitation and poor rehabilitation of agriculture workers is also discussed in detail. The author also discusses attack on Janjagriti Kendra by vested interest and its response by the poor.

To the author, the area is highly pro-migration because of uncertainty of agriculture, indebtedness, land alienation and unemployment. Also, the role of industrialization on deforestation and the consequences of deforestation on local economy is discussed in detail. Against this background the protest of Kisan Sabha (KS) in 1960s and its slogan against *sarkari, sahukari* and *sahakari* credit is well explained.

The author discusses the process of formation of Chhattisgarh Mines Sharmik Sangh in 1977 and its role in the protection of human rights of workers of Bhilai Steel Plant with reference to the special contribution of Late Shankar Guha Niyogi. There is also a case history of the murder of Shankar Guha Niyogi and the role of a number of sister organizations which promised to carry on the dream of Niyogi into action.

Besides the above, there is an intensive documentation of the role of Chhatisgarh Mahila Jagriti Shagthan, Ekta Parishad, Parivartan, etc., in the restoration of human rights of tribals. Parivartan is a sister branch of Ekta Parishad and in Bastar it has mobilized people on land issue along with the questions of wages, access to forest, use of stone and consumption of outside liquor. They have strongly opposed the role of several top politicians and bureaucrats involved in corruption in land allotment and deforestation.

On the basis of the above description of the nature and process of natural resources based exploitation of local and the role of local initiatives in dealing with such exploitation with the help of outside civil society bodies it seems that exploitation of any type can significantly be addressed if there is people's movement, dedicated local level leadership and support from the sister organizations working in any part of the country. The paper is based on an integration of both "book view" and "field view" experiences.

Anoop Singh (2002) also discusses agrarian issues in his paper, which is partly based on secondary source information and partly on primary information. It deals with the process of land alienation due to industrialization and construction of dam, social and economic consequences of land alienation on poor and the role of Chhatisgarh Mukti Morcha in mitigation of these problems. More specifically it deals with the following issues:

(1) Distribution of land to landless under different Land Ceiling Acts.

(2) Land grabbed by the neo-rich.

(3) Ruthless exploitation of neo-rich and industrialists.

(4) Construction of dams for storage of water for factories and land alienation among the masses; and

(5) Role of CMM against the ruthless exploitation by Bhilai Engg. Corporation, Kedia Distillery Ltd., and so on.

The author observes that : "Prolonged apathy of the ruling elite, the rampant debauching of the capitalists and an underdeveloped region, have had one good effect. They have aroused the people and taught them to fight not only for their land but also for a development agenda that is ecologically sustainable and socio-economically more equitable" (P. 59).

R. K. Sail (2002) discusses the practice of inequitable distribution of land in Chhattisgarh. He observes that the largest number of absentee landlords are from the districts of Bilaspur, Durg, Raipur, Rajnandgaon and Sarguja. According to him, a majority of land is still held by a small number of households which are necessarily non-tribals. He also discusses the ongoing land *satyagarh* in about 700 villages in the district of Raipur. This *satyagarh* is broadly addressed to five land related problems, which are as under:

1. Many landless have been provided *patta* without physical occupation of the allotted land. Many of them do not know about the physical location of land.

2. Many are occupying government land without *patta.* Needless to mention that the government has open spaces under its direct control, which have been forcefully occupied and are being cultivated by the rich and powerful. They have been provided *patta* for such land but not the poor.
3. Under section 170 (B) of Land Reforms Act, there is a provision of restoration of land for tribes. The government official/magistrate is empowered under the above section to restore the land of the tribal if such an affidavit was not filed by the landlords by May 1985 or if the filed affidavit was declared false. Unfortunately such laws were not implemented on behalf of the tribals.
4. Some of the revenue land has been shown on land records as forest land, although there is hardly any plant on it. The displaced and uprooted tribals have been forced to leave this so-called forest land and under the process they have suffered constant harassment by the forest officials and the middle man.
5. Thousands of dalits and tribals have been forced out from their ancestral land in Chhattisgarh. They have not received any government support. They are forced to become bonded labourer.

The author has not only highlighted these land related problems but also discussed a number of protests such as land *satyagrah, jail barao andolan,* etc., to store rights of poor dalits and tribals. The scholar has systematically discussed the impact of slogan like.

(A) *jamen ka faisla, zamin par hoga* (All land issues will be settled on the very land itself).

(B) *zamin do ya jail do* (Give us land or imprisonment).

(C) *hum jail police se darte nahin, apna adhikar chorte nahin* (We are not afraid of either prison or police and do not leave our rights).

(D) *janun khet mein nagar chalahi, wohi khet ke malik hoh* (Land to the tiller).

Partly depending on historical facts and partly on empirical evidences, the author has discussed land based eploitation of poor dalits and tribals and examined the collective role of civil society organizations in meeting their human rights. The author has very clearly documented how through collective consciousness the victims are ready to sacrifice their lives for a better tomorrow.

Land Reform Unit (2002) of Lal Bahadur Shastri National Academy of Administration conducted a study on land reforms in Madhya Pradesh. This study is based on a case study of different villages. One of the studies was conducted in a village of Rajnandgaon of Chhattisgarh. The study says: "The allottees lost control of the land allotted to them due to the strong-arm tactics of the landlords. There were several instances of violent clashes between the land owners and allottees. Finally, the allottees were given possession by use of police force in 1989."

This report also examined the extent of distribution of government land to weaker sections and its socio-economic impact on them, the extent of encroachment steps taken to regularize the genuine encroachers and to evict the illegal occupants. By using simple random sampling technique, villages and beneficiaries were identified in districts of Madhya Pradesh; from Chhatisgarh, districts like Bilaspur, Durg, Raipur, Rajnandgaon, and Bastar had participated in the study. The study is based on integration of both primary and secondary source data. The findings reveal the following:

(1) No government land was allotted for the purpose of homestead in the districts of Durg, Raipur, Rajnandgaon and Bastar.

(2) As per the central norms at least 50% of the land is to be allotted to the persons belonging to the SC and ST category and only after covering them it has to be allotted to other category. It emerges from the study that 31.53% and 35.06% of SC and ST were allotted land respectively. Hence, a majority of the beneficiaries belonged to the reserved category.

(3) So far as the physical security of the allotted land is concerned, in a majority of cases, land was used by those who were allotted it.

(4) Encroachment of government land was very common in all the districts under study.

(5) Records pertaining to government land are available very unsatisfactorily.

In short, the finding reveals that of course land reform measures have been taken but on many fronts it is not satisfactorily working due to the fault on part of the government.

Harsh Mandar (2002) also examined the problem of land alienation among the tribes of both Chhattisgarh and Madhya Pradesh. He said that in a majority of the cases, court decisions are in favour of tribals but they have not secured the actual possession of land because of violence by the non-tribals. To him, due to protective legislation, the cases of land alienation have gone down but restoration of land already lost is tardy. He also prepared the case study of displaced tribals through development projects and contractors and its consequences on the victims. The following three case studies reveal this point.

(1) The case study of village Bada-Bacholi in village Bastar, located close to the Bailadilla Iron Ore Project, highlights some individual cases of land alienation such as: A Baniya obtained 0.05 acres of land from a Gond family on a yearly rent of Rs. 240, to open a grocer's shop. The family used to make purchases from this shop on credit basis. After some years, the Gond family was told that they owed Rs. 1500 to the shopkeeper, after the deduction of rent for the period. Ultimately the land was grabbed by the Baniya.

(2) In a second case, 4.37 acres of land was grabbed for establishing a private dairy by a few persons. The tribal owners of the land were not paid any compensation. Similarly, 13.30 acres of land of a tribal family was taken over for opening a grocer's shop and dairy, without paying any compensation.

(3) In some other cases, a liquor contractor acquired 0.05 acres of land, a Bengali acquired 0.19 acres of land. There are many such examples. In all, about 30.02 acres of tribal land was alienated by non-tribals in the village. In addition, 20.27 acres of land of the tribals was officially permitted to be purchased by non-tribals in this village. In the process, 75 tribal families became landless. The various provisions

of the Land Revenue Code of that period have been ineffective in providing protection to the tribals. The paper also examined the historical causes of land alienation and made a number of recommendations to address the land questions.

III

Tribal Studies

One of the strategies to examine the pattern of tribal studies with reference to Chhattisgarh followed in this study is to examine the publication of Bhopal based Tribal Research Institute (TRI) as well as to explore details published in professional journals. The Tribal Research Institute, established in 1957, has done significant research and survey work in the area of tribal development. Its publications can be grouped under three headings.

(1) Articles published in the Bulletin of Tribal Research and Development Institute;

(2) Impact studies conducted by the Institute which are available in report form; and

(3) Unpublished anthropological studies conducted on tribes.

So far as the journal is concerned, from 1990 to 2000 it has published 118 articles on tribal issues. 20 articles were published on the tribes of Chhattisgarh. The details are as under:

If we categorize these articles on the basis of issues covered, it is clear that most of the articles deal with either their social life, political life and health. This is clear from the following table:

Health/Disease/Medicinal Plants	4
Social Institutions/Organizations/Social Profile	6
Food/Nutrition	2
Education	1
Political Life	3
Development/Displacement	2
Total	*20*

Author	*Year*	*Title*	*Methodology used*	*Findings*
M. R. Goel	XIX (1&2), 1991	Specific Diseases among the tribes of Surguja regions	Simple impressionistic description of journalistic variety.	The study is based on tribes like Gond, Baiga, Kawar, Oraon, Pardhan, Mahar and Kaul living in the remote and dense forest villages of Surguja district. To them diseases are due to misfortune. Therefore, modern health practices are meaningless for them. For cure they are totally dependent on local traditional health managers.
Anju Goel	-do-	Tribes of Surguja District of M. P. and their medicinal plant	-do-	The study deals with special precaution taken by the tribes of Surguja district to collect about 34 variety ofherbs and medicinal plants. People depend more on the use of these medicinal plants and herbs for cure in comparison to modern medicine. It is used in three ways, i.e. vegetable, juice, dried mixture with water.
M. Y. Khan	XX (1&2), 1992	Marriage in Gadbas of Bastar	-do-	Gadbas have migrated to Bastar from Orissa. They follow settled marriage system. Marriage by elopment is still followed. They discourage marriage. with lower groups and encourage marriage with higher status tribe. Traditional panchayat still plays role in marriage settlement.
Aruna Palta	XXI (1&2), 1993	A study on the Food Consumption pattern and nutrient intake of the Oraons of Jashpurnagar	The study was conducted on 62 males and 46 females with the help of an interview schedule. Calorie, protein, mineral and vitamin intake were computed using standard tables. Additional information relating to	Objective of the study was to map food consumption pattern and nutrient intake among Oraon of Jashpur district. The study reveals undue preponderance of cereals in the diet of Oraons while some important food groups as milk, fats and oils, sugar, animal foods are grossly neglected.

			housing, ventilation, lighting, water supply, cooking practices, types of utensil used for cooking, kitchen facility, fuel used, kitchen garden, cattle rearing and poultry, etc, were collected with the help of semistructured interview schedule.	
U. S. Patnaik and P. Toppo	XXII (2), 1994	Employment for tribals through construction work in Pharsabahar Block of Jashpur Project, Raigarh	The study was conducted in Pharsabahar tribal block of Jashpur district to examine as to what extent the expenditure on construction work has generated employment for tribals. The time span of the study was 12 years, i.e. from 1979-80 to 1990-91. The data was collected from unpublished records, registers and annual reports of the block.	The findings reveal (a) that there is discrepancy between tribal and non-tribal wage rate. Former receive less than the latter; and (b) more money is spent in purchasing materials and less is spent as labour wage. Hence, construction projects provide employment to local tribals without improving their socio-economic status.
U.S. Patnaik and P. Toppo	XXIII (1), 1999	Impact of scholarship on tribal education in Jashpur project,	Purpose of the study was to know disbursement of pre-and post-matric scholarship and	The findings reveal that in spite of some delay, in many cases thousands of tribal students have availed scholarship facility but the quality of teaching is not upto the mark. The scheme has increased

		Raigarh District.	its impact on tribal students of Jashpur district. The period of study was from 1975-76 to 1989-90.	education and scholarship.
A. Palta, N. Sharma and M. Vishwakarma	XXIII (2), 1995	Socio-economic profile of the Kamars, a primitive tribe of M. P.	Of 2866 identified Kamar families residing in 249 villages, the study was conducted on 10% households (286) from 32 villages. 1355 persons were covered in the study Interview schedule and observation were the two techniques of data collection.	The study disclosed poor socio-economic condition of Kamar. Their education, housing and sanitary conditionis low. They do not have economic asset. Water supply is very poor. The study suggested effective planning for their development.
B. G. Singh	XXIII (1), 1995	Exposure to community development programms and development of locus of control	Purpose of the study was to know the interface between CDP and the tribals. 10 villages, i.e. 5 each from the limited exposure villages, participated in the study. 240 households from four different categories participated in the study. Locus of control scale was used to conduct the study.	The findings reveal (a) intense exposure led to greater internality than limited exposure; (b) unmediated group showed greater internality than mediated group; and (c) due to interaction of intensity and medication unmediated intense exposure group showed highest internality while other group showed lowest internality.

B. M. Mukherjee and N. Khatua	1996	Political Organization of Pandos in Surguja district	The study aimed to examine the traditional caste council of Pandos and its relationship with village panchayat as well as the nature of their integration with the state politics. The study was conducted in five villages of Surajpur Block of the district. Interview guide and participant observation were the two techniques of data collection.	Pandos have faith and admiration for their traditional panchayat. They approach the statutory panchayat for aid and material support but they go to caste panchayat for intra-group dispute.
O. P.Agrawal	XXIV (1&2), 1996	Primitive tribes and their development in Madhya Pradesh: A review study of Pahari Korba	Of the 7 Primitive Tribes in the undivided M.P., Pahari Korba is one among them. They live in the districts of Raigarh, Sarguja and Bilaspur of Chhatisgarh. The study was conducted in 10 villages, i.e. 2, 7 and 1 from the districts of Raigarh, Sarguja and Bilaspur respectively. Interview schedule, group interview, government registers were the instruments of data collection.	The study underlined the near failure of development projects by projecting that there is a lack of proper communication with the tribals, schemes were not proper, fund not adequate and timely inadequate response from tribes and improper execution of schemes. Accordingly development measures were recommended.

K. K. N. Sharma	XXV (1), 1997	Prevalence of protin calorie malnutrition among the tribal school children of Shankarpur and Churcha villages of Baikunthpur tehsil of Sarguja district.	To know the dimensions and magnitude of malnutrition among the school children (age 6-9 years, the study was conducted on 46 students of two schools of Baikunthpur tehsil of the district. The conclusion was drawn on the basis of measurement of weight and height.	The study revealed that of 46 children, 42 were suffering from malnutrition. The factors identified for this state of affair were lack of health awareness, health education, lack of health check-up and so on.
T. K. Vaishnav	XXV (2), 1994	Bhaina : A lesser known tribe of M. P.	Based on 1981 data/ information, attempt was made to describe their social and demographic life by following continuity and change model.	The author discussed the population of this tribe alongwith its origin, physical characteristics and language, clan and kinship, vital demographic events, economic life, political life and folk dance and song.
Indumati lakra	1997	Health status of women of Khairwar tribes of Surguja District	The study was conducted on 100 women from Kahirwar tribe of Wadraf Nagar Block of Surguja district. Purpose of the study was to know their health and nutritional status. Pre-tested questionnaire was the instrument of data collection.	The author observed that due to a number of local and outside factors, which are historical in nature, women have very poor health status. Author also suggested different measures to deal with all these historical constraints.

Arun Palta, M. Vishwakarma and N. Sharma	XXVI (1), 1998	Impact of nutrition and health education on the Kamars: A primitive tribe of Madhya Pradesh	The study was conducted on 286 households of Kamar belonging to 32 villages of Raipur district. Interview schedule consisting of 45 questions was used to collect data. Purpose of the study was to map their nutritional status, cooking practices and belief, immunization, hygiene and health and environmental sanitation.	The finding reveals that after availing health education programme their opinion favourably changed and their effort for achieving and retention of proper health status also increased. In short, the intervention had positive impact.
M. Y. Khan	XXVII (2)	Panchayats in the Murias of Bastar	By depending on secondary source information published from 1938 to 1975 the author discussed changing patterns of traditional panchayat system	The study reveals that in spite of increasing interation with the outside forces and significant change in the outside forces and significant change in the panchayat, even today going to court for dispute resolution is discouraged. Those who negate are citicized.
K. Chaubey	XXVII(2), 1999	Life Style and Avenues among Population of Bastar, M. P.	The study was conducted to capture various aspects of life with the help of field survey and personal observation.	The finding disclosed that tribals do not maintain cleanliness, they are kind hearted, they have special houses, follow eating festival, take different drinks, suffer from common diseases. To them illness is due to the will of god. They follow traditional practices to celebrate vital demographic events.
F. Mollick and B. M. Mukherjee	XXVII (1), 1999	Impact Displacement	The study was conducted in the Gevra Area of South Eastern Coal Field limited. 22 vilages were affected by this project.	Authors explained social and economic life of villagers before the introduction of this project and after the introduction in a comparative manner. They also suggested some precautionary measures for effective rehabilitation.

			The study is based on factual information and is journalistic in nature.	
A. Palta and M. Aghaniwanshi	XXVII(1), 1999	Anthropometric Profile of the Hill Korwas of Surguja district	The study was conducted on 294 males and 266 females (560) persons from 266 Korwa families belonging to 5 development blocks and 13 villages of the district. Respondents were selected with the help of simple random sampling method.	The findings reveal their poor nutritional status. Their height, weight, mid-arm circumference, BMI and relative body weight percentage values, though are comparable to the Kamar, but are much lower than their urban and rural counterpart. The study also suggested measures.
R. Biswas, P. K. Patra and A. K. Kapoor	XXVIII (1&2), 2001	Demographic Profile of Kamar: A Primitive Tribe of M. P.	Purpose of the study was to know various demographic variables of the Kamar. Interview of different types of respondent; was the main technique of data collection.	The findings reflect decreasing population size, high fertility, low age at marriage, high child mortality, poor sanitary condition and so on. The author suggested a detailed study to capture the reality.
K. R. Sharma	XXVIII (1 & 2) 2001	An Evaluation of Ashram schools in Madhya Pradesh	Objective of the study was to know status and functioning of Ashram schools in three districts of Chhatisgarh. Observation, interview, questionnaire and intefview schedules were the techniques of data collection. 12 schools were covered in the study.	Except library other required infrastructural facilities are available in these schools. However, the problem related to under utilization of resources, drop-out decreasing number of hostel inmates are there. Further the problem of quality is serious. Only 30% students could solve the basic mathematical questions.

Anthropological Studies

Between 1985 and 2000, 6 anthropological reports were prepared by the TRI of which 20 were conducted on different tribes or sub-tribes of Chhatisgarh. This included studies on tribes like Halwa, Dorla, Bison-Horn Maria, Hill Maria, Oraon, Abujmaria, Muria, Pahari-Korba, Raj Gond, Durwa, and so on. In most of these studies besides secondary sources, observation technique was used.

Impact Studies

From 1984 to 2000, 189 reports relating to impact studies were prepared by the TRI. About 50 reports were prepared on the tribes or sub-tribes of Chhattisgarh. Some of the specific issues covered in these reports are: tribal development through cooperative movement, impact of ICDS, drinking water project, impact of ITD, impact of Kamar Vikas Abhikaran, evaluation of welfare schemes. Impact of NGOs, functioning and impact of education promotion schemes. Impact of food for work, functioning of girls', hostel, development of Pahari Korba, education and scholarship, identification of area-specific diseases and number of its victims, impact of minor irrigation schemes, tribals in home-based cotton industry, indebtedness, and barter system.

Most of these studies are empirical with no links either with the model of development or socio-economic background of the conditions in the historical perspective, which led to the introduction of these schemes. Most of these studies lack cross-cultural and comparative analysis of the phenomenon. Further, these studies are based on semi-structured interview schedules with maximum concentration/dependence on data provided and experience shared by the local level bureaucracy. The sampling procedure adopted in conducting the study lacks depth and direction. From 1989 to 2007, 9 articles and observational notes relating to tribal questions were published in the *Economic and Political Weekly*:

(1) Bastar: Development and Democracy (1989) in two parts by PUCL.

(2) Forest Policy for Bastar: A Story of Tribal Exploitation (2003): B. K. Ganguly and K. Chaudhary.

(3) Physiognomy of Violence (2006): K. Balagopal.

(4) Poverty and Income Distribution in Rainfed and Irrigated Ecosystems (village studies in Chhatisgarh) (2000): A. Janaiah and others.

(5) The New Tribal States : Can They Survive in the Modern World? (2000): Daya Krishna.

(6) Open reply to Independent Citizens Initiative on Dantewada (2007): Ganapathi.

(7) Open Letters to Government and Maoists (2006): Independent Citizens Initiative.

(8) The Spring and its Thunder (2006): Sagar.

(9) Bastar, Maoism and Salwa Judum (2006): Nandini Sundar

The content analysis of these articles is as under:

The first article deals with the trauma of infrastructural development in Bastar and the complete lack of democratic values in the introduction of development work. It deals with exploitation of tribals by contractors and state functionaries. It also deals with the cases of atrocities on the tribes of Bastar. The second article deals with exploitation caused due to introduction and functioning of state-centric forest polícty in Bastar. It explains how the forest management practices led to erosion of bases of livelihood of tribals by the forest department. The third article deals with violence both by the state as well as the so-called Naxalite movement. The author has argued that in the midst of violence, erosion of human rights of tribals remained in practice since long. The fourth article is economic in nature based on case studies of some of the irrigated and rainfed villages and its impact on both poverty and income. The authors have concluded that other things remaining the same, the degree of income has increased in the irrigated villages and the degree of poverty has increased in the rain-fed villages. The fifth article deals with the question of the very survival of tribes with reference to their both material and non-material culture in an era of globalization when in the name of tribe the separate Chhatisgarh state was formed. The sixth contribution explains in greater detail the extent of exploitation and state violence against the so-called Naxalities.

The seventh contribution deals with an appeal by the ICI to both the government and Maoists to forget the process of retaliation and violence in the interest of poor citizens of Bastar. The eight contribution deals with the nature and magnitude of ongoing violence in Bastar. The ninth article shows how because of the introduction of Salwa Judum (peace restoration scheme) by the government there is confusion among all and instead of giving relief to the people it has contributed to rural violence. It is also an explanation of life conditions of those living in the camps organized by the government. It also deals with crime against women and violence against those who are still living in the villages and for practical reasons have not gone to the camps for so-called safety purposes.

IV

Conclusion

On the basis of description of some of the studies conducted either today or during the last some years, both by the students of sociology and social anthropology and others, it seems that the old trend of monographic study is now no more a dominant trend of research on tribes. Only few students of social anthropology are conducting monographic studies today. Most of the studies conducted today are interdisciplinary in nature. While sociologists and anthropologists study with emphasis on culture and social structure the other study political economy of tribal societies.

Most of the studies on tribal issues now deal with their conditions, impact and participation from the point of view of empowerment, human rights, and basic need approach. In the recent past, violence and its aftermath in Chhattisgarh have been studied by a significant number of researchers, most of whom are neither sociologists nor social anthropologists. With a change of priority area of research there is not only change in the disciplinary background of the researchers but also the methodology has changed significantly.

Interview schedule, case study and group discussion are the three main instruments to collect primary data. However, interview schedules of different types are used, viz. main schedule on households, perception of other villagers, institutional leaders at the village level (panchayat representatives, school teachers, health workers), NGOs, and change agents at the Block/Tehsil level. Unfortunately, most of the studies are descriptive in nature. Case study is still a very effective technique. But most often, it is constructed mainly with the support of properly filled interview schedule. In many cases such case studies lack depth and direction.

Group discussion (also know as FGD) is also organized in a formal manner using tape recorders to comprehend information relating to common issues. There is also an emerging trend, particularly among social work students, to use PRA technique for resource mapping among tribals. Except for issues of social movements and agrarian question, the use of history and "book view" are now missing.

Two approaches have emerged in the recent past to get government information. These are : through assembly question and through Right to Information Act. However, these two techniques are seldom used by the researchers. Staying for longer period in the field is now a thing of the past. Principal investigators make only occasional visits. Even Ph. D. scholars do not undertake long field visits. One of the reasons provided is that now the trend of tribal studies has moved much above the exploratory stage and huge qualitative and quantitative information are now available in print form. Internet facility has also contributed to this thinking. As a result most of the researchers do not feel essential to stay in the field for longer period as it was done in the past. Disappearance of language problem coupled with increasing degree of acculturation have also contributed to above thinking.

References

Land Reform Unit (2002): "A Report on Land Reforms in M. P.," in *Land Reforms in India* (ed.) P. K. Jha, Mussoorie: Lal Bahadur Shastri National Academy of Administration, Vol. 7.

Mandar, Harsh (2002): "Issues in the Opposition to Big Dams," in *Land Reforms in India, op. cit.*

Mukherjee, G. (1983): "Paper on Chhattisgarh at the First Workshop on Local History of Bhopal," Eklavya, Bhopal.

Roy, Dunu (2002): "Land Reforms, People's Movements and Protests" in *Land Reforms in India, op. cit.*

Sadgopal, Anil and S. B. Namra (eds). (1985): *Sangharsh aur Nirman: Shankar Guha Niyogi aur Unke Naya Bharat Ka sapna,* Delhi: Rajkamal.

Singh, Anup (2002): "The Land Question in Chhattisgarh," in *Land Reforms in Indian, op. cit.*

Sail, R. K. (2002): "People's struggle for Land–A Case Study," in *Land Reforms in India, op. cit.*

3

ANTHROPOLOGY OF NORTH BENGAL: An Appraisal

Sekh Rahim Mondal

The northern region of West Bengal is popularly known as North Bengal. It is the abode of several groups of people of diverse ethno-social backgrounds. They have been living in this place since time immemorial and largely integrated with their habitat. The place is the meeting ground of races, ethnicities and cultures. The Tibeto-Mongoloids, Indo-Mongoloids, Proto-Australoids, Indo-Aryans and many others as well as the mixture of them are the major inhabitants of North Bengal. Owing to racial, ethnic, social and cultural diversities of North Bengal, the place is regarded as the "living museum" and a natural laboratory of anthropologists and sociologists. As a matter of fact, the expert of human sciences have done commendable work among the peoples of this region. But unfortunately these works are not much known to the wider academic world. Moreover, the life ways of the peoples of North Bengal are changing very fast. Under such a situation the region demands more anthropological and sociological studies not only for documentation of vanishing cultures but also for information required for development of the peoples of this region.

Places and Peoples of North Bengal

The portion of West Bengal which spreads from the Ganges on the south and the Himalayas on the North is physically called North Bengal. This region consists of six districts, viz. Darjeeling,

Jalpaiguri, Cooch Behar, Uttar Dinajpur, Dakshin Dinajpur and Malda. The region covers the vast Himalayan and sub-Himalayan tract as well as Barind plains stretching over 21,332 sq. kms. It is surrounded by Bhutan, Nepal and Sikkim to the North, Bihar to the west, Assam to the east and rest of West Bengal and Bangladesh to the south. The region shares international borders of Bhutan, Nepal and Bangladesh and as a matter of fact has tremendous strategic significance.

There are three broad geo-ethnic zones within the region of North Bengal. These are hills, foothills and plains. The region of North Bengal is considered to be the place of floral, faunal, ethnic and cultural diversities. The hill areas consist mainly in Darjeeling Himalaya. The foothill areas comprise the entire Terai and Duars areas of Darjeeling and Jalpaiguri districts as well as parts of Cooch Behar district. The deltic or Barind plains consist of the districts of Cooch Behar, Uttar Dinajpur, Dakshin Dinajpur and Malda.

The region of North Bengal has a complex history. The place was ruled by the Palas, Kambojas, Khens, Kochs, Mohammedans, and many others. The influence of Tibet, Bhutan, Nepal, Sikkim and Assam was very crucial in social and cultural formations of North Bengal. The impact of British colonial rule was also conspicuous. The partition of India caused the immigration of a large number of Hindu Bengali refugee population from earlier East Pakistan (now Bangladesh) to several parts of this region. The immigrants from Tibet, Bhutan, Nepal and earlier Sikkim state were quite notable. A majority of these immigrants had settled permanently in this region and had shown a remarkable adaptive capability to this place. Virtually the peoples of North Bengal were less exposed to the outside world prior to the mid-nineteenth century. But the construction of railways since 1854, the growth of tea plantation in hills and foothills from 1874 to 1920, and the emergence of trade and commerce as well as gradual urbanization and development in various parts of north Bengal have caused the movement of several groups of people to this region from various parts of the country.

The six districts of North Bengal have a combined population of 1,47,24,940 as recorded in 2001 census. The average density of settlement in the region is as high as 690 persons per sq. km. There has been a tremendous growth of population in the region after independence of the country.

North Bengal is the abode of a number of colourful ethnic and social groups consisting of tribes, castes, regions, minorities and other ethnic communities which have been living in this place since historical times. The place is the meeting ground of different racial, social and cultural groups. Different ethnic and social groups live in North Bengal with their distinct cultures. Due to close interaction with each other, the people of this place have developed some common cultural traits, distinguishing them from the peoples of other regions. In the formation of ethnic and social groups as well as their cultures, some regions have greatly contributed since historic times. Tibet, Butan, Nepal and Sikkim contributed to the formation of peoples and cultures of hill areas of Darjeeling Himalaya. The South-East Asian region, more specifically the North-Eastern regions of India, contributed to the sub-Himalayan foothill places. Eastern Bengal, Bihar and Southern Bengal contributed to the plains (or Barind areas). The Tibeto-Mongoloids, Indo-Mongoloids, Indo-Aryans, Proto-Australoids and a mixture of them are the inhabitants of North Bengal. The indigenous peoples of North Bengal are mostly of *kirati* stock. The peoples of present North Bengal consist of tribal groups, caste groups, ethnic and linguistic groups as well as religious minorities. Among the peoples of North Bengal there are about 12 percent scheduled tribes, 34 percent scheduled castes, 22 per cent Muslims and 32 per cent other castes and communities.

The native born and other indigenous groups of North Bengal constitute four distinct categories based on their ethnic, social and cultural backgrounds. The mongoloid peoples of hill (Himalayan) areas are commonly identified as *paharias*, while the inhabitants of foothill (sub-Himalayan) areas are commonly regarded as *desias* and the early migrant Proto-Australoid tribal groups of tea plantations at *duars* and Terai areas are designated as *modesias*, while the immigrant *bangalis* of earlier East Pakistan who settled in the entire North Bengal region are commonly referred to as *bhatias* (Chaudhury 1998; Mondal 2006).

Social Anthropology and Sociology in North Bengal

Anthropological and sociological studies of North Bengal were initially started by some non-professional scholars followed by trained researchers of research institutes like Culture Research Institute of the Government of West Bengal, Anthropological Survey of India, Government of India, and Indian Statistical Institute, Government of India, and several universities located outside of North Bengal region. But the interest of studies on this region got a tremendous speed after the creation of the departments of (a) Sociology and Social Anthropology in 1976 under the leadership of Prof. Niren Chandra Chaudhury (since 2001 the department is renamed as Sociology); and (b) Anthropology in 2001 under the leadership of Professor Sekh Rahim Mondal. Both the former and the present faculties as well as the research scholars of the Department of Sociology and Anthropology have made valuable and significant contribution towards the study of peoples, societies and cultures of the region.

Through village and community study programmes on varied topics for preparation of master's dissertations, Ph.D. theses, and research projects, both the departments have initiated the trend of field studies on various groups living in North Bengal. The field studies conducted on rural and urban areas in different parts of North Bengal have created a data base in both the departments for studies and research. The faculties and scholars of anthropology and sociology disciplines associated with the Center for Himalayan Studies (created in 1978) of the University of North Bengal have also made a significant contribution towards empirical studies on various socio-cultural issues among the peoples of North Bengal, particularly on Himalayan and sub-Himalayan areas of this region. The departments of sociology, anthropology and the Centre for Himalayan Studies have laid the solid foundation of empirical studies on the peoples of North Bengal, although the initiation of which was started by a few freelance and outside professionals. In addition the works of some teachers and scholars of several other social science disciplines of the University of North Bengal deserve special mention as these studies have some sociological and anthropological significance in the context of this region.

Tribal Studies

In ethnographic studies on tribal communities of North Bengal the works of the scholars associated with the Cultural Research Institute (CRI) of the Government of West Bengal deserve appreciation. The

CRI scholars have done significant research and survey in the area not only on tribes but also on scheduled castes and other backward communities of this region. The works of CRI on tribal communities of North Bengal made a landmark by virtue of publication of some notable monographs. In addition to the scholars of CRI some other researchers have also worked on tribes of North Bengal on their own interests. The ethnographic studies of Das (1969) on Lepchas, Das and Raha (1967) on Rabhas, Roy Burman (1955) on Totos, Sanyal (1973) on Totos and Meches are still considered as classics to the students of anthropology and sociology. Roy Burman's famous concept of bridge and buffer was derived from the study of the Totos, a small tribe which lives on the borders of West Bengal and Bhutan.

Studies on Tea Plantation Workers of Hills and Plains

North Bengal is noted for its gardens located both in hills as well as in foothills and plains. In hills, the plantation labourers are mostly the tribes and castes of Nepalese origin, while in foothills and plains the tea garden labourers are exclusively the tribes of central Indian origin. There are some significant studies on tribal plantation labourers of North Bengal. Among these studies the works of Rai (2004) and Sharma (2000) in hills and Bhowmick (1981) and Bhadra (1997) on Plains deserve special mention.

Village, Peasant, Agrarian and Community Studies

In the areas of village, peasantry and agrarian studies in North Bengal, the works of Subba (1989) in hills and Chattopadhyay and Chatterjee (1984), Roychudhuri (1987), Som (2001), Taniguchi (1977), and Xaxa (1980) in the plains are most notable. In village and community studies in North Bengal, the most significant contribution was made by Sanyal (1965). His study of Rajbansis (a major scheduled caste community of North Bengal) is still considered as a handbook in ethnographic study. The village studies of Bogra district in the province of Bengal (which now belongs to Bangladesh) by Ramkrishna Mukherjee during the 1940s (published in 1971) is also very notable. Village studies conducted by Mukherjee clearly revealed the social situation of rural North Bengal of the late colonial era. North Bengal is inhabited by many religious communities. Mondal (1994, 1996, 1997) conducted several studies on Muslim minority of this region. His studies on Nashya Shaks (an indigenous and an OBC Muslim group) of North Bengal is a significant contribution in the field of community studies of this region. In recent times, some faculties and scholars in the department of anthropology and Centre for Himalayan Studies of the University of North Bengal have started work on some little known and small communities of North Bengal. The works on Dhimals by Biswas (2007) and Roy (1999), on Bhujels by Mollick (2005) and on Dhunias by Chatterjee (2007) need to be mentioned here.

Urban and Industrial Studies

The region of North Bengal is devoid of large scale industries, but its characteristic features are trade and commerce, and rapid urbanization. In urban studies in North Bengal, the works of Chaudhury (1985, 1988) and Mondal (1997) are notable. The works of Bhowmick (1996) and Bhadra (1992) on tea plantation labourers of North Bengal are very important.

Studies on Ethnic Identities and Socio-Political Processes

Due to geographical and strategic location and also for higher social complexities, the areas of North Bengal have witnessed several socio-political movements. The ethnic movements based on the issues of migration and immigration, land and agrarian questions including identity and social relations have been examined by some noted scholars. In the field of socio-political movements of North Bengal, the works of Bhadra and Bhadra (2007), Danda (1991), Misra (1985, 1986), Mondal (1988, 2000, 2007), Mukherjee (1992), Mukhopadhyay (1987, 1995, 2005), Sarkar (2000) and Subba (1999) are very important.

Gender Studies

Women and gender studies constitute an important field of studies in North Bengal. Bhadra (1992), Begum (1992, 1998), Mondal (2005), Roy (2005) and others have made notable contribution to this field.

Studies on Ethnic, Social and Cultural Matrix

Several significant studies have been conducted on social and cultural profile of the peoples of North Bengal as a whole or on some places of this region. The most notable studies on this important area have been conducted by Chaudhury (1999), Mondal (2000, 2006) and Mukhopadhyay (1999).

Studies on Cultural Syncretism

A few studies are available on the process of cultural and religious syncretism among the peoples of North Bengal. Among these studies the works of Mukhopadhyay (2003, 2006) and Mondal (1996) may be noted.

Development Studies

The positive and negative impacts of development programmes implemented in North Bengal region have also been examined (Biswas 1985, Chaudhury 2003, Chaudhuri 1982, Das 2007).

Studies on Refugees and Human Rights

North Bengal is a land where refugees from neighbouring states like Bangladesh and Tibet have settled down and got accommodated with the local situation (Roy 2001, Mondal 1998, 2001, Dutta 2001).

The students of the Department of Human Rights of the University of Calcutta, under the leadership of Professor Buddha Deb Chaudhuri, have conducted several significant studies on the issues of refugees and human rights of some places of North Bengal. In the University of North Bengal, Biswas and Bhattacharya (2003) have also contributed to this field.

Studies on Culture and Health

There are many significant studies on social and cultural dimensions of health care practices prevalent among various groups of people living in North Bengal. In this context the works of Bhadra (1997), Biswas and Bhattacharya (2007), Bagchi and Biswas (2005), Das (2007) and Tarafdar (2007) are important. Gerontological problems have also been highlighted by a few scholars. These studies have been able to set a solid foundation for the growth of medical anthropology in this region.

Studies on Bio-Social and Bio-Cultural Issues

Some scholars of the newly created anthropology department of the University of North Bengal have started to work on bio-social and bio-cultural aspects of the issues relating to food habits, nutrition and health condition of tribals of North Bengal. A few studies are also available on culture and reproductive health of women among some folk communities. In this respect, the works of Bagchi and Biswas (2005), Sen (2007), Sen and Ghosh (2007), and Mitra (2007) deserve special mention.

North Bengal is known in the academic circles of anthropology and sociology for two well known personalities of this region, namely Dr. Charu Chandra Sanyal and Dr. Benoy Kumar Sarkar. The social thoughts, ideas and works of these two noted scholars have a great relevance in shaping the anthropological and sociological researches of North Bengal. Two Chair Professor posts (one in the Centre for Himalayan Studies and another in the department of sociology of the University of North Bengal) are dedicated to and designated after the names of these two noted personalities.

Gaps and Scope

Due to ethnic, social and cultural diversities and also for several forces of change in North Bengal, the place is considered as the most virgin field for anthropological enquiry. Although several studies have already been conducted on various dimensions and issues on the peoples and societies of North Bengal, there are still wide gaps on certain issues of anthropological significance. Due to paucity of information and also for emerging situation more studies have to be conducted not only on new and emerging areas but also on topics that have already been touched upon. Future studies on the peoples of North Bengal have to be conducted not only for documentation of vanishing and emerging life ways of the regional population but also for the sake of planning policies for this region.

Following topics have been identified as the gaps and the most crucial areas of anthropological investigation from the point of view of regional significance. This is because of the fact that information on these fields is either meagre or not easily available. The suggested areas for urgent anthropological research are:

1. Study of tourism–problems, prospects and consequences.
2. Study of indigenous knowledge system and intangible cultural heritage of the region.

3. Study of forest, forest dwellers and biodiversity management.
4. Study of reserve forest, park and biosphere reserve in the context of indigenous rights.
5. Survey of border villages–conflicts, conflict resolutions and peace processes.
6. Study of border identities and inter-cultural dialogue.
7. Strategic studies and the study of human rights.
8. Study of new social formations and emerging social complexities.
9. Study of sustainable development and change–the role of government and non-government organizations.
10. Study of local artifacts and regional museum movements.
11. Study of AIDS epidemic and other emerging bio-social problems.
12. Study of women and gender issues.
13. Study of global local interface.
14. Study of identity, ethnicity and politics of culture.
15. Study of urban, rural and disaster management.
16. Study of aging and problems of elderly.
17. Analysis of fieldwork experiences and problems.
18. Study of linguistic, ethnic and cultural minorities.

Concluding Remarks

According to available information on social anthropological and sociological studies of North Bengal, it may safely be said that some notable ethnographic studies were conducted among the indigenous tribes and castes of this region. Some studies were also conducted on socio-cultural life of tribal and non-tribal tea plantation labourers living in plains and hills of North Bengal. The focus of these studies primarily was on economy and social organization of the concerned folk communities. In recent past, some young scholars devoted their attention to explore the socio-cultural life of some little known indigenous and marginalized groups of North Bengal with the objective to analyze the processes of detribalization and re-tribalization among them. Considerable studies were taken up on religious minorities (especially Muslims). Various aspects of the local Muslim society consisting of their social structure, problems of development, social processes and gender issues were taken into consideration.

The studies conducted by the scholars on the peoples of North Bengal were usually guided by the classical structure-functional or functional paradigm. However, in recent times there has been an awakening for the importance of subaltern, post-modern and reflexive perspectives to analyze regional societies. It is interesting to note that most of the studies conducted on the peoples of North Bengal were interdisciplinary in orientation to which an interaction between social anthropology, sociology and other social sciences was highly conspicuous. Hence, the studies on North Bengal regional societies and cultures were cross-disciplinary in character. Methodologically, a majority of the studies grew out of field investigations based on classical anthropological tools and techniques, like census survey, interview, case history, genealogy and observation. However, the studies that had been conducted in recent past were primarily based on survey work on the basis of interview schedules, focus group discussion and key informants interview. The classical holistic approach of micro-study has gradually been replaced by the study of sample households for the sake of macro perspective. The scholars involved in development studies relied more on PRA technique. Most of the earlier studies on North Bengal were based on long term intensive field investigation. But the studies of recent past are mostly completed through short term field work and occasional field visits. This may be due to the fact that contemporary studies have moved much above the exploratory stage. The scholars of recent times are not simply depending on field studies for the sake of their research data, rather they are more inclined to obtain information from internet and other secondary sources. The age old etic perspective is now been gradually shifting towards emic perspective. So far as the trends of studies is concerned, it is very clear that traditional descriptive and ethnographic studies of folk societies are now gradually been replaced by the analytical and problem oriented studies of complex societies. The contemporary studies are more focused emerging issues and problems which the people of several places of North Bengal have been facing in recent times.

It is to be admitted here that the anthropological studies on the peoples of North Bengal are still meagre. Hence, more studies have to be conducted for the sake of basic information required for academic necessities and also for regional and local policy formations. Some gaps in research have been identified not only in the emerging fields, but also in the fundamental areas of anthropological research. Several new areas of research on emerging issues have also been pointed out on the basis of their regional significance. Considering the unique geographical and strategic location of the place and also for socio-cultural peculiarities of the region, it is necessary to encourage the promising scholars to devote their attention on the study of peoples, societies and cultures of this region.

References

Bagchi, D., and Subir Biswas (2005), "Women in Stone Crushing–Aspects of Their Fertility Behaviour", Unpublished Research Project Report; Centre for Women Studies, University of North Bengal.

Begum, Rokaiya (1992), "Women in Muslim Society of Rural West Bengal", Unpublished Ph.D. thesis, Department of Sociology & Social Anthropology, University of North Bengal.

Begum, Rokaiya (1998), "The Social Situation of Muslim Girl Child in Rural West Bengal", ICCR Major Research Project Report, Department of Sociology & Social Anthropology, University of North Bengal.

Bhadra, R. K. (1997), *Social Dimensions of Health of Tea Plantation Workers,* Dibrugarh: N. L. Publications

Bhadra, R. K. and Mita Bhadra (eds.), (2007), *Ethnicity, Movement and Social Structure: Contested Cultural Identity,* Jaipur: Rawat Publications.

Bhadra, Mita, 1992, *Women Workers of Tea Plantation in India,* New Delhi: Heritage Publications.

Bhowmick. S. K. (1981), *Class Formation in Plantation System.* New Delhi: People's Publishing House.

Biswas, Saswati (1985), "Impact of Development Agencies on the Eastern Himalayas with Special Reference to the West Bengal Himalayas – A Study of Two Villages", Unpublished Ph.D. Thesis, Centre for Himalayan Studies, University of North Bengal.

Biswas, Samar Kumar and S. Bhattacharya (2007), "Health Situation among the Stone Crushers of Balason River Bed in Siliguri, West Bengal,

India", in B. Chaudhuri and S. Chowdhuri (eds.) *Health, Environment, Development and Other Essays– Anthropological Perspectives,* IUAES Inter-Congress, New Delhi, Inter India Publications. [A Publication of IUAES Inter- Congress].

Biswas, Samar Kumar and S. Bhattacharya (2005), "The Stone Crushing Women of Balason River Bed : An Appeal from Humanitarian Perspective", in A. Bhuimali (ed.) *South Asian Journal of Human Rights,* Vol. I, No. 1 & 2, pp. 141-157.

Biswas Subir (2007), "Anthropological Profile of the Dhimals of North Bengal", UGC Minor Research Project Report, Department of Anthropology, University of North Bengal.

Chaudhury, N. C., 1998, "Uttar Bange Janogosthi : Kristi-o-Sanskriti" (in Bengali), in *Bulletin of the Fifth West Bengal State Science Congress,* University of North Bengal.

Chaudhury, N. C. (2003), *Impact of Minor Irrigation Schemes in the Life of the Women in the Terai Region,* Report of the North Bengal Terai Development Project.

Chaudhury, Namita (1985), "Growth of Siliguri, A Study in Urban Migration", *Journal of the Indian Anthropological Society,* Vol. 20, No.1, pp. 13-31.

Chaudhuri, Namita (1988), "Urbanization in North Bengal–in the Post-Independence Period", Unpublished Ph.D. Thesis, Department of Sociology & Social Anthropology, University of North Bengal.

Chaudhuri, Namita (1999), "Darjeeling–Sikkim Himalayan Region: an Ethnographic Overview", *The Glimpses of the Eastern Himalayan Culture,* Kolkata, Centre for Communication and Cultural Action.

Chaudhuri, Buddhadeb (ed.), (1982), *Tribal Development in India: Problems and Prospects,* New Delhi: Inter India Publications.

Chatterjee, Rajib (2007), "Socio-Economic Profile of the Dhunias of Sub-Himalayan Darjeeling–Study of a Little Known Muslim Occupational Group (OBC) in West Bengal", *Islam and Muslim Societies* (in press).

Chattopadhyay, M. and Chatterjee, A.K. (1984), "Agrarian Relations in a North Bengal Peasant Movement Belt", *Man and Development,* Vol. 6, No. 2.

Danda, A.K. (1991), *Ethnicity in India,* New Delhi: Inter India Publications.

Das, A.K. (1969), "The Lepchas of West Bengal", *Bulletin of the Cultural Research Institute,* Special Series, No. 11, 1996.

Das, A.K. and M.K. Raha (1967), "The Rabhas of West Bengal", *Bulletin of the Cultural Research Institute,* Special Series No. 9.

Das, Samhita (2007), "Impact of Changing Health Care Policies and Rural Society: A Study in the Darjeeling Plains of West Bengal",

Unpublished Ph.D. thesis, Department of Anthropology, University of North Bengal.

Datta, K. and R. Chakraborty (2001), "Freedom in Exile: The Tibetan Refugees of India in Pursuit of Rights and Identity", in S. Roy (ed.) *Refugees and Human Rights*, Jaipur: Rawat Publications.

Misra, B. P. (1985), "Sannyasi Rebellion: Sociology and Economies of a Conflict in Sub-Himalayan Bengal", Occasional Paper, Centre for Himalayan Studies, University of North Bengal.

Misra, B. P. (1986), Behind Gorkhaland Agitation, *Mainstream*, 25:7, pp. 15-20.

Mitra, Kapil (2007), "Rajbansis of Darjeeling District in West Bengal–Some Dimensions of Nutrition and Health", Ph.D. Research Proposal, Department of Anthropology, University of North Bengal.

Mondal, Sekh Rahim (1994), *Dynamics of Muslim Society*, New Delhi: Inter India Publications.

Mondal, Sekh Rahim (1996), "The Nashyas of Sub-Himalayan Bengal", M.K.A. Siddiqui (ed.) *Marginal Muslims Communities in India*, pp. 73-89, New Delhi: Institute of Objective Studies.

Mondal, Sekh Rahim (1997(a)), *Educational Status of Muslims*, New Delhi: Inter India Publications.

Mondal, Sekh Rahim (1997(b)), *Muslims of Siliguri*, New Delhi: Institute of Objective Studies.

Mondal, Sekh Rahim (1998), "Immigration, Adaptation and Ethnicity: A Study of Refugees in Northern Districts of West Bengal", *South Asian Anthropologist*, Vol. 19, No. 2, pp. 71-78.

Mondal, Sekh Rahim (2000), "Ethnic Profile of Himalayas–Some Observations", *Science and Culture*, Vol. 66, No. 1-2, January-February.

Mondal Sekh Rahim (2000), "Tribal Profile of Himalayan and Sub-Himalayan West Bengal: Ethnicity and Emerging Identity" in S. Sengupta (ed.) *The Tribes of Eastern Himalaya*, New Delhi: Mittal Publications.

Mondal, Sekh Rahim (2001), "Tibetan Muslim Refugees in India: The Problem and Prospect" in S. Roy (ed.) *Refugees and Human Rights*, Jaipur: Rawat Publications.

Mondal, Sekh Rahim (2005), *Rural Muslim Women–Role and Status*, New Delhi: Northern Book Centre.

Mondal, Sekh Rahim (2006a), "Ethnic, Social and Cultural Matrix in the Hills and Plains of North Bengal", in Buddhadeb Chaudhuri and Sumita Chaudhuri (eds.) *Indigenous People, Traditional Wisdom and Sustainable Development*, New Delhi: Inter India Publications [A Publication of IUAES Inter-Congress, Vol. 4].

Mondal, Sekh Rahim (2006b), "Social and Cultural Dynamics of Indigenous People", *The Eastern Anthropologist*, Vol. 59, No.2, pp. 229-238.

Mondal, Sekh Rahim (2007), "Emerging Ethnic Identity Among the Nashya Shaik of North Bengal", in R.K. Bhadra and Mita Bhadra (eds.) *Ethnicity, Movement and Social Structure: Contested Cultural identity*, Jaipur: Rawat Publications.

Mallick, Gonesh Chandra (2005), "The Bhujels of Darjeeling Himalaya–A Bio-Social Study", Ph.D. Research Proposal, Department of Anthropology, University of North Bengal.

Mukherjee, Ramkrishna (1971), *Six Villages of Bengal*, Bombay: Popular Publication.

Mukherjee, P. N. and B. B. Sahoo (1992), "Agrarian Structure, Contradiction and Mobilization–A Framework for the Analysis of Emerging Rural Power", *Social Scientist*, Vol. 2, No. 9 & 10, Sep.-Oct., 1992, pp. 77-86.

Mukhopadhyay, R. S. (1987), "Uttar Khand Movement: A Sociological Analysis", Special Lecture, No. 8, Centre for Himalayan Studies, University of North Bengal.

Mukhopadhyay, R. S. (1995), "Socio-economic Transformation of the Rajbansis and Kamtapuri-Uttarkhand Movement in North Bengal", *Journal of the Indian Anthropological Society*, Vol. 30, No. 3.

Mukhopadhyay, R. S. 1999, "Social Counter of Darjeeling Hills", *The Glimpses of the Eastern Himalayan Culture*, Kolkata: Centre for Communication and Cultural Action.

Mukhopadhyay, R. S. (2003), "Adaptation and Blending of Religious Traits and Cultural Revivalism: The Rajbansis of North Bengal" in N.K. Das (ed.) *Culture, Religion and Philosophy*, Jaipur: Rawat Publication.

Mukhopadhay R. S. (2005), "A Note on the Cultural Background of Kamtapur Movement in North Bengal", R.K. Das and D. Basu (eds.) *North East India in Perspective*, New Delhi: Ananda Publishing House.

Mukhopadhay, R. S. (2006), "Fusion of Cults Among Some Indigenous Communities of Sub-Himalayan North Bengal", *Humankind*, Vol.2, 2006.

Rai, Indumati, (2004), *Women at Work in Cultural and Community Context: A Case From Darjeeling Tea Gardens*, Unpublished Ph.D. Thesis, Centre for Himalayan Studies, University of North Bengal.

Roy, Ranjit Kumar (1999), "The Dhimals– A Little Known Community of Sub-Himalayan Bengal: An Ethnographic Overview", Unpublished M.Phil. Dissertation, Centre for Himalayan Studies, University of North Bengal.

Roy, Sanjoy (2001), "Stateless World of Bengali Refugees: A Question of Rights", S. Roy (ed.) *Refugees and Human Rights*, Jaipur: Rawat Publications.

Roy, Sanjoy (2005), *Tribes– Education and Gender Question*, New Delhi: Northern Book Centre.

Roy Burman, B. K. (1959), "Dynamics of Persistence and Change of a Small Community–The Totos", Unpublished Ph.D. Thesis, University of Calcutta.

Roychaudhury, T. K. (1987), "Land Control, Class Structure and Class Relations in Western Duars (1871-1905)", *Journal of the Asiatic Society of Bangladesh*. Vol. XXXII, No. 1, pp. 23-49, June.

Sanyal, Charu Chandra (1965), *Rajbansis of North Bengal*, Calcutta: The Asiatic Society Publication.

Sanyal, Charu Chandra (1973), *The Meches and Totos-Two Sub-Himalayan Tribes of North Bengal*, University of North Bengal, Darjeeling.

Sen, Jaydip (2007), "Health, Disease and Nutritional Status Among the Rajbansis of North Bengal– An Anthropological Study", UGC Major Research Project Proposal, Department of Anthropology, University of North Bengal.

Sen, Jaydip and Amit Ghosh (2007), "Prevalence of Hypertension Among Santal Individuals Addicted to Alcohol–A Study at Dakshin Dinajpur", *Journal of Human Ecology* (in Press).

Sarkar, Satahsiddha (2000), 'Ethnicity, Community and Identity: A Study of Gorkha Land Movement in Darjeeling Hills", Unpublished M.Phil. Dissertation, Centre for Himalayan Studies, University of North Bengal.

Sharma, Khemraj (2000), *The Himalayan Tea Plantation Workers*, Dibrugarh: N.L. Publications.

Som, Bijoybihari (2001), "Agrarian Social Structure–A Case Study of Some Villages of Cooch Behar, West Bengal", Unpublished Ph.D. Thesis, Department of Sociology & Social Anthropology, University of North Bengal.

Subba, T.B. (1989), *Dynamics of Hill Society: Nepalese of Darjeeling and Sikkim Himalayas*, New Delhi: Mittal Publications.

Subba, T.B. (1999), *Politics of Culture: A Study of Three Kirata Communities in the Eastern Himalayas*, New Delhi: Orient Longman Limited.

Taniguchi, S. (1977), *Agrarian Structure of North Bengal*, Unpublished Ph.D. thesis, University of Calcutta.

Tarafdar, Pinak (2007), 'Health Development: Displacement of Traditional Culture", in B. Chaudhuri and S. Chaudhuri (eds.) *Health Environment; Development and Other Essays: Anthropological Perspectives*, New Delhi: Inter India Publications, [A Publication of IUAES Inter-Congress].

Xaxa, V. (1980), "Evolution of Agrarian Relations in Jalpaiguri", *Sociological Bulletin*, March.

4

ANTHROPOLOGICAL RESEARCHES IN JHARKHAND

Vijoy S. Sahay

At the very outset, I would like to state that this paper is neither an exhaustive account nor a complete record of all the researches of anthropological nature relating to the newly carved out state of Jharkhand. Rather, in this cyber age, it is not even possible to do so. A couple of days before, I attempted to search in the website about the recent articles and books written on the tribes and castes of Jharkhand. To my utter surprise, I found ninety-four thousand five hundred references. There were articles written by scholars of all disciplines, including anthropologists. There were articles written by scholars of whom I had never heard. Many such articles were presented in different international conferences at different places in the world; to name only a few, for example, the articles written by Stuart Carbridge, S. Sewell, S. Devalle, R. Zone and K. Thangaraja presented at Syracuse University, U.S.A. After going through several articles on the tribes of Jharkhand in the website, I wondered that perhaps the foreign scholars were more interested in the study of tribesmen of Jharkhand than the scholars of our universities and research institutions; though, I am a little skeptical of the ulterior motive of many such writers, of whom I have discussed in the later part of this article. After my browse into the Internet, I thought that to take a complete stock of all the anthropological literature relating to Jharkhand tribes and castes was a difficult task, if not impossible.

Therefore, when I received a call from Professor Sachchidanand to attend the conference relating to the aforesaid theme, I thought that owing to time limitation, instead of presenting a quantitative account of the entire anthropological literature available on Jharkhand, I would better interpret the trends of anthropological researches in Jharkhand in three phases; first, during the pre-independent era, secondly, from 1950s to 1976, and thirdly, post 1976 researches. Why I choose to present the post-1976 anthropological researches on Jharkhand, because the exhaustive account of almost all the researches done before 1976 on the tribes and castes of India in general, and Bihar or Jharkhand in particular, have been furnished by late Professor L.P. Vidyarthi in two of his significant books, viz, *The Tribal Culture of India* (1976) and *The Rise of Indian Anthropology* in two volumes (1977). Whereas *The Tribal Culture of India* specifically deals with tribal studies, both the volumes of the *Rise of Indian Anthropology*, besides the tribal and caste studies, cover various other dimensions of anthropological researches in the country. Professor Vidyarthi wrote and edited more than 50 books and, hundreds of articles in national and international journals. He is better known by the concepts of *sacred complex* (1961) and *nature-man-spirit complex* (1963); however, I consider the aforesaid two books as the most valuable contributions of Professor Vidyarthi to Indian anthropology.

The state of Jharkhand, with its headquarters at Ranchi, has twice led the anthropological researches in the country. It has been the home and the workplace of two veteran anthropologists of international repute, namely S.C. Roy and L.P. Vidyarthi. Besides Vidyarthi and Roy, it has produced yet another doyen in Indian anthropology of the same caliber and repute, namely, Professor Sachchidananda. While Roy is remembered as the *father of Indian ethnography/anthropology*, Professor Sachchidananda laid the very foundation of anthropological teaching and researches at the university level in Ranchi; first, as the founder Head of the Department of Anthropology, Ranchi (then Bihar University) and later, as the Director of two premier research institutions of the state of Bihar, viz., Bihar Tribal Research Institute at Ranchi and A.N. Sinha Institute of Social Studies at Patna, respectively.

It was Professor Sachchidananda who first sowed the seeds of anthropological teaching and researches in Jharkhand. The seeds of anthropological learning sown by him sprouted in the anthropologically fertile soil of Jharkhand. In course of time, it assumed the form of a great banyan tree with hundreds of roots under which Professors A. B. Saran, K. N. Sahay, B. N. Saraswati, Narayan Mishra, V. S. Upadhyay, and many others flourished and contributed to anthropology. S. C. Roy, L. P. Vidyarthi, and Sachchidananda, with a band of disciples, brought to light many of the hitherto unexplored fields of tribal and rural life and culture.

While Roy focused his attention on the tribes of Chotanagpur and the adjoining states of Orissa, Madhya Pradesh and Bengal, Vidyarthi's interest ran throughout the length and breadth of the country, i.e. from the sacred complex of Rameshwaram in the south to the Khasa (Jaunsar Bawar) of the Himalayas in the North and from the tribes of the state of Meghalaya in the east to the sacred city of Dwarka in the west. His manifold anthropological interest went as far as to the island culture of Andaman and Nicobar archipelago. If Roy brought international repute to India by being a member of Council d' Honour of the International Congress of Anthropological and Ethnological Sciences (I.C.A.E.S.), Vidyarthi's selection as the President of the Tenth I.C.A.E.S. and I.U.A.E.S. (International Union of Anthropological and Ethnological Sciences) from 1973 to 1978, marked the advent of a new era in Indian anthropology. However, the basic differences among these three geniuses of Indian anthropology lie in their intellectual background and general anthropological outlook.

From 1898 till his death in 1942, Roy lived in Ranchi. By profession he was a lawyer yet he was a self-styled anthropologist. In course of his ethnographic works, he came in contact with British social anthropologists like Sir James Frazer, W.H.R. Rivers, A.C. Haddon and many others. Therefore, Roy's researches in anthropology reflected the British influence. The greatest contribution that Roy made to Indian anthropology was his persistent persuasion to Sri Ashutosh Mukherjee to initiate anthropological teaching at the University of Calcutta in 1920. It would not be an exaggeration to say that it was at the behest of Roy that the teaching of anthropology first began in the country. It may be considered as a landmark in the history of social sciences in India. Today, Roy is remembered as a meticulous monographer, author of several papers, editor of an epoch making anthropological journal, *Man in India,* and also as a teacher and supervisor in anthropological researches. It was Roy who initiated several professional anthropologists, including late D.N. Majumdar into ethnographic studies of several tribes of Jharkhand and Orissa.

Thus, Roy dominated the Indian anthropological scene for over three and a half decades. However, we find that his work was purely of monographic nature and in line with colonial anthropology. He did not initiate any conceptual framework in his anthropological investigation. It was, perhaps, so because he lived at a time when anthropology in India was still in infancy. The diversification and proliferation of the discipline had not taken place in the country. Nevertheless, living in a small town like Ranchi in Jharkhand, Roy laid down the foundation of anthropological researches in the country. Besides his book, *The Munda and their Country* in 1912 and the journal *Man in India* in 1921, Roy wrote several monographs and papers on the Oraons, the Birhors, the Bhuinyas and the Kharias.

Vidyarthi received initial anthropological training under D.N. Majumdar in Lucknow. He joined the Department of Anthropology in 1953. He soon left for Chicago, from where he obtained his doctorate. In America, he worked with Julian Steward, Robert Redfield, Sol Tax, and many others. Therefore, we find that initially Vidyarthi seems to have been influenced by American anthropology. His concepts very clearly reflect the influence of the Chicago School of Anthropology. However, in his later years, Vidyarthi emphasized *Indianness* in social sciences in general, and anthropology in particular. In his Presidential Address, during the Tenth I.C.A.E.S. in 1978 in New Delhi, he said, "India's ancient scriptures like the *Vedas,* the *Upanishads,* the *Puranas,* and the other great epics provide sensitive insights into social realities. Therefore, the Indianness in social science has to emerge with a proper appraisal of these ancient texts, whose influences on the behavioural patterns of our countrymen cannot be neglected". To quote him further: "These ancient scriptures reflect the wisdom and provide guidelines for shaping the socio-cultural life in India. The patterns of *nature-man* relationship, *man-man* relationship, and *man-spirit* relationship are explained in great depth. The basic elements of Indian lifestyle in their traditional practice of the four *ashramas,* four *purusharthas,* and sixteen *sanskaras,* etc., still continue to influence the ethos, worldview, and the life of an average Indian. *Dharma* (wrongly translated as religion) is the first of the four fundamental principles of social ethics of man in the form of *purushartha*, which literally means '*the meaning of man*' or '*the aim of being man*'. The other three principles are *artha* (wealth), *kama* (desire), and *moksha* (salvation). It is man's duty to fulfill the first three in order of priority and live with purity to achieve the last".

The above quote from his presidential address during the Tenth I.C.A.E.S. suggests that Vidyarthi focused his attention on different aspects of tribal life, including the impact of industrialization, tribal politics and leadership in Jharkhand. On the other hand, at the macro-level, his researches covered the geographical, philosophical, cultural, and religious aspects of entire India. Vidyarthi made Ranchi his home from 1953 till his death in 1985.

Another doyen of Indian anthropology, Professor Sachchidananda began his career from Ranchi. First, he founded and headed the Department of Anthropology, Bihar University, and then headed the Bihar Tribal Research Institute, both at Ranchi. Finally, he joined and headed the A.N. Sinha Institute of Social Sciences at Patna. During this period he carried out a large number of projects relating to change in tribal culture, agrarian studies, education, woman studies, etc. Though I have not extensively gone through his entire works, as I understand, all his works can be attributed to the rubric 'Changing Dimensions of Social Anthropology in India'. For five decades he has extensively toured every nook and corner of Chotanagpur and Santhal Pargana. Professor Sachchidananda has his home in Patna; however, I understand he is the most versed scholar today on the tribes of Jharkhand.

His first book was a study of culture change among the Munda and the Oraon. It detailed changes in living condition, the dynamics of tribal economy, patterns of family and marriage, folk beliefs, religion, the impact of community development and tribal panchayats. The book attracted a great deal of attention at that time since it had culture change as a distinctive focus.

His next book entitled *The Tribal Village in Bihar* was not a village study in the traditional sense. The author tried to explore the extent to which the tribal village could be viewed both as a unity and its extensions in various fields. It was not a study of an isolated community, the village was being transformed into a part of society interacting vigorously with its neighbourhood. The entire social process was analyzed in the background of the history of the region extending over a century. The third book was a restudy of the Munda. The author's attention was not only on the themes covered by S.C. Roy. It included the concerns of contemporary social anthropology.

Since Chotanagpur is fast becoming the centre of industrial enterprises, Professor Sachchidananda along with Dr. B.B. Mandal studied the impact of industrialization in areas close to Ranchi and Jamshedpur. The problem was whether industrialization has created disorganization in tribal society. Although there was a loosening of tribal solidarity and weakening of family ties and the traditional mechanism of social control and appearance of such maladies as beggary, prostitution and juvenile delinquency, the tribal can still be distinguished from others. He has not been dissolved in the mass society. They have maintained a distinctive identity. People have adjusted their social system with the industrial ethic. They have made peace with the new order. This is a tribute to their resilience of tribal society in the vortex of change.

Out of a large mass of anthropological writings on Jharkhand, I believe the landmark publications are as follows: *The Munda and their Country* (1912), and the journal *Man in India* (1921) by S.C. Roy; *A Tribe in Transition: A Study in Culture Pattern* (1937) by D.N. Majumdar; *Encyclopedia Mundarica* (1912) by Father Hoffman; *Sacred Complex of Hindu Gaya* (1961) and *The Maler: A Study in Nature-Man-Spirit Complex* (1963) by L.P. Vidyarthi; *Under the Shadow of the Cross* (1976) by K.N. Sahay, and *The Changing Munda* (1979) by Professor Sachchidananda. In this connection, mention of three other scholars may also be made, first W.G. Archer's *Blue Grove and the Dove,* and *The Leopard* that contains Oraon poetry, and *Hill of Flute* that deals with the Santhal life and culture that Archer saw in mid 1940s. K.K. Leuva, Assistant Commissioner of Scheduled Castes and Tribes, Bihar, also published a book on the Asur in 1963. Lastly, I would like to mention the book of Kumar Suresh Singh, *Dust Storm and Hanging Mist: The Study of Birsa Munda and His Movement* (1966). While discussing the landmark books and articles on Jharkhand and its tribes, mention can be made of hundreds of articles published in the *Journal of Social Research* edited by Vidyarthi and the *Bulletin of Bihar Tribal Research Institute* (B.T.R.I.). The B.T.R.I. also published *Land and People of Tribal Bihar* (1964), *Life and Times of Birsa Bhagwan* (1954) and report on *Land Alienation in Chotanagpur, Culture Change Studies on Chero and Paharia Tribes*, etc.

A.B. Saran made a detailed study of murder and suicide among the Munda and the Oraon. It was not only a statistical analysis of murder, suicide and human sacrifice but also of the motives of tribals, the role of police, lawyers and the judiciary in dealing with these problems. Manohar Lal studied the recruitment network attitude and perception of the Munda elite and their role in social transformation of their own society. Mohan Kumar Gautam studied the Santhal in two villages of Santhal Paragana. His main focus was the search by the Santhal for an identity of their own community. The Santhal society was able to maintain its social organization, religion, mechanism of social control, although it was surrounded by a number of Hindu castes. They have been able to achieve integration with the wider society while preserving their distinctiveness and identity. Some fresh light has been thrown on the Oraon in two books published by Abhik Ghosh. In the first study published in 2002, he explores the aspects of symbols and the philosophy behind the use of particular theoretical approaches. The symbols are grounded in their everyday life. The ethnography of the Oraon is seen through this lens. The world view inherent in such reinterpreted multivocal symbols is then visualized as a valid possibility used in decision making. In his second book, the author expands his theoretical approach to include fifteen villages in three districts.

After 1976, the important books that have appeared are *The Chero of Palamau* (1978) by B. Mukherjee et. al.; *The Passing Scene in Chotanagpur* (1988) by P. Das Sharma; *Santhals: Religion and Rituals* (1987) by A.B. Chaudhury; *Jharkhand Movement* (1994) by Sajal Basu; *Birjiya; Society and Culture* (1994) by Sameera Dasgupta; *Santhali: A Look into Santhali Morphology* (1994) by T. Hembrom; *Folklore of the Santhal Parganas* (2001) by Cecil Henry Bombas; *Documentation of Jharkhand Movement* (2004) by William Ekka and R.K. Sinha; the *Chik Baraik of Chota Nagpur* (2005) by Shyamal K. Nandi and a book in Hindi about *Ethnomedicine of Oraon* by Birendra Toppo in 2006.

If we examine the trend of anthropology literature on the tribes and castes of Jharkhand (or for that matter Bihar), we find it can be broadly divided into four phases. Firstly, the British administrators like Dalton, Risley, O'Malley, Bradley-Birt and Bainbridge, P.O. Bodding, etc., wrote on the tribes and castes of the region. It is generally believed that these British scholars-cum-administrators studied the indigenous and local people and their culture with a motive to understand them in order to consolidate their colonial rule. Whatever may have been the ulterior motive of the British administrators, it is no denying the fact that their books and articles still serve as baseline data on the respective tribes and castes.

The second phase of anthropological researches in India in general and Jharkhand in particular began with the entry of S.C. Roy with his monumental work, *The Munda and their Country* in 1912.

Then India achieved independence. After independence, the teaching of anthropology started proliferating in various universities of the country. The first generation of anthropologists after independence, like Professor L.P. Vidyarthi and some others received training in America, and the impact of American anthropology was felt in India. Because of Vidyarthi, it was mostly felt in Jharkhand. A series of studies on *nature-man-spirit-complex* and *sacred complex* on the tribes and religious places of Jharkhand were done by the scholars, mainly from the Department of Anthropology, Ranchi University. These works are of pure anthropological nature. During this period, the works done by the Bihar Tribal Research Institute and the A.N. Sinha Institute of Patna are also academically of great sociological and anthropological interest.

Post-Vidyarthi period in Jharkhand also witnessed tremendous social, cultural and political upheavals. The demand for a separate sate of Jharkhand began to take shape as a violent movement. The divide between the tribal and non-tribal worlds widened considerably. The Christian missionaries began to proselytize tribesmen. The influx of population from outside caused demographic imbalance in the region. The migrants outnumbered the locals. Because of unemployment, the tribesmen began to migrate to Punjab, western U.P. and other states. Gradually, a fertile ground for the emergence of extremism got ready in the soil of

Jharkhand. On the one hand, greater potential of natural and mineral resources was realized, on the other hand, discontentment among the local tribal and non-tribal people was smoldering.

Under the above circumstances, the tribal studies in Jharkhand also took a turn. A number of highly educated tribal leaders attended the conferences organized by the Indigenous Population Group, an internationally organized forum. They began to launch movements in favour of the Indian tribesmen to be considered as indigenous population; and they demanded not merely tribal autonomy but to the extent that the right of self-determination may be granted to them. A number of such writings by motivated scholars could be found today in the form of books and articles. Such literature on Jharkhand tribes has been serving as a disintegrating factor in Jharkhand life and culture.

In a recent seminar, which I attended, I could see the separatist flavor and elements in the writings of many scholars. Their papers, in my opinion, were prejudiced against the non-tribesmen living in Jharkhand. Incidentally, this seminar was also attended by a number of anthropologists from Kolkata, Ranchi, and other places. There are a few well-known anthropologists also, who write such provocative books and articles in order to gain political mileage. Such writings neither serve the purpose of anthropology nor of academy. After 1980s, a flood of such books has appeared on Jharkhand.

There is yet another trend of writing books and articles on Jharkhand tribes by tribesmen themselves. Such tribal scholars, in order to assert their identity and to boast of their glorious past, either distort their history, or without any evidence, make a conjectural history about the migration of their group. A couple of weeks before, I came across one such book by Sri Joseph Kandulna on Munda tribe. According to his book, Mundas belonged to the Middle East. They were the architects of the Egyptian, Mesopotamian and the Indus Valley civilizations. Because of incessant Aryan invasions, they took resort in the woods of Jharkhand. Such books have gained enormous popularity in Jharkhand.

The need of the hour is to re-establish the tradition of anthropological studies in Jharkhand. It is no denying the fact that the situations in which the founding fathers of anthropology in

Jharkhand worked have completely changed now. It is not very easy and safe to work continuously in the interiors of Jharkhand, especially in Chotanagpur. One cannot stay with a team for a very long period in rural or tribal areas because of the menace of extremism. But anthropologists have always devised new strategies for anthropological researches. For example, during the Second World War, when the American and European anthropologists where forbidden to go to the Pacific or the African nations for researches, they adopted the methods of study of culture at distance.

Indian anthropologists in general and anthropologists interested in the study of Jharkhand in particular must also pay attention to it. I would like to mention one or two cases in this connection. A couple of years back, I sent one of my research scholars to Betla National Park in Palamau and Mahuadar area of Netarhat. His topic of research was wildlife vis-à-vis tribal life. He had hardly spent a week in the field when one day he was intercepted by the activists of the People's War Group (PWG). With great difficulty he was able to convince them that he had no other motive of his visit, but academic. However, he was so scared that he left Betla National Park and came to Mahuadar. On the second night of his arrival, he was intercepted by the members of the MCC (Maoist Coordination Committee) group. Ultimately, he left the field and stayed for a couple of days in Daltonganj, and only through the secondary sources collected data and completed his thesis. Though he was finally awarded the degree, such a work would definitely lack the quality.

Under such circumstances, teamwork in Jharkhand appears to be difficult. Even the Department of Anthropology, Ranchi University, prefers to do fieldwork in other states than in Jharkhand. Barring a few districts, the entire Jharkhand has been reeling under the influence of extremists. It poses a challenge to anthropologists to study the causes and the extent of extremism prevailing in the state, and also measures for its amelioration.

Such social and political atmosphere of the state has been giving shelter to such writers who advocate separatism and are opposed to any developmental plans of the government. I experienced it in a recent seminar at Chaibasa, referred to earlier. I found that most of the papers presented in the seminar were of negative nature.

They were either against the developmental plans in Jharkhand or the presence of non-tribesmen in the state.

Anthropologists should not merely be mute and passive spectators of such phenomena. It is also their task and the ethics of their discipline to point out the negative forces operating in society and culture. If they refrain from doing so they would prove themselves to be escapists. The state of Jharkhand has been undergoing unprecedented changes. After the formation of the state, it enjoys the maximum amount of natural and mineral resources in the country. It is home of 32 tribal groups, ranging from gathering and hunting economy to shifting cultivation and intensive agriculture. In spite of education, development of the means of communication, and proselytization to Christianity, it still maintains the colorful tribal life and culture. Though Jharkhand has never been a 'seat of power' at the national level, there are a number of anthropological sites that require proper study and preservation.

There is a lot of scope for ethno-archaeological and fundamental researches in social and cultural anthropology in Jharkhand. For example, one such study being conducted under my supervision is of 'Munda and their Killis'. Over twenty-five years back, I was sent by Professor Vidyarthi to study the *sasandiris* of the Mundas in Torpa area. I was struck to know that only the clan members received a place in the *sasan* of the Mundas. Ever since then it was in my mind to examine the clan system of the Munda, and how the clan organization was conterminous with its territorial organization. This work is in progress and one of my research scholars, Neeraj Kumar Thakur, has mapped out the territories of sixteen major clans. We have planned to carve out a *killi* map of the Mundas on a geographical map of the region.

Customary laws of the tribesmen need to be studied and defined. We should be aware that the customary law happens to be in existence for hundreds or thousands of years. Such customary laws emerge under certain ecological, economic and technological levels of the group. Obviously, ecology, economy, and technology have witnessed unfathomable changes during the past few decades in Jharkhand. Now the question arises, whether the same customary laws are still useful for the tribesmen? It is a moot question. Restudy of such laws is needed.

In this connection, I would also like to point out that the tribal movements that took place should also be objectively restudied. It has been found that a number of such movements in tribal areas have been depicted, particularly by the historians, as freedom struggles, or wars for independence against the British. What I presume is that at least some such movements against the British were merely because of the clash of the concept of property between the British and the tribesmen, and not because of any overwhelming sense of patriotism among the tribals. The tribesmen, particularly the Mundas, held communal property. The land and forest of a village belonged to all the members of the clan. On the contrary, the British had the concept of individual property. After establishing their rule when they started land survey and a particular piece of land was allotted to particular individual, it certainly disturbed the mind of the tribesmen, which ultimately resulted into revolts and movements.

I would also like to draw your attention to totem and totemism among the tribes of Jharkhand. Recently, I was working in the Munda area. All the Mundas I found were well aware of their clans, but they had little concept of totemism. They did not seem to attach any observance or significance, especially the youngsters, to their totems. Needless to say, the Mundas have totemistic clan organization. This suggests that there is a need to study the Jharkhand tribes with a viewpoint of continuity and change. Finally, I would like to suggest that there are innumerable archaeological sites scattered all over Jharkhand. They need our attention, preservation, and documentation. Thus, besides anthropological studies there is a lot of scope for historical, archaeological and ethno-archaeological studies in Jharkhand.

References

Basu, Sajal (1994), *Jharkhand Movement*, Indian Institute of Advanced Studies, Simla.

Bihar Tribal Research Institute, Ranchi (1954), *Life and Times of Birsa Bhagwan*.

Bombas, Cecil Henry (2001), *Folklore of the Santhal Parganas*.

Chaudhury, A. B. (1987), *Santhals: Religion and Rituals*, Anthropological Survey of India, Kolkata.

Dasgupta, Sameera (1994), *Birjiya: Society and Culture*, Firma Klem, Kolkata.

Das Sharma, P. (1988), *The Passing Scene in Chotanagpur.* Anthropological Survey of India, Calcutta.

Ekka, William and R. K. Sinha (2004), *Documentation of Jharkhand Movement,* Anthropological Survey of India, Kolkata.

Gautam, M. K. (1977), *In Search of an Identity: The Case of the Santhals of Northern India.* Leiden.

Gautam, M. K. and A. K. Singh (eds.) (1986), *L.P. Vidyarthi: Contributions to the Development of Anthropology.* Concept Publishing Company, New Delhi.

Ghosh, Abhik (2002), *History and Culture of the Oraon.* Mohit Prakashan, Delhi.

——(2006), *The World of the Oraon.* Manohar, Delhi.

Hembrom, T. (1994), *Santhali: A Look into Santhali Morphology,* Anthropological Survey of India, Kolkata.

Hoffmann, John and A. V. Emelen (1950), *Encyclopedia Mundarica.* Patna: Government Printing Press.

Lal, M. (1983), *Munda Elites.* Amar Prakashan, Delhi.

Majumdar, D. N. (1937), *A Tribe in Transition.* Longman Green & Co., Calcutta.

——(1950), *Affairs of a Tribe,* Universal Publishers, Lucknow.

Mukherjee, B. *et al.* (1978), *The Chero of Palamau,* Anthropological Survey of India, Kolkata.

Nandi, Shyamal K. (2005), *Chik Baraik of Chota Nagpur,* Anthropological Survey of India, Kolkata.

Oraon, P. C. (2004), *Land and People of Jharkhand.* Ranchi; J.T.W.R.I.

Porteous, Shelley (1986), *Experiencing Vidyarthi:* In *L.P. Vidyarthi: Contribution to Development of Anthropology,* by M.K. Gautam and A.K. Singh (eds.).

Roy, Sarat Chandra (1970), *Munda and Their Country.* Bombay: Asia Publishing House. (First published in 1912 from City Bar Library, Ranchi)

Sachchidananda (1979), *The Changing Munda.* Concept Publishing Company, New Delhi.

——(1964), *Culture Change among the Munda and Orason.* Bookland, Calcutta.

——(1968), *The Tribal Village in Bihar.* Munshiram Manoharlal, Delhi.

——(1984), *Industrialization and Social Disorganisation.* Concept Publishing House, New Delhi.

Sahay, K. N. (1976), *Under the Shadow of the Cross.* Calcutta: Institute of Social Research and Applied Anthropology.

Sahay, Vijoy S. (1981), In Search of Ranchi School of Anthropology. In L.P. Vidyarthi and V. S. Upadhyay (eds.), *The Development of Anthropological Researches in India.*

Sahay, Vijoy S. (1988), My Guru As I Saw Him. *South Asian Anthropologist,* Vol. IX (I), Ranchi.

Sahay, Vijoy S. (1988), My Guru As I Saw Him. (Revised). *The Oriental Anthropologist,* Vol. I No. I, Allahabad.

Saran, A. B. (1974), *Suicide among Munda and Oraon.* National Publishing House, New Delhi.

Toppo, Birendra (2006), *Ethnomedicine of Oraon,* Anthropological Survey of India, Kolkata.

Vidyarthi, L. P. (1963), *The Maler: Nature-Man-Spirit Complex in a Hill Tribe of Bihar.* Calcutta: Book Land Pvt. Ltd.

——(1976), *Tribal Culture of India,* Concept Publishing Company, New Delhi.

——(1978), *Rise of Indian Anthropology.* Concept Publishing Company, New Delhi.

——(1978), *Presidential Address:* Xth International Congress of Anthropological and Ethnological Sciences. New Delhi.

5

TRENDS OF SOCIAL ANTHROPOLOGICAL STUDY AND RESEARCH IN BENGAL

Buddhadeb Chaudhuri

I

There is a long tradition of anthropological study and research in India and the Department of Anthropology, University of Calcutta, is the oldest university department in India and one of the oldest among such departments in the world. Apart from the first university anthropology department, which has contributed in the development of anthropology in the region, the presence of a few other research organizations like the Asiatic Society and Indian Statistical Institute in Calcutta immensely helped in the growth of the subject. Besides, the Anthropological Survey of India, one of the largest anthropological organizations in the world, has its head office in Calcutta with a number of regional centers. Being a Government of India organization, it played a significant role in the development of anthropology, both in theory and practice, considering all the sub-disciplines of anthropology. It also provided the general background of Indian population to formulate the various strategies or policies initiated by the government. Besides, particularly after independence, in research organizations (such as the Centre for Social Sciences), anthropological studies formed an integral part. Again organizations (like Cultural Research Institute) were also established to initiate studies and research on disadvantaged people (like scheduled castes and scheduled tribes).

These studies have also significantly contributed in the development of anthropological knowledge. In this paper, however, I shall cover certain specific issues of social anthropology.

II

Before discussing the trends of social anthropological studies and research in this region, it may not be out of place to discuss briefly about the different universities/institutes and research organizations where anthropology is formally taught or research studies are conducted, particularly in social anthropology.

University of Calcutta: Department of Anthropology–one of the oldest anthropology departments–postgraduate and Ph. D. teaching and research; anthropology department at the undergraduate level in eleven colleges.

Vidyasagar University: Department of anthropology–teaching and research at the postgraduate and Ph. D. level; anthropology department at the undergraduate level at four colleges.

Viswabharati University: Department of Anthropology–teaching and research-postgraduate and Ph. D. level started as a part of Centre for Rural Studies (Palli Charcha Kendra)

Apart from these university departments and colleges where anthropology is taught as a distinct discipline at the undergraduate and post-graduate levels and for Ph. D., issues related to social anthropology are also taught in the Department of Sociology at Burdwan, Kalyani and Jadavpur Universities.

Institutes and Research Organisations

As mentioned before, the Anthropological Survey of India is one of the largest anthropological organizations in the world. Its head office along with its Eastern Regional center are all located in Calcutta which have immensely promoted the study and research of anthropology in this region.

The Indian Statistical Institute, one of the most prestigious research organizations of India, is located in Calcutta and there are different units through which anthropological studies are conducted. A number of distinguished anthropologists were and are attached to many of these units.

The Centre for Social Sciences, Calcutta, is another relatively smaller but prestigious research centers dealing with different branches of social sciences, including anthropology. It was established in early 1970s supported by the Indian Council of Social Science Research (ICSSR) and Government of West Bengal and a number of distinguished social anthropologists (like late Professor Surajit Chandra Sinha) were attached to this Centre. Besides these institutes, social anthropologists are also working in a number of organizations in and around Calcutta working on different issues using anthropological approaches. A number of social anthropologists were and are attached to the Behavioural Science Unit of the Indian Institute of Management, Calcutta. Social anthropologists were and are associated with the Agricultural Extension Wing of Bidhan Chandra Krishi Viswavidyalaya (Agricultural University) to study the socio-cultural dimensions of agricultural development following anthropological approaches. Social anthropologists are also working in the All India Institute of Hygiene and Public Health and in the Census Department, Government of India. Anthropologists are also working in Cultural Research Institute, Government of West Bengal, to study and formulate policies of development of the disadvantaged people (particularly of scheduled castes and scheduled tribes).

Besides, anthropologists are also working in many non-governmental organizations (like CINI, Vivekananda Society, Centre for Alternative Research in Development, Rural Development Association, etc.) to formulate policies for development and empowerment of the vulnerable sections of the population, like women, children, scheduled castes and tribes, drug addicts, displaced persons, etc.

III

If we examine the history and development of anthropology and the socio-political context, its close link with colonial rule is quite evident. All over the world, the colonial rulers, for more effective administration and in order to protect the colonial interest, felt the need to have adequate knowledge and information about the subjugated peoples. India was no exception and there were a number of studies and publications during the colonial period and Calcutta being the capital of colonial rulers, a number of important publications were there from this place. *The Tribes and Castes of Bengal* published in 1891 by H. H. Risley and *The People of India* by the same author in 1915 may be mentioned here. It may not be out of context to mention about an interesting government document of that period. At the time of collection of data for the people of India project, a special instruction was given to select a particular caste having certain physical features. The intention was quite clear: to project that peoples of India are not only socially differentiated, physically also they are quite distinct. It may not be out of context to mention here that during the colonial period, the ICS officials had to undergo training in London to know about the people whom they were going to rule. Interestingly, after the second World War, with the decline of British imperialism and the rise of US neo-imperialism, the importance of information about people based on field work is still very much there. A few years back, when I had an opportunity to discuss with an academician about this training programme and wanted to know whether they still have any such programme, I was told that still now such programmes are organized for the senior executives of multinational companies. Thus, the need of anthropological knowledge and undertstanding based on uniqe anthropological field work is still there even in the changed socio-political and historical context. Long back, in the first International Congress of Anthropological and Ethnological Sciences held in London in 1934, the importance and use of anthropological knowledge in colonial administration and the need of training in anthropology were emphasized. However, it would be wrong to think that anthropology only serves the colonial interest. As the colonial rulers tried to use it in their own colonial interest, the nationalist scholars through their field research tried to focus on the uniqueness of pluralistic Indian society and culture and emphasized its unity in diversity.

Anthropology, Sociology and Research Methodology

It has already been mentioned that the oldest university anthropology department in India is located in Calcutta University, one of the oldest universities in India. Even though there were a number of brilliant sociologists in this region and there was a well-known sociology unit in the Indian Statistical Institute, sociology as a separate distinct discipline at the university level started much later. As a result, though sociology flourished much earlier in the University of Bombay or in the University of Delhi, it was only in late seventies when a separate sociology department was established in Calcutta University.

It may be added here that even though there was a long anthropological tradition in this region, unlike in the North (Delhi University) or West (Bombay University), it was not much influenced by anthropology in terms of theory, research methodology and area of research. Most of the sociology departments of this region were more influenced by political science as is evident from the nature and type of research. Interestingly, the sociology department of Calcutta University is not the first university sociology department in this region and developed much later.

It is known that social anthropologists are more preoccupied with studies made on small communities or rural areas and mostly depend on case studies and observation for data collection and follow qualitative method of data analysis. The Department of Anthropology, University of Calcutta, has a long and rich tradition of field research. Late L. K. A. Iyer, who joined the department when it was established in 1920, was a famous ethnographer during his time and had a number of important publications on tribes and castes. The name of T. C. Das may also be mentioned here who became famous for his study on Purum Kuki (1945) and Bengal famine of 1943 (1949). After the publication of the monograph on Purum Kuki, one issue of the *American anthropologist* was fully devoted to further interpreting and re-interpreting the findings of this study. This was perhaps the only occasion when one whole issue of the *American Anthropologist* was devoted after the publication of any volume. It attracted so much attention as it represented a new trend of research. Surajit Sinha, one of Das' students commented after his death; "India lost one of her most devoted specialists on tribal ethnography and a great teacher who was ever experimenting with methods for training the students in field work during his long tenure as a teacher in the Calcutta University (1921-63)."

The name of K. P. Chattopadhyay, another teacher of this department, may also be mentioned. He initiated study and research on some unconventional areas like jute workers. He also played a crucial role in the study of and research in social anthropology. The name of Nirmal Kumar Bose, another distinguished anthropologist, may also be mentioned here even though he was attached to the geography department of Calcutta University. He was also the Director of the Anthropological Survey of India and influenced research of social anthropology not only in this region but also in India as a whole. His books, *Hindu Samajer Garan* (1949), *Peasant Life in India* (1961) and *Calcutta. A Social Survey* (1964) may be mentioned here. His study on Calcutta city marks a departure from conventional social anthropological study. He also initiated studies of some unconventional areas as a part of studying Indian civilization. These scholars really influenced a large number of students of this university and shaped the future research of social anthropology in this region as new university departments or research centers were established. Thus social anthropological study became more diversified and complex societies or urban areas were also studied following typical anthropological approaches. Thus, though the appropriateness and adequacy of anthropological tools in the context of studying complex societies are sometimes made, in the last three decades such studies have been made quite competently.

Tribal Studies

Anthropological studies are diverse in nature. Calcutta was and has become a center for anthropological studies. As the anthropologists, at the initial stage, were more pre-occupied with studies on simple-folk people, ethnographic studies on the tribals predominated. However, a few of them may be mentioned. Notable anthropologists (like N. K. Bose) contributed to the undertstanding of tribal societies in relation to the Hindu civilization. His important work in this regard was the "The Hindu Method of Tribal Absorption". Tribals and non-tribals are coming into contact through socio-cultural interaction since time immemorial. This socio-cultural process is unique in two senses. First, it sometimes brings together two cultural groups and sometimes there are some revivalist outlooks among the tribals who respond unfavourably to the interactions of non-tribal counterpart. The study on Purum Kuki of Manipur by T. C. Das can also be mentioned in this content. He has described vividly the kinship and social organization of the Purum Kukis of Manipur. He also made explicit the prescriptive marriage system among the Purums.

The Anthropological Survey of India, Calcutta, is a repository of tribal studies. It attempts to preserve the diverse nature of our culture by orienting its programme to national tasks and by covering major gaps in developing programmes of nationwide continuance of anthropological studies of human groups. It conducts researches on biological and cultural aspects of Indian populations with emphasis on tribes and weaker sections of the population. Activities of the Survey also center around the preservation and documentation of the diverse nature of our culture and in that context studies on tribals and development with reference to industrialization were also made. Studies on the impact of industrialization on the life of tribals were also made by the Cultural Research Institute, Government of West Bengal. It may be added here that even though most of these studies are academic many of them have development implications. The study by Roy Burman on the Totos may be mentioned here. P. K. Bhowmick, who worked on the Lodhas (1963), provided a development model for them and initiated some programmes for their upliftment. This is an interesting case of how anthropological knowledge can help and contribute to the development process.

Tribal studies are of diverse nature. The interest of anthropologists ranges from basic cultural studies to narratives of civilizations of different origin. Tribal studies include studies on ethnography of tribal economy as well as tribal politics and movement. Overall tribal studies can broadly be classifed into:

(a) Ethnographic studies;

(b) Tribal economy;

(c) Forest, environment and tribals;

(d) Tribal development policy and planning;

(e) Tribal religion and festival;

(f) Tribal politics, movement, identity and socio-political system;

(g) Tribal education;

(h) Tribal women;

(i) Tribal demography, nutrition, growth and health; and

(j) Tribal society, culture and change.

Urban Studies

The pace of urbanization is quite fast in most of the developing countries, including India. It has obvious social, economic, political and environmental implications. There is a growing importance of mega cities and decreasing importance of small towns. There is an urgent need to examine it with reference to cross-cultural situation. What are the socio-economic and political implications of this trend? Again, is it possible to conceive urban development in isolation? How plausible is the achievement of success regarding urban development without considering the regional context? Interestingly, even though Calcutta is one of the mega cities in India, the growth rate has gone down indicating significant rural development in the region. Migration is a major factor contributing to rapid urbanization. What happens when people of different cultures migrate to cities? Do they still maintain their distinct identities? Many of the Asian countries are pluralistic in nature and have their own characteristics based on ethnicity. Tension and conflict result in different parts of the world when the expectations and aspirations of the people are not fulfilled. These are important issues requiring urgent attention and social anthropologists have responded to them and initiated studies on many of these issues.

It is true that hardly there was any study on urban anthropology worth mentioning as this was a new area of research to social anthropologists. But after the very interesting study by Nirmal Kumar Bose on the city of Calcutta and publication of the book in India and the article in *Scientific Americana*, gradually studies on various urban issues were initiated with anthropological perspective and approaches. Thus studies were made on different communities in Calcutta, to study their nature of change after migration, identity issues and cultural change. The melting pot theory of the west provided a model for approach in the context of the migrant population. Besides the earlier study of Nirmal Kumar Bose, a recent study by S. Chaudhuri (2007) has also indicated how people often try to maintain their distinct social identity even after migration to the city. This is often done through cultural activities, clubs, libraries, traditional festivals, newspapers and educational institutions. It does not mean that people are all living in isolated enclaves. They do have opportunities to interact with others at different levels, at the place of work, for political activities, in clubs, games and sports and many other activities. In reality, people have multiple identities and respond and interact accordingly. Thus there are different places of religious activity for people belonging to different religious groups; caste organizations are functioning in the context of some communities and provide help and support to people belonging to that group. Languages, regions often become an important consideration. However, there are many occasions when people join hands cutting across religion, region, language or caste. Class is often an important cementing force.

There were also studies on the poverty stricken people, the slum dwellers, pavement dwellers and the beggars. Three processes were noted after migration or in the context of such poverty stricken people, continuation of certain traditional norms, modification of traditional norms and emergence of distinct adaptive norms in such limiting situations. An interesting seminar on the city of Calcutta was also organized where besides anthropologists, people from other disciplines contributed interesting papers to discuss the different facets of city life. Subsequently a volume on socio-cultural profile of Calcutta was also published. Anthropologists have also studied the religious places or community festivals in urban areas. In fact, the number of visitors has also increased in urban temples. The number of community festivals has also increased considerably in the recent past. What does it indicate? A rise in *bhakti* or devotion or better travel facilities or certain secular demands? It has been noted that to meet secular demands, there is a modification in religious activities. It has also been noted how it is articulating with the growing or changing demands of the society. In fact, study with anthropological perspectives has provided interesting insight about these changing situations. Anthropological studies have also been made on important religious places of Calcutta like the Kalighat temple. It has been noted that the number of visitors has increased considerably. This does not always mean that there is a rise in devotion. It may be related to better travel facilities. The increasing economic implications of such important temples have also been noted.

Studies on the Aged

Though the problems of the aged have already assumed importance in developed countries of the West, in India, the problems of aged persons has assumed much greater importance since independence. Due to overall scientific and technological developments, life expectancy of the people has also increased and naturally their number has increased considerably.

Of late social anthropologists have shown keen interest in this problem and studied the aged in different areas including in urban areas and in slums, focusing on various problems of the aged: (a) socio-cultural; and (b) the behavioural. Among the socio-cultural variables, loss of income, authority, status, social contact, health, role, status and intensification of familial control are important. The behavioural problems of the aged include changes in personality, needs, expectation, and intereaction.

A syllabus for old age care has been designed by the Ministry of Labour, Government of India, in collaboration with the Central Staff Training and Research Institute, Salt Lake, Kolkata. They have prepared a syllabus for old age care trade which includes some training on craft.

Other studies have pointed out the problems of the aged in the context of three important parameters, family, health and behavioural aspect. Need for care of the elderly at home has also been emphasized. Family plays a pivotal role in the absence of adequate health care system in caring for the elders. The institutional medical support is neither adequate nor available to the elderly in India. So, their dependence on family becomes inevitable.

Gender Issues

The role of women in society is not negligible. But since it is male dominanted, the position of women in society has come down. The gender issue has been a great concern in contemporary world. The heroic role of women was found in many countries including India. During the Vedic period, we find notable women (like Gargi) who had participated in learning and debate. But the issue of gender has not been given such importance as it is given today. The UNO declares Women Day every year. Sociologists and anthropologists have pointed out the importance of gender equality in advancing society.

Gender studies are held in different locations. Apart from university departments, there are centers for research where gender studies are conducted.

In Kolkata also, a number of scholars of various disciplines are conducting gender studies. There are two centers of women studies in Kolkata. One is located at 1, Reformatory Street, Kolkata (Alipore Campus) in Calcutta University. Another center for women studies is located in Jadavpur University.

The Institute of Development Studies, Kolkata, has also conducted a gender study. Another publication from 'STREE', Calcutta, 'Guilt Without Trial' is a book written by Carolyn Sleightholme on Calcutta's sex workers. The study deals with the helplessness of women in sex trade in Calcutta.

Anthropology and Rural Development

Changes in rural societies have been especially prominent since the Industrial Revolution. In the history of human civilization, depending on the local ecology and natural resources and also due to subsequent technological development, different types of rural societies with varied cultures, levels of development and economic life gradually emerged in different parts of the globe. In fact, though agriculture is the main economy in rural areas, all are not always involved in agriculture and could survive by following varied other occupations or supporting the primary economy. It may be added here that in spite of the fact that the rural people are more homogeneous in nature, there do exist considerable variations in levels, of development, economy, and socio-cultural tradition, not only among different countries of the world but also in the context of a particular country. Apparently though rural society is homogeneous, it is also very varied and naturally the policy for rural development must articulate with such varied context.

A new development paradigm is also needed that puts people at the center of development, considers economic growth as a means and not an end, protects the life opportunities of future generations as well as the present one and respects the natural systems on which all life depends. Growth does not mean development. Unless and until there is growth with justice, where peoples have equal share and access to resources, there cannot be true development. It is well known that Green Revolution has increased crop production, but it is also responsible for the concentration of holdings and increasing inequality. Proper development strategy may evolve with experience and experiment where traditional wisdom can contribute much. Technology is required but not the domination of technology over its creator.

The anthropologists have classified villages in a number of ways: thus there can be (a) migratory agricultural villages where people stay in a particular village for a few months depending on the period of cultivation; and (b) semi-permanent agricultural villages where people stay for generations, even centuries. Again on the basis of settlement and location of cultivable land, the villages can be (a) nucleated type, where the residential houses are located in clusters surrounded by agricultural land; and (b) dispersed villages where cultivators live separately along with their farm lands. It is obvious that social life differs greatly between the first type of nucleated villages where people live in close proximity and the second type of dispersed villages where people have less social contact or interaction.

On the basis of social differentiation, stratification and land ownership, villages can be classified into (a) villages composed of peasant joint owners; (b) peasant joint tenants; (c) peasants including some tenants and labourers; (d) tenants; (e) employees of a big private landowner; and (f) labourers and employees of the state, church, public landowner. Immediately after the colonial rule in many countries, there was an acute shortage of food and the government of the concerned countries desperately tried to increase food production at any cost. Maybe an increase or growth in production was the goal at that moment and maybe the objective was achieved in a given context, but is it possible to equate it with development? Any increase in production is growth but development is a broader and wider term and has other connotations too. It not only includes growth, but an equitable distribution of facilities and resources and reduction, if not elimination, of exploitative practices.

However, during the twentieth century, social science became increasingly concerned with economics, economics with wealth rather than people, with economy rather than society, with maximization of income rather than improving the quality of life. The dominant contemporary tradition of focusing exclusively on such variables as per capita gross national product or national wealth is really a continuation of the above approach. However, gradually there is a shift from this approach. It has been observed that wealth is important, but to concentrate on it exclusively is wrong. Valuable social and cultural traditions can be and are maintained at all levels of income. The richness of culture can be largely independent of the people's wealth. Again, unless societies recognize that their real wealth is their people, an excessive obsession with the creation of material wealth can obscure the ultimate objective of enriching human lives. It is not the level of income alone that matters–it is also the use that is made of this income. Much depends on how the fruits of economic growth are shared, particularly on what the poor get, and how much the additional resources are used to support public services, particularly health and education. What is decisive is not the process of wealth maximization but the choices that individuals and societies make. Sustainable development is concerned with models of material production and consumption that are replicable and desirable. These models do not regard natural resources as a free good, to be plundered at free will of any nation, generation or individual. The close link between poverty and sustainability must be analyzed carefully if the concept of sustainable development is to have any real meaning. The poor, struggling for their survival, often lack the resources to avoid degrading their environment. In the societies of the poor, what is at risk is not the quality of life, but life itself.

In the approach of rural development, different models are available: (a) community approach where certain communities, which are generally considered as backward groups in the concerned country, like the tribes in may countries, scheduled castes and tribes in India, get special support, (b) region based– where certain areas, generally backward in the concerned country get special support for development. In some cases, special development inputs are provided to a region already developed to create a developed region which can provide an example to be replicated by other areas; (c) community and region based–It is really a combination of the first two, where certain communities of a particular region get special support, and special facilities are also enjoyed by other people living in that particular area. The best example is Intensive Tribal Development Blocs in India; and (d) in many cases, while extending facilities, the economic condition is also considered beforehand. This is done considering the constraints of the resources, and generally the facilities and development inputs are provided to poorer families. Ideologically, three groups or models are available in the context of rural development:

(a) Those who turn their backs on modernization altogether, looking towards a revival of a pre-colonial village centred order.

(b) Marxists, who see social redistribution as logically prior to sustainability. Thus they suggest more equitable distribution and sharing of resources through land reform.

(c) Groups proposing appropriate technology, which seek to develop and apply technical and institutional alternatives to the centralizing, iniquitous and often environmentally destructive processes of development.

During the 1960s Green Revolution was introduced in many countries by means of government propaganda, subsidy and inputs in order to increase crop production. Cultivating these new seeds, no doubt, required considerable departure from the prevailing practices of traditional subsistence or near subsistence agriculture. In fact, the traditional system of farming is not only inappropriate for cultivating HYVs, but the practice of the Green Revolution also demanded the deliberate and systematic breakdown of the traditional system.

Within a space of two decades, the varied agricultural systems of the third world and the social system were replaced by a new western model in many countries. The poor peasants, cultivating the new varieties of HYVs were exposed to new uncertainties and new opportunities for being exploited and dominated. Simultaneously with pauperization, Green Revolution also brought a process of perpetuating dependencies. The rich not only increased the size of their landholdings, but also increased their share of benefits from the distribution of inputs and infrastructural facilities. Many of these consequences were not entirely unintentional since the target group in Green Revolution was typically the middle-class or well-to-do farmers. The Green Revolution was not only responsible for pauperization but also resulted in the malnutrition of peasants. Besides, genetic erosion is a result of Green Revolution and as old varieties disappear, and as genetic uniformity spreads in the third world, an increasing incidence of devastating crops disasters are bound to occur. The extensive use of chemical herbicides and pesticides hastens the process of pest mutation. The Green Revolution technology is biased. Although high yielding, non-sterile varieties could be developed, the seed companies have a disincentive for doing so since it would mean large-scale loss of markets and, consequently income and profits. Again, transnational elites were quick to find partners among the elites in the third world countries. Green Revolution enabled the introduction of technical inputs into an unequal system of landholding, thereby not only reinforcing the gap between rich and poor, but even increasing it. In spite of limited variations from the perspective of the third world countries, appropriate technologies in seeds will give special emphasis to hardiness, disease resistance and the capability of reproduction of the seeds. The basic problem of Green Revolution is that the impact of technology is powerfully influenced by contemporary social, political and economic relationships.

Some Emerging Areas of Anthropological Studies

It may not be out of context to discuss here some emerging areas attracting attention of the social anthropologists in this region:

1. Environment, development and forest
2. Indigenous wisdom and knowledge
3. Anthropology and human rights

The world today is deeply concerned with ecological issues. Man for his ever-growing needs uses resources in nature. In this way, he promotes development. The use of natural resources and the initiation of development produces changes in ecology. The nature of changes in ecology manifests the character of development. The character of development, again, determines the use of resources. The pattern of use of resources reflects to a certain extent the path of development that a governing group decides to follow. Although the issues have to be analyzed from different points of view, the role of human being as an agent of change has to be taken as a focal point. In the relationship between development and environment, adjustment is the need, but conflict is generally the outcome. The development programs of many countries like India or Malaysia are guided mainly by governmental issues. This is now regarded as too costly to be avoided. The process of planning and concomitant administrative decisions should attach top priority to a resolution of the contradiction between development and environment.

With end of the colonial rule in South and South east Asia, a number of nation states were created, a process, which often resulted in a large-scale migration of people. These migrations, quite often, were a response to political pressures and policies in post-colonial states. Development programs initiated in tribal dominated areas often adversely affected the tribal way of life, economy and habitat resulting in displacement. This was frequently followed by the encroachment on traditional tribal areas by non-tribal and the exploitation of natural resources became more intense, generally affecting the ecosystem of a tribal area. These are the inevitable difficulties of development policy in a situation where the component programs are funded by international agencies and one often supervised by them. Quite often greater emphasis and attention are given to the interests of the developed sectors of the country, such as the industrial sector and the interests of the backward tribals are often treated as secondary. Actually with the formation of new nation states and increase in population, the exploitation of natural resources has become more intense. There is tremendous competition to have access and command over natural resources and this has often created conflicts and tensions at different levels. The developed countries (or rather the multinational organizations) try to control the resources of the less developed countries, while the dominant sections of the developing countries try to manipulate in such a way that they can enjoy the major share of the national natural resources, often depriving the local population, mostly the tribals.

Different natural resources (namely forest, land, water) have their own specificities and ecological characteristics. A discourse on the relationship between human being and these natural resources in different geographical regions will contribute to an understanding of man-nature balance, marked by both adjustments and conflicts. Perhaps of all natural resources, the most critical situation prevails in the context of forests. Degradation, deforestation and desertification are conspicuous in developing countries, particularly in south and south east Asia. In India, for example, forest has become an issue of common concern in recent past mainly for three reasons: firstly, due to ecological consideration; secondly, for its commercial value; and lastly in view of the growing unrest centering forest and exploitation of forest resources. There were a number of clashes and conflicts between forest dwellers (including the tribals) and the governmental officials as the forest policies or programs were reported to go against the interest of tribals. This again was not always directly related to forest policies or programs, but sometimes a big development project (like the construction of a river valley project, dam) adversely affects forest ecology, indirectly the tribals. Many of the river valley projects were opposed by local people. This perhaps is not limited to India only. Indigenous people of Sarawak, Malaysia, have set up barricades across logging roads to protect against damage of their land and forest caused by timber companies. The big Nam Chom Dam Project in Thailand was ultimately dropped in March 1988 in face of strong opposition. Quite often these types of big development projects were planned in the name of national interest. The opposition from the local population in the context of such big development projects naturally raises a vital question. In a welfare state, can there be a basic contradiction between the local interest and national interest? One very important component of knowledge to be generated in the sphere of man-nature relationship is the perspective of local inhabitants. It may so happen that what planners and decisions-makers consider significant is subordinate to other factors in view of local people. But one should understand and know the experiences and problem solving ideas of local people. Some voluntary organizations (or social activists), in addition to governmental agencies, engage in intimate interaction with people on crucial ecological isues in different areas, They may be in a position to appreciate and communicate the people's aspirations and experiences. These experiences are extraordinarily valuable in understanding the man-nature relationship from below. If one gives more emphasis on only one issue, without considering the socio-economic factors, a somewhat unbalanced view of the whole ecological issues may emerge. Adequate emphasis should be given to linking the ecological factors with economic, political, social and historical forces as well.

The health situation in most of the countries in SAARC region is really critical. Despite all our technological breakthroughs we still live in a world where a fifth of the developing word's population goes hungry every night, a quarter lacks access to a basic necessity, like safe drinking water and a third lives in a state of abject poverty. In developing countries, the major causes of death are infections and parasitic-diseases, which kill seventeen million people annually, including 6.5 million from acute respiratory infection, 4.5 million from diarrhoeal diseases, and 3.5 million from tuberculosis. Most of these deaths are linked to poor nutrition and unsafe environment, particularly polluted water, which contributes to nearly one billion cases of diarrhoea a year. In both developing and industrial countries, the threats to health security are usually greater for the poorest. The disparities between the rich and the poor are similar for access to health services: in developed countries, there is 1 doctor for 400 persons, whereas in developing countries, it is 1 : 7000. Spending on health programmes is also very different and it is quite low in the developing countries; for example, it is only $7 per individual per year in Bangladesh. The situation is not much better in many other developing countries. Considering this alarming situation, out of the seven important targets put forward for human development in the Agenda for Social Summit, four were related to health. They are as follows:

1. Primary health care for all with special stress on the immunization of children.
2. Severe malnutrition to be eliminated and moderate malnutrition rates to be halved.
3. Family planning services for all willing couples.
4. Safe drinking and sanitation for all.

Need for an Alternative

The prevailing health and medical system, the western system, has unfortunately failed to meet the need of the world's majority. The failure of the Alma Ata Declaration in fulfilling its objectives of achieving Health for All by the year 2000 gives more urgency to looking for an alternative. In most countries, a very frightening policy change is being manoeuvred by agencies like the World Bank and International Monetary Fund to give less and less emphasis to the social and welfare sectors and higher emphasis to the economic and infrastructure sectors. As such the financial allocation for health is going down in most Asian countries. The implication of such a trend in countries where health insurance is unaffordable to the majority is unimaginable. Based on current trends in health care financing and the failure of the Alma Ata Declaration to take a grip of the situation, the condition of the poor has become more critical and difficult.

Generally, when we talk or think about science, we refer to the western or industrial society. In the context of scientific development, we prefer to discuss more about the so-called modern scientific innovations assuming that science is only there in those societies and quite often implying that scientific rigour or interest is absent in other societies. The role of science is to help mankind to meet various demands exploiting the natural resources in the best possible way without adversely affecting the environment. Thus, in the given socio-economic and historical context, the knowledge of making fire revolutionized human society. People have developed their own science and technologies based on the demands of the concerned societies, but quite often these are ignored. What I want to impress here is that we need to look at indigenous science and technology, particularly when an existing body of knowledte is available. Perhaps it is better to develop it instead of replacing it in the name of scientific development and modernization. A number of social anthropologists in this region are now deeply involved in studying the traditional wisdom and knowledge of the people, particularly the tribals. A Post-Graduate course on Human Rights has been introduced in Calcutta University attached to the Department of Anthropology, Calcutta University. Human Rights are now a topic of pressing concern in a world of conflict, competition and seemingly relentless globalization. But how do we deal with the tension between a concern for 'local cultures' and the existence of 'universal rights'? Over the last decade anthropology–with its rich understanding of local cultures–has been centrally involved in these wider discussions and debates. This new M. Sc. in Anthropology and Human Rights provides a robust exploration of anthropology's contribution to human rights work. Is the widespread practice of child foresterage in West Africa a normal aspect of West African kinship or is it the thin edge of the wedge of child trafficking? Where do we draw the line between 'indigenous peoples' or 'natives', and 'outsiders'? In addressing these and other issues anthropologically, the course will enable students to develop theoretical and practical skills for analyzing human rights issues in context. It will equip participants with a reflective understanding of their own cultural and professional practices, whether they work in organizations that increasingly concern themselves with human rights issues, or are seeking a socially aware approach to a pressing topic of our time.

The course provides a lively and stimulating look at key human rights issues and the way anthropology's unique cross-cultural perspective has contributed to its understanding and debate. Particular attention is given to case studies from India and around the world, in order to explore how rights operate in social life and are shaped by wider cultural forces. We explore important topics relevant to the critical study of human rights such as the limits of relativism, the nature of individuals and humanity, the legacy of colonialism and the nature of legal pluralism. Students will gain grounding in the anthropology of law, power and rights and consider how globalization is linked with the rise of human rights and other rights-based concerns, including indigenous rights; environmental and land rights; child, health and medical rights; war violence and social justice; and cultural and intellectual property rights. The programme offers a broad-based approach, with options on public health, children, international human rights law, as well as intensive training in ethnographic research methods.

6

SOCIAL ANTHROPOLOGY OF ORISSA: A Critique

N. K. Das

Orissa is a meeting place of three cultures, Indo-Aryan, Dravidian, and Munda, and three ethno-linguistic sections. There are both indigenous and immigrant components of the Brahmans, Karna, who resemble like the Khatriyas, and others. The theory that Orissa did not have a viable Kshatriya varna has been critically considered by the historian-anthropologists. We will also see endogenous and exogenous processes of state formation. The tribespeople had generally a two-tier structure of authority-village chief level and at the cluster of villages (*pidha*). Third tier of authority was *raja* in some places. Brahminism remained a major religion of Orissa throughout ages, though Jainism and Buddhism had their periods of ascendancy. There is evidence when Buddhism showed tendencies to merge into Hinduism, particularly into Saivism and Saktism. Buddhism did not completely die out, its elements entered into the Brahmanical sects. The historians see Hinduisation process intimately associated with the process of conversion, associated with the expansion of the Jagannatha cult, which co-existed with many traditions, and which led to building of Hindu temples in parts of tribal western Orissa. We notice the co-existence of Hinduisation/peasantisation/Kshatriyaisation/ Oriyaisation, all operating variously through colonisation. In Orissa, according to Kulke, it was a continuous process of 'assimilation' and partial integration. The tribe-Hindu caste intermingling is epitomised in the Jagannatha worship, which is today at the centre of Brahminic ritual and culture, even though the regional tradition of Orissa remains tribal in origin. Sanskritization, Aryanization and Hinduisation are widely used concepts in available literature denoting the social change process. In their study of culture change in western Orissa in 2004, N. K. Das and Santanu Mitra observed that there is a strong tendency towards de-Sanskritization and re-tribalization, which appears to be a thriving force of cultural change. Indeed the tribespeople did adopt some traits of more popular Hinduism but continued to pursue religions of the tribes concerned (Nagbansi, Gonds, and the Binjhal, Gond, Savara, Sounti, Bhuyan, Kisan, Bathudi, and Mirdha).

Orissa has a rich tradition of anthropological studies. Historians, archaeologists, political scientists and linguists have also dealt with the anthropological themes in Orissa. Right from the colonial era, Indian anthropologists/ scholars have been engaged on Orissa communities, their culture, language, architecture and social change. Thus while N. K. Bose studied the Juangs of Orissa (1928), S. C. Roy studied the Bhuiya (1935). The Orissan ethnography witnessed a turning point when Verrier Elwin published works on Juangs (1942), Bondo (1950) and the Savara (1955). Utkal University, Sambalpur University and research and training institutes of the Orissa state have brought out several works from time to time. At university level, we may mention contributions of A. Aiyappan, L. K. Mahapatra, N. Patnaik, K.K. Basa, Jagannath Dash and N. K. Behura. Work on pottery techniques by N. K. Behura remains an important contribution. In more modern times the contribution of the German scholars has been phenomenal. A. Eschmann, H. Kulke (1978, 1986), and Schnepel (1993-94) have brought out a number of books on the Jagannatha cult of Orissa. H. Kulke (1978,1979) has particularly dealt with the historical dimensions of spread of this cult and state formation. A significant contribution of this team is compilation of a volume *The Cult of Jagannath and the Regional Tradition of Orissa*, edited by Anncharlott Eschmann, Hermann Kulke, Gaya Charan (2005). One Oriya scholar, G. C. Tripathy, has collaborated with this team in bringing out this volume. Another German scholar, Dr. J. Lidia Guzy, from the Freie university of Berlin has studied the Mahima cult and more recently the Dalit folklore in western Orissa. She has sung Oriya folklore in her own style and brought out a cassette of folk-songs too. Georg Pfeffer and D.K. Behera have brought out a series of tribal studies. Anthropological Survey of India's People of India data on Orissa's 279 communities have shown that in all forty-three languages are spoken in Orissa. Orissa is the meeting ground of three language families (Indo-Aryan, Dravidian and Austric) which are present in higher proportion than in other states, making Orissa linguistically one of the most heterogeneous states of India. They have diverse modes of linkages between them. The Oriya speakers show a wide range of bilingualism as they are found conversant in many languages.

Review of Literature

Orissa has a rich tradition of anthropological studies. However in any review of anthropological research in Orissa, it will be inappropriate to ignore the contributions of the historians, archaeologists, political scientists and linguists. They too have often touched upon some or the other themes of social anthropology.

In this review however we will basically focus on the anthropological works, though for comparison some works of the historians/linguists will also be refereed to. We may start with the colonial ethnography/ anthropology. Dalton's *Descriptive Ethnology of Bengal* (1872), *Ethnographic Notes* of W.W. Hunter (1872-73) and *Tribe and Caste Volumes* prepared by British officers during 1891-1937 covered numerous communities of Orissa and neighbouring states. Some British officers like E.L. Samuel (1856), J. P. Frye (1860) and J.A. May (1873) wrote first hand ethnographic notes on the Orissa communities such as Juangs, the Khond (Kandha) and the Bondo. These volumes were meant for administrative purposes mainly. Most of the early writings were replete with value-loaded annotations, often discourteous in naming and even describing the life styles of the communities. S. C. Roy wrote the monograph on the Bhuiya of Orissa in 1935. The Orissan ethnography, according to Vidyarthi (1972), witnessed a turning point when Verrier Elwin started his work among the Juangs in 1942. He published several papers and books on the Juang (1948), Bondo (1950) and the Savara (1955). By 1952, a research institute was established in Orissa to collect information on ethnographic situations, mainly tribal. In 1957, F. G. Bailey published his highly acclaimed book *Caste and Economic Frontier* using data on the Kandha tribe and the Pana caste of south Orissa. Using this data, Bailey also wrote the famous paper for the *Contributions to Indian Sociology*, wherein the concepts of 'tribe' and 'caste' were delineated. In fact, the Juangs have been one of the best-studied tribes of Orissa. Dalton wrote about the Juangs of Keonjhar that "they are still semi-nomadic, often changing the sites...they cultivate in the rudest way. They thus raise little early rice, corn, pumpkins, ginger and pepper seed". Professor N.K.Bose studied the Juangs of Orissa as early as 1928. In Dhenkanal, he observed two divisions among the Juangs. He also found the existence of Darbar and dormitory among them. He noted only two clans, *bandhu* and *kutumba*, among them. In 1945, Verrier Elwin wrote a full monograph on the Juangs of Orissa. He covered Keonjhar and Dhenkanal districts in the monograph. He too found the dormitory as also the practice of bride price in settling a marriage. He also described the headmanship among these people. There is a Juang Development Agency working for economic development among them. In 1956 the Podu (shifting cultivation) Prevention Act was enforced which forced them to go for labour work. Urbanization has now affected them considerably. Besides Dalton, Elwin (1945, 1948), and Bose (1929), N. Patnaik (1963) has also studied the Juangs.

The Cult of Jagannath and the Regional Tradition of Orissa (2005) is an important multi-disciplinary contribution. It deals with the role and significance of regional Hindu traditions that emerged in the beginning of the early medieval period out of an interaction of elements of classical Hinduism with autochthonous local religious practices and belief. *State Formation in Ancient Orissa* by Prafulla Kumar Mohanty (2002) is a general study of the state formation process in Orissa from the earliest time to the beginning of the twelfth century. *Forest Tribes of Orissa:* Vol. I: *The Dongaria Kondh,* edited by Klaus Seeland and Franz Schmithusen, attempts to document the Dongaria's traditional knowledge of their natural environment; how they classify trees, plants, hills, forests, crops and soils and how so far they have been managing their forests. *They Sing Life: Anthology of Oral Poetry of the Primitive Tribes of India* by Sitakant Mahapatra (2002) is an anthology of the oral poetry of selected tribes of Eastern India. These songs combine the sensibility of a major poet and the insight of an anthropologist. However it is unfortunate that the scholar uses the redundant notion of primitive to describe the tribes. *Tribal and Indigenous People of India: Problems and Prospects,* edited by R.N. Pati and J. Dash (2002), includes several articles dealing with Orissa situation.

Some articles devoted to Orissa are titled as *Tribes of Orissa and Their Population*/Jagannath Dash and Suresh Chandra Pradhan, *Tribal Languages of Orissa*/K. Mohapatra, *Status of Tribal Communities of Orissa*/N. K. Behura , *Classification and Enumeration of Scheduled Tribes in Orissa*/L. K. Mahapatra, *Atrocities against SC and ST: Some Remedies and Ramifications*/Raghunath Patnaik, *Problems and Welfare of Orissa Tribes*/L. K. Mahapatra, *Profile of Bonded Labour System in India with Special Reference to a Primitive tribal Community of Orissa*/ R. P. Mohanty, *Undone Ujias and Their Tribal Identity*/Jagannath Das, and *Food and Nutrition Situation in 10 Tribal Dominated Villages of Lamtaput Block, Koraput district, Orissa*/R. N. Pati. Some other titles are the *Concept and Treatment of Diseases among the Dongria Kondhs of Orissa*/Jagannath Dash and Suresh Chandra Pradhan, *Problems in Tribal Education with Special Reference to Orissa*/N. K. Behura, *Impact of Forest Policies on the Indigenous Peoples: A Case Study of Hill Kharias in Similipal Hills, Orissa (India)*/Jagannath Dash, *Customary Right in Land and Forest and the State*/L. K. Mahapatra, *Entitlement for Food and Social Security and Environment Management*/ L.K. Mahapatra, *Impact of Industrialization in Socio-cultural Frontiers: A Case of Oraons*/Nilakantha Panigrahi and Prakash Ch. Parida, *Tribes of Orissa and their Development*/B. Chaudhury, *The Saora View of "Good Life", "Happy Life" and Development*/ G. Mohapatra and *A Kondh View of Good Life and Development*/Gopinath Mohanty. Fact remains that the issues addressed in this book are of practical applied value such as unequal access to and inadequate educational opportunities, persistent and increasing burden of poverty, inequalities in access to health. Focussing on another applied aspect of research, Nilakantha Panigrahi deals with the issue of development of eco-tourism in tribal regions of Orissa. Eco-tourism, both at conceptual and empirical levels, is significant in a number of respects. Traditionally it encapsulates scientific, aesthetic, and philosophical approaches which reflect the structure and function of society. Over the decades numerous changes have been observed both in the content and context of eco-tourism. With globalisation, the processes of change not only widened and multiplied, but also gained in importance. The present research paper in observing the treasure of tourism of the Orissa region in eastern India, emphasises the potential of eco-tourism in the scheduled areas which are largely dominated by tribal communities. It argues and concludes by way of recommendations that if eco-tourism is properly developed it can not only attract tourists from far and near, but can also generate more revenue for the inhabitants of the region and for the state.

Angana Chatterji and Mihir Desai have come forward with "An IPT Enquiry" (September 2006) which sheds light on the issue of Communalism in Orissa. The report of the People's Tribunal on communalism in Orissa documents the growth of communalism in Orissa, highlighting the criminal activity and human rights violations; the consolidation of these forces and their relationship to state and civil society, and the related growth of social and gendered violence against disenfranchised groups and religious minorities, such as Adivasis, Dalits, Christians, and Muslims. Based on its findings, the Tribunal recommends that the Government of India and the Government of Orissa treat the communal situation in the state on par with an emergency, and act promptly to address the injustices perpetrated on minority and disenfranchised persons and groups as a preventive measure against future injustices. K. Suresh Singh in his review 'A perspective on the ASI', *Seminar* issue on 'Situating sociology' [November 2000] observed that the People of India Project (PoIP) launched in 1985 in terms of the parameters of a rapidly emerging postcolonial ethnography extends beyond the territorial limits of colonial ethnography. Orissa is exhaustively covered under this project. Unlike British colonial ethnographic surveys, the People of India Project did not generate first-hand anthropometric data but drew on its earlier surveys and studies to cover biological dimensions. In short, the new People of India study sought to present a composite bio-linguistic, cultural profile of all communities of India. The concerns for environment, resource use, gender relations, impact of change and development, market and technology were appropriately reflected in a 15 point format which was uniformly canvassed for all groups. The project also involved the updating and publication of the old data sets generated by all India projects in the 1960s. While the continuity of ethnographic tradition was stressed by using the previously gathered information as a benchmark, the focus of PoIP was on change.

Bailey went to work in the southern tribal area of Orissa, which he conceived analytically as an "encapsulated region" and also as a zone in which the national state and local villages constituted intersecting political fields, populated with brokers and fixers in middle getting things done (lobbying projects, mobilizing votes, through exchange/transaction). He conducted 38 months of field work between 1952-1959, from which he then produced three volumes of ethnography: 1957: *Caste and the Economic Frontier: A Village in Highland Orissa*. Manchester: Manchester University Press.1960: *Tribe, Caste and Nation: A Study of Political Activity and Political Change in Highland Orissa*. Manchester: Manchester University Press.1963: *Politics and Social Change: Orissa in 1960*. Berkeley: University of California Press. As the title of his 1960 monograph suggests, he analyzed politics at three arenas or levels. In each, he located a political structure that contributed to the environment of local political action: the encapsulated village of Bisipara, a tribal village in the Kond Hills of highland Orissa, whose Kond inhabitants were organized in a segmentary lineage system, the Orissa state and the caste system of the Oriyas, which entered the highlands from the surrounding plains, the nation of India and the rules and regulations of the British colonial order and, later, the Indian nation-state. These political systems (lineage, caste, and state) coexist and offer alternative concepts and normative rules. His studies are of *"the ways people in one setting, the village of Baderi, respond, and fail to respond, to the different possibilities of action that these structures provide"* (Jacobson 97-98).

Bailey extensively uses cases of decision and dispute—events that he then situates in a context of multiple structures. His 1960 *Tribe, Caste, and Nation*, for example, is largely focused on the extended analysis of a single argument that arose between the Konds and Oriyas living in Baderi village at the time he was doing fieldwork. Bailey also distinguished three levels of explanation: the cultural model, which is the actor's own model of his political action; the sociological model of groups and interrelations within village; the external view of relations outside village, "demonstrating how certain groups within the village are enabled to challenge, and to some extent to overthrow, the established order" (Vincent, 346-347). Bailey went on to elaborate his individualized view of politics as strategizing, manipulating norms, maximizing advantage, seeking power, etc., into general propositions about politics, power, and structure as emerging out of that maneuvering. He presented a general statement of his position in his *Strategems and Spoils* in 1969, which he intended as a kind of handbook of the universal rules of the game of politics. Like Barth, Bailey's version of an individualist political anthropology engendered sharp critiques. One of the early influential critics was Sydel Silverman. Unlike Barth, whose career has been marked by serial ethnography in different locations, Bailey has been productive as an essayist, producing a number of short studies that extended and modified his position (and several books that revisit and rework his 1950s field materials).

The synthetic cultural traditions, Jagannatha tradition and fascinating tribal and caste communities of Orissa attracted several foreign scholars. For a long time the German team has been contributing towards the Orissan research in a serious manner. Izskowityz (1953) from Sweden, F. G. Bailey (1955, 1958, 1960) from England and Herman Neiggermeyer (1964) studied different aspects of life in Orissa. Herman Neiggermeyer (1964) wrote a monograph on the Khutia Khond tribe. Izskowityz (1953) presented an ethnographic account of Gadaba tribe. Bailey worked in two villages, Bisipara (1952-54) and Baderi (1955), in Koraput and Phulabani areas. Iravati Karve studied the Oriya kinship system in her celebrated work *Kinship Organisation in India* (1965). M.C. Behera and Premananda Panda have also brought out some studies recently. N. K. Das made a three dimensional comparative study among the Dongaria Kandhs mainly measuring and evaluating the social realities as depicted by the noted Oriya writer Gopinath Mohanty in his novel *Amrutar Santana* by comparing with the old ethnographic writings and ethnographic facts collected in the field (Das, 1973). N. K. Das as part of Master's degree in anthropology made this comparative study under guidance of Professor T. B. Naik at Raipur University. Nabakrishna Chaudhury Centre for Development Studies at Bhubaneswar is constantly contributing to enrich the tradition of anthropological research of Orissa. Contributions of N. K. Behura and Nilakantha Panigrahi of this centre are noteworthy.

The Anthropological Survey of India and the state level Scheduled Caste and Scheduled Tribe Research and Training

Institute (SCSTRTI), established in 1955, have conducted several studies in Orissa. SCSTRTI has published a large number of monographs on several caste and tribal communities of Orissa. It also publishes a scientific journal *Adibasi,* which contains research findings of the Institute. One of the earliest works of the ASI is Data on Orissa brought out by N. K. Bose. S.Bose of the ASI conducted a land survey in quantifying the carrying capacity of land in relation to the cultural setting of people. K. A. Razeq (1989) studied acculturation among the hill Saora of Ganjam and Koraput. Weekly markets played important role in bringing social and cultural change among the Saora. S. Das (1989) studied the Gadabas of Koraput, south Orissa. He found that the Gadabas have been exposed to a dam, new Bengali refugee settlements, and hydroelectric project. Gitanjali Misra (1989) studied the Juangs of Keonjhar district. She observed that the Juangs indulge in shifting cultivation, which they call *taila,* or *dahi* cultivation. She also observed the custom of bride price and the headmanship. N. K. Das has studied the ethnicity factor and electoral politics in tribal belts of western Orissa (Das, 1997). He has also written about the Simko movement led by Nirmal Munda, a lesser-known freedom fighter, who launched his movement against imposition of unjust British colonial laws and taxes on poor tribes who enjoyed jural rights over their land in the then princely state of western Orissa (Das 1990). Das studied the identity issue and culture change in contemporary era in the aftermath of the process of state formation in the Binjhal community.

The Anthropology Department of Utkal University has been very active in social, physical anthropological and pre-historic-archaeological researches in Orissa. L. K. Mahapatra prepared a doctoral thesis, A Hill Bhuiya Village: An Empirical Socio-Economic Study, at Hamburg University, Germany in 1960. Professor N.K. Behura has made significant contribution in the fields of pottery technique and its relation with wider caste system in Orissa. He has written several books on theoretical anthropology, ethnographic accounts of Orissa tribes, tribal development, quality of life, etc. Professor Behura also brought out a journal called *Manav* on behalf of the Anthropological Society of Orissa. Professor P.K. Nayak of the same department has brought out a book "Blood, Women and Territory: An Analysis of Clan Feuds among the

Dongaria Konds". K.K. Basa has published several books dealing with the pre-historical and archaeological sites of Orissa. N.Patnaik has evaluated the impact of community development blocks on tribes. As director of State Tribal Research, he had brought several monographs on tribes of Orissa. As fellow of Indian Institute of Advanced Studies, Shimla, he brought out a critical study of Jagannatha phenomenon in Orissa. S. N. Ratha of Sambalpur University has brought out several important publications. D. K. Behera of the same department and Georg Pfeffer have brought a series of volumes under the common title of *Contemporary Society: Tribal Studies.* Georg Pfeffer, a German professor of ethnology at the Freie university of Berlin, has studied the cults and kinship of scheduled tribes in Koraput region of south Orissa. Nabakrishna Chaudhury Institute of Development Studies at Bhubaneswar has been conducting several important works among different populations and regions of Orissa. Nilakantha Panigrahi is currently working on poverty related issues among the tribals, displaced populations, and other communities facing economic crises. P.K. Mohanty and Jagannatha Dash have written books on foraging, and other tribal communities of Orissa. The Census Organisation of India has studied some villages and it also studied the uprooted tribal families of Rourkela (Tondon,1970). Archaeological and historical researches have been prominently carried out in Orissa, crafting its identity. V. Ball (1876) had initiated prehistoric studies in Orissa. Acharya (1923) and Banerjee (1930) and then N.K. Bose and Harani Sen (1948), in 1940s, were responsible for excavating palaeolithic sites at Kuliana (Mayurbhanj). It was the excavation at Kuchai by B.K. Thapar where evidence of neolothic culture in Orissa in general and in Mayurbhanj area in particular was established on a firm footing (Thapar 1985). Orissa underwent a metal age (a protohistoric phase) before emerging into the early historic phase. Copper double axes are reported from Mayurbanj region during early part of the last century (Basa 1999). Although the first written account in Orissa is known from the Asokan inscriptions at Dhauli and Jaugarh in the third century BC as in the case with the Gangetic valley. This is because Kalinga figures in the list of sixteen Mahajanapada. Recent excavations of Lalitgiri have thrown light on early culture and also transition from Hinayana to Mahayana form of Buddhism (Basa

1999). Since hunting, fishing and gathering were the primary modes of subsistence, such hilly terrains of Neolithic, central and southern Orissa were appropriate places for pre-historic men with regard to raw materials for manufacturing tools as well as abundant plant and animal resources as well as forest for hunting, fishing and gathering activities (Basa 1999). K. Ravi and Rammana have recently studied the status of traditional knowledge in parts of Orissa and Bastar.

Culture Zones, Etymology and the Oriya Identity

Orissa is divided into three eco-cultural zones: the coastal plains, the northwestern highland or plateau and the southwestern region, Dandkaranya. Orissa has the highest proportion of the scheduled castes and tribes too. K.S.Singh observed that abundance of toddy trees in the coastal area explains the presence of toddytapers, Siyal, Pasi and the links with distillers, Sundi and Kalar. Geographically, Orissa is regarded as a state of the eastern region of India, but culturally it is as much a part of northern India as it is of southern India.

This cultural synthesis has influenced the course of its social history to a considerable extent. South Orissa feels some sense of homogeneity with the southern states and the coastal districts have affinity with the North. Western Orissa on the other hand has strong linkage with its tribal past, which characterises its folk culture. The state of Orissa is thus a confluence of the multiple strands of Indian culture. The names Kalinga, Utkal, Odra and Kosala have found mention in ancient Sanskrit and Pali literature. Except Kosala, the other three geographical names are still applied to modern Orissa (Panigrahi 1981: 4). However a Kosala identity is in existence in western Orissa particularly in terms of a political demand for a separate state forming the Sambalpur region. The name Kalinga occurs in the Puranas in association with Anga, Vanga, Pundra and Sumba. The evidence furnished by Asoka's Inscription thus clearly proves that Kalinga in his time included the entire region now known as Orissa. It seems that its southern boundary extended upto the river Godavari (Panigrahi 1981: 5). In one of the earliest copperplate records of Orissa, known as Sumandala Copper Plates of Prithvivigraha, Kalinga as a *rashtra* (kingdom) has found mention. Orissa can be broadly divided into four natural regions, viz. (a) the hilly areas in the north and northwest, (b) the Eastern Ghats, (c) the central and western plateau, and (d) the coastal plains. The hilly areas in the north and northwest and the central and western plateau constitute the mineral belt of the state. Most of the tribal population of the State lives in this region. The important rivers of Orissa are the Mahanadi, the Brahmani, the Budhabalanga, the Subarnarekha, the Salandi, the Rushikulya, the Banshadhara, the Bada, the Bahuda and the Indravati. The Chilika Lake is about 64 kilometres long and 16 to 32 kilometres wide. Climate of Orissa is equitable; it is neither very hot in summer nor very cold in winter. There are three well-marked seasons in the State. They are summer, rainy and spring. The summer continues from March till June when the temperature rises very high, though not as high as in northern India. There are occasional showers during this season. The rainy season continues from July till October and there is heavy rainfall in the month of August. Gopalpur-on-Sea, Puri, Bhubaneswar and Chandipur, on account of their pleasant weather, are good summer holiday resorts (Dash 1997: 30).

In Orissa, people live in 50 5,734 villages and 81 towns which cover an area of 155, 701 sq. km. The coastal areas of the state are thickly populated (47.33%) while Koraput district is very thinly populated. There are 91 Scheduled Castes and 62 Scheduled Tribes in Orissa, as per official records of which 3,310,850 (71) are Scheduled Caste persons. The proportion of rural population to total population in Orissa according to 1991 census is 86.6 per cent which is much higher than the national average of 76.30 per cent showing more population of Orissa as rural. The literacy rate in rural Orissa is 60.44 per cent and that in urban areas is 80.95 per cent, as per 2001. The Scheduled Tribes in Orissa constitute 22.21 per cent of the total population of the state which is much higher than the national average of 8.01 (1991 census). The literacy rate among the Scheduled Tribes in Orissa is 22.31 per cent (34.44 per cent among male and 10.21 per cent among females) which is lower than the national average of the literacy rate of the Scheduled Tribes, i.e. 29.6 per cent as per 1991. The female literacy rate among the Scheduled Tribes in Orissa being only 10.21 per cent is very low when compared to their national average, i.e. 18.19 per cent. Of the total population of the Scheduled Tribes 40.24 per cent (57.51 per cent males and 23.00

per cent females) are returned as main workers and 9.12 per cent marginal workers as per 1991.

Orissa lies across routes of migration of peoples and cultures from north and east to south. Orissa and Andhra have had a strong relationship in history, polity and culture. Developments in Indo-Ganga plains too impinged on Orissa, as did developments in central India. An extraordinary range of diversities marks Orissa. Oriya identity has evolved over centuries. It is now marked in Oriya language, the territory, many elements of culture, vibrant folk and oral traditions, flourishing crafts and the majestic presence of Jagannath. In all parts of the country, all communities, particularly the tribal and non-tribal have interacted. Both Buddhism and Jainism had strong influence in Orissa, as they were associated with political authority, trade and business, mining and metallurgy, religion and rituals. Some of the features of Oriya society such as equality and vegetarianism could be traced to these religions and Bhakti movements through which these ideas percolated to the people.

Orissa derives its name from "Odra Vishaya" or "Odradesa". The fragmentary concepts of Kalinga, Utkla, Odra, Kosala, etc., are from time to time, homogenised through Asoka, Kharavela, Kapilendra Deva, Utkala Sammilani, and even the British (Patnaik, 2002). Orissa may have been known as Kalinga, Utkal or Odradesh, but it is Odissa /Orissa that synthesizes the region's ancient past with a vibrant presence in a dynamic manner. A unique feature of Orissa is its rather uninterrupted cultural development. Even during the heyday of Muslim rule in India under the Mughals, inaccessibility allowed Orissa to preserve its tradition till 1803, when the East India Company defeated the Marathas, who had ruled Orissa since 1751. An uninterrupted tribe-caste Hindu inter-communion characterizes the cultural history of Orissa. This feature finds its lasting manifestation in the Jagannath tradition of Puri. The crucial role played by the Oriyas in spread of Indian cultures and religions in vast South East Asian regions generally remains less noticed. Seaports flourished along the Orissa coast as early as fourth and fifth centuries BC, when Oriya Sadhabs went to the islands of Java, Sumatra, Borneo and Bali with their merchandise. Not only did they bring home wealth, they also carried glorious Indian civilization with them and helped its spread abroad. The

Odras and Utkals were Austric people. They derived their names from two kings, who were brothers, known as Gaya and Utkal (Dash 1997: 5).

Linkages of Languages and Growth of Syncretism

People of India data have shown that more than ninety per cent of the people of Orissa have Oriya as their mother tongue and thus Orissa is predominantly a unilingual State. In the southern districts, Telugu is also used as the official language for limited purpose (Dash 1997: 66). Asoka's inscriptions in Orissa, like those of other parts of India, are in Pali. Asoka's invasion of Kalinga not only influenced its language, but also its culture. The Chedis of whom Kharavela was the third member were a people of northern origin and were a branch of a dynasty of the same name originally ruling in Madhyadesa or Magadha. The language, in which the Hatigumpha Prasati has been composed, is also of Sanskrit origin. Jainism, which Kharavela professed, was a religion of northern origin with a sacred language of Sanskrit origin. The ruling dynasties of Orissa like the Vigrahas and the Matharas have all used Sanskrit in their charters. A change in the official language from Prakrit to Sanskrit took place from the fourth-fifth century A. D. The revival of Hinduism and of Sanskrit in the Gupta Empire had its repercussion on Orissa also. A great work like *The Panchatantra* was composed in Orissa during the rule of the Matharas. Sanskrit, Prakrit and Pali were never the spoken languages of Orissa, but the Orissan people ultimately adopted a language derived from all of them (Panigrahi 1981: 283). Most of the ancient Sanskrit and Oriya literary works are in the shape of palm leaf manuscripts.

The development of Oriya script is ascribed to a period from the 6th century A. D. to the 12th century A. D. The Natha and Siddha literature are the earlier works in Oriya. Serious writing in Orissa started in 14th century during the times of Gajapatis. The demand for Mahabharata and Ramayana in Oriya grew at this time and the Oriya Mahabharata of Sarala Dasa could meet the demand substantively. Balarama Dasa is famous for his Ramayana, which is to be found in Oriya home. Vilanka Ramayana, which contains the episodes of Sahasrasira Ravana, is available in Orissa. Apart from Ramayana, Bhagavata is another popular work. The sixteenth century Vaishnava poet Atibadi Jagannatha Dasa had composed Bhagavata for the first time in an Eastern Indian language. Jayadeva was a wandering ascetic. It was at the lotus feet of Sri Jagannatha at Puri that Jayadeva composed his famous Gita Govinda. The tribes of Orissa are ethno-linguistically classified into three groups: Munda (Austroasiatic), Dravidian and Indo-Aryan. The tribal languages began to appear in written forms only in the last century. The Christian missionaries took initiative to study the languages and to produce and publish Biblical texts in Roman script. However, due to certain historical factors from 1930's onwards, some tribal leaders and writers attempted to shape their literature and even invent scripts to provide indigenous writing systems for promoting literacy and literary activities in their languages. Publication of more and more books in many tribal languages during the last few years by adapting Oriya writing system has greatly expanded literary activities in the tribal languages (Mahapatra, K., 1998).

The Oriya speakers show a wide range of bilingualism as they are found to be simultaneously conversant in Telugu (73,338), Hindi (1,540,159), Kui (36,776), Sanskrit (14,481), Santali (7,199), Khond (6,721), Ho (5,313), Bengali (3,476), Munda (3,842), Parji (3,791), Savara (3,387), Urdu (1,850) and English (1,661). The Telugu speakers are bilingual in Oriya (3,23,198), Hindi (29,163) and Kui (1,006). On the other hand, Hindi speakers are bilingual only with Oriya (346, 816), Gondi (1,930) and Urdu (1,807); the Urdu speakers in Oriya (135,191) and Hindi (31,335); the Bengali speakers in Oriya (12,266) and Hindi (10,386). The tribes are bilingual, mostly so, in Oriya, Telugu, and Hindi or other tribal languages. The speakers of Bhumij (16,227), Gadaba (12,774), Halabi (3,048), Juang (11,136), Koda/Kora (1,588) and Konda (2,042) are mostly bilingual in Oriya. But Parji speakers are mostly bilingual in Telugu (1,350); Gondi speakers are bilingual in Hindi (4,191) and Oriya (15,607); the Ho are bilingual in Oriya (89,654), Hindi (3,715) and Santali (1,792); the Kharia are bilingual in Oriya (41,564) and Hindi (8,802). The Khond/Kondh are bilingual in Oriya (122,126), Telugu (6,157) and Parji (382). The Kisan are bilingual in Oriya (94,882) and Hindi (4,790). The Koya are bilingual in Oriya (33,498) and Telugu (1,296). The Kui speakers are bilingual in Oriya (251, 581), Telugu (9,333) and Parji (212). The Munda speakers are bilingual in Oriya (96,946),

Hindi (16,666) and Santali (1,208). The Mundari speakers are bilingual in Oriya (46,761), Hindi (5,969) and Santali (742). The Santali speakers are bilingual in Oriya (1,96,781), Hindi (4,692), and Ho (1,370). The Savara speakers are bilingual in Oriya (1,16,388) and Telugu (7,301). An interesting case is that of the Gadaba who speak three languages belonging to the three language families, namely, the Dravidian language of Gadaba, the Austric language of Gutolic, and the Indo-Aryan languages of Oriya and Halbi.

An admixture of scripts called Kalinga or later Kalinga script existed in the Eastern Ganga dynasty during the period from the 7 to 11 century. Earlier, Gaudi script derived from Siddhamatrika prevailed from the 10 to the 14 century. The Oriya and the Perso-Arabic scripts are commonly used in Orissa. There are two tribal scripts, one invented by Pandit Raghunath Murmu called Ol Chiki for Santhali language and the other by the Savaras who claim to have transited from (Jagannath) to *akshara brahma* (script). The tribal scripts have been used as identity markers. The beginning of Oriya literature is traced to the 8th century and its flowering to the 14th century when an enormous range of creative output appeared with a dozen variety of the Ramayana and four versions of the Mahabharat and translation of the Bhagavat Purana of Jagannatha Das. Among the contributors to the literary heritage of Orissa were people from all sections of society, *sudra* muni, Sarla Das, a weaver Gangadhar Meher, a Brahman Jayadeva whose Geetgovind is sung at the temple everyday, a Khond poet, Bhima Bhoi, a Khandayat Fakirmohan Senapati (1843-1918), father of modern Oriya literature. A feature has been the incorporation of rich tribal material into Oriya literature.

The origin and development of Sanskrit and Oriya languages can also be gleaned from the inscriptions. The sculptures supplement our knowledge of the social life of Orissa in ancient and medieval times. There are also sculptural representations of dress, ornament and coiffure of both men and women as well as toilets used by both the sexes. The Puranas such as the Visnu Purana, the Vayu Purana, the Skanda Purana, the Brahma Purana throw much light on the caste system of Orissa in ancient and medieval periods. The dramas like Anarghaaghava and Prabodhachandrodaya depict the theatrical performances that were popular in Orissa. The Sahityadarpana mentions some games of the people of Orissa. The Manasollasa reveals the caste system as well as the food habits of the people of Orissa during the period under survey. The Gitagovinda indicates the status of the *devadasis* as well as the dance and music that were popular in Orissa during the period (B. Das 1985). In addition to the aforesaid Sanskrit works some Oriya works also can be relied upon to reconstruct the social history of Orissa in ancient and medieval periods. The Sarala Mahabharata and the Adalapanji contain stray references to various aspects of social life such as caste system, position of women, food and Siddha food habits, musical instruments, the position of weavers, Hadis, Dombas, Savaras, etc. The chewing of betel is more widely in vogue in Orissa than in other states. In fact, the Orissan epigraphs refer to betel nuts and betel-leaves at several places. Jayadeva is among the central most figures in Oriya culture. It is an established fact that Jayadeva's works have spread to southern India, where verses of the poet's work have been incorporated into Kathakali and Bharatnatyam classical dance forms respectively. It is Jayadeva's *ashtapadis* that are sung in dance performances of Odissi, the classical dance of Orissa. Oriya *bhajans* (devotional songs) are based on *ragas* and *talas* specified by Jayadeva's hymns. The Gita Govinda composed by Jayadeva is one of the popular themes in the traditional *patachitra* paintings of Orissa. Jayadeva's *ragas* do not match the lyrical patterns of Bengal, which unlike Orissa, does not possess a classical vocal tradition. Even earlier, the first English translation of *Gita Govinda*, published by Sir William Jones in 1792, identified Kalinga (Orissa) as the saint poet's birthplace. The government of Orissa, through the Odissi Akademi, has initiated an annual Jayadeva Utsav (festival) in Bhubaneswar and New Delhi to commemorate the great poet's birth in Orissa, through classical music and dance. The people of Orissa have now been able to establish the fact that the 12th century saint-poet Jayadeva indeed belonged to their state.

Classical and Popular Folk Performances

Orissa has a rich tradition of folklore, theatre and theatrical presentations consisting of music, dance and dramatics in many varieties and forms. Jatra groups of Orissa move from place to place. There are many items which are performed solo like the Bohurupi, Ghantapatua, Mundapota Kela, Janughanta, Jogi, Ghuduki,

Dhankoila, Galpasagara, Kathaka, Harikatha, etc. There are items which are enacted in duets, like Ghata Kalasi, Dhoba Nacha, Sabara Sabaruni, Kela Keluni, Dasakathia and such others. There are items, which need four to eight persons such as Gotipua, Sakhinata, Ghudukinata, Dhumpa Geeta, Nachuni Nach, Mahari Nacha, Naga Nacha, Patua Jatra, Chaiti Ghoda, Pala, and such others. Dhankoila Jatra, Humo, Dalkhai and other Jatra items need a term of twenty to sixty persons. They are the Leela, Suanga (Titinatya, Gitabhinaya), Dandanata. The Pala and Dasakathia are most popular forms of folk performances of Orissa. In Dasakathia a colourful and popular performance is rendered by two-member, one singer (Gayaka) and the other accompanist (Palia). This performance is ritualistic and secular. The dramatic performance includes verbose stanzas of various types including pauranic episodes. The origin of Pala goes back to Muslim-Mughal period, when assimilation of Satya Narayan of Hindu pantheon with *pir* of Mohammedanism brought about a synthetic cult known as Satyapir (H. C. Das 1978). We have two types of *pala* in Orissa—the Baithaaki (sitting) and the Thia (standing). The *thia pala* is taken to be the developed form of *danda nata*. The group of performers consisting of six persons is including the Bayak or the drummer (who plays on the Mrudanga), the chief singer known as Gayaka. In *pala* performance songs of various types in different styles predominate the dance to the tune of music. Patua Jatra, similar to that of *pala*, is a well-known form prevalent among the low caste people (Das 1978). Jhoomar dance named after the accompanying Jhoomar songs is current among the Mahanta and Munda communities of the Sundargarh district. Among the Mahantas the men perform the dance. Among the Mundas the singers who accompanying the dancers sing songs and the dancers follow them in chorus in accompaniment of Madal. The Mundas are especially experts in this dance particularly in intricate footsteps, movement of hip and wrists, and body (H. C. Das 1978).

The tribes of Orissa have a very rich tradition of folklore, songs and dances, which often have secular, religious and seasonal character. Among tribal dances may be included the colourful spring time dance of the Santals with their musical instrument, Madal performed by the maidens, their pastoral dance during ripping of grain, the dance of the Kolha at the time of planting of seeds in honour of their deity performed by men and women, the dances of the Gonds done in dedication to their deity Bhimsen, at harvesting festival time, marriage celebrations, accompanied by several musical instruments like the horned-drums, flutes and clarinets, the spring dance of the Bhatra with beautiful dresses, silver ornaments of women. Karma is a folk ritual based on folk dance in honour of the deity Karam sani or Kararani, ritualistic in character. This dance type is confined to the Binjhal, Kharia, Kisan and Kol tribes who perform it in the month of Bhadrab from the eleventh day of the full moon day. The boys and girls chop off a branch of Karam or Sal tree and bring the same to a well decorated place of the village where the priest locally known as Jhankar performs the ritual such as pouring liquor, offering fowl, sweet meats, etc. This is followed by singing and dancing in accompaniment of drum (*madal*), cymbal, etc., with colourful costumes in exuberance of red cloth, set in peacock feathers skilfully designed ornaments made of small conch shells. Both men and women take part and continue to engross themselves for the whole night. The technique of the Karma dance varies from tribe to tribe. The Sua dance of the Sambalpur tribes is performed by young girls in the spirit of adventure and romance accompanied by drummers and musicians, and the ring dance of the Oran performed during all festivals and in the spring and autumn seasons are other popular dances in a circle. The women dancers placing their arms at the back of their neighbours and clasping the hands of the next in the courtship dances of Ho is worth seeing.

Chhow dance is a famous dance form of Orissa. It has earned its name and fame in the international arena for its famous martial art based Chhow dance. This variety of dance is prevalent in the Mayur-Bhanja, Nialgiri and Sareikala (now in Jharkhand) regions. Exclusively men perform this dance. The steps and movements, the attack and defence, the performers each holding a sword and shield, dividing themselves into two parties, the drums and their mode of play, the huge kettledrum known as 'Dhumusa', being must in the orchestra, its reverberating powerful beats energizing the dancers, all signify that Chhow dance has unmistakably originated from martial practices. Puppet dance known as Kandei or Sakhi Nata, a rare and unusual type of stylised indigenous drama and dance based on mythological stories, is performed in various parts of Orissa.

The puppetry of Orissa may be classified into three categories, such as hand puppets, string puppets, rod puppets (H. C. Das 1978). In western Orissa, we find different types of folk dances and music. An important folk dance of the area is Dalkhai. The unmarried grown-up girls form a semi-circle and dance outside the village. We have another form of dance -song-worship all combined in the Karma or Kelikadam dance. This dance is generally performed on the Ekadasi (the eleventh day), which is known as the Bada Ekadasi (the big eleventh day) of the month of Aswin (September) every year. N. K. Das and Santanu Mitra observed Karma performed in great style in western Orissa. Das and Mitra observed that among the Binjhal it is celebrated with much pomp and ceremony. After completion of the rituals and offerings to Karmasain the Binjhal priest narrates to the village folk the miraculous deeds of Karmasain in form of stories. Dance takes place only at the completion of the narration of the story by Jhankar (the Binjhal priest). The Karma dance is also performed when natural calamities occur or disease persists. Male and female take part in the dance. The drummer plays the drum at the centre of the dancing group. The Madal (drum) used in the Karma dance is an earthen made leather drum. This drum is bigger than Mridangam. The tune of the Madal reaches a radius of three to four kms. and attracts people of nearby villages with its sweet and scintillating music. The Madal is the central piece of musical instrument of this dance. Ghumara dance also portrays love, joke and the pangs of separation. Tal, Ghumara and Nisan Tal, these three musical instruments accompany the dance sequence. The dancers wear tight trousers and loose shirts, a long piece of cloth is tied around the head in the form of a turban and peacock's feathers are fixed to it. The origin of the Danda dance has been ascribed to the kingdom of Boud (modern Boud district of Orissa), where Buddhism was the cardinal religion. The Prabha dance resembles that of Lord Siva's Tandab dance (the dance of destruction). Musical instruments like Mardala, Gini, Flute and Mahuri accompany the chief musical instruments of the Danda dance, Dhol (drum) (Panda 1978). Dhapa dance is generally performed in a majority of tribal villages. Samprada is a Mridangam type drum, but it is different in its process of construction from the Mridangam and is biggest in size. One individual, who becomes the centre of attraction, performs the Samprada or Bahak dance and his assistant simply repeats his songs and sayings. Spiritual and devotional *prayers,* chanda and *choupadi* find place in the songs of the dancer. An assistant (Palia) helps the dancer with a Khol (a flattened drum). This dance is generally performed on the eve of the spring festival (Panda 1978). Danda Nata is performed with great religious fervour. An artist dressed in multi-coloured skirt and tight-fitting attire of local design appears and announces the opening of folk theatre in a jovial manner. Dhol, a double-sided drum, and Mahuri (Shahanai) are the only musical instruments used at that time. Lately, this typical dance drama, Danda Nata, assumed the character of *yatra* performance on mass scale. The dance-drama continues for a period ranging from 13 to 21 days (C. B. Patel 2002). Dhap folk dance was prevalent in western Orissa. It derives its name from Dhap, a musical instrument of the shape of typical Khanjani. This folk art medium is operformed mostly by the Kandhas. Unlike Danda Nata, in Dhap both men and women participate in equal ratio (C. B. Patel 2002).

Odissi dance, which has earned world reputation for its elaborate grace and charm, is the continued tradition of ancient *Odra nrutya,* a highly civilised dance that existed 2,000 years ago. The history of Odissi dance is largely the history of the Devadasis (dancing-girls) attached to important shrines of Orissa. The practice of dedicating dancing-girls in honour of gods was at one time prevalent throughout India. There are quite a few anthropological studies on this tradition. In Orissa it began with the growth of Siva temples at Bhubaneswar. History also proves that the powerful Ganga rulers first attached the dancing-girls known as Maharis in Orissa to the shrine of Jagannath at Puri in early 12th century. Prataprudra Deva, the son of Purusottama, in an inscription, dated July 1499 A.D. regulated the performance of dance. It was ordained that the dancing-girls were to dance and sing only from Jayadev's *Gita-Govinda* at the time of food-offerings (*bhoga*) in the Jagannath temple. Dancing was not only confined to the Devadasis as an art of honour. Princesses also practised it. Gradually the Devadasis ceased to be respected as they took to easy virtues. The dances of the "Gotipua" and "Sakhipila" (young boys dressed as girls) took its place catering to the taste of the general public. Abhinaya Chandrika, the code of Odissi dance written in 15th century by Sri Maheswar Mohapatra, gave the ground for re-establishment of

Odissi dance. Within few years Odissi could be revived and put in the rightful place in the classical dance map of India. Odissi, with a religious import and devotional intent has a rich and varied repertory embracing both Nritta (pure dance) and Nrutya (interpretative dance). The theme is rooted in religion; the urge is as much spiritual as aesthetic. A performance of Odissi opens with Mangalacharan, an invocatory piece of dance followed by singing of a *sloka* in obeisance to lord Ganesha or Jagannatha. Batu Nrutya is an item of pure dance laying stress on sculpturesque poses. A piece from *Gita Govinda* is indispensable, Dasavatar being the most popular item. Odissi is a highly stylised dance, with strict rules governing every aspect of its rendering. Odissi is full of sculpturesque poses known as Bhangis. Mostly these Bhangis are based on the "Tribhanga' or three-bend concept of Hindu iconography (Panda *et al.* 1999).

Orissa Cultural History and Linkages with South East Asia

By the time of Mahavira and Buddha, Kalinga-Utkal regions on the eastern coast of India had acquired recognition and fame (M.N. Das 1962). The political history of Orissa opens with the rule of the Nanda Emperors of Magadha. The Hatigumpha Inscription of Emperor Kharavela at Udaygiri refers to a Nanda King twice, that the Nandaraja constructed an aqueduct in Kalinga, and that he took away to Magadha the sacred seat of the Jina, which belonged to Kalinga (Kalinga Jinasana). However, when Chandragupta Maurya succeeded to the throne of the Nandas, Kalinga did not form a part of his empire (M. N. Das 1962). Ashok's Kalinga invasion was an epoch-making event of ancient times, an event of far-reaching consequence in history. Kalinga was conquered but the conquest changed the heart of the conqueror. The change in Asoka changed the course of religious and cultural history of Asia. It is in his Kalinga Rock Edicts that Asoka enunciated some of the finest principles of a good government and declared, "All men are my children". The next great epoch of Orissan History was the reign of Kharavela. The history of this emperor is recorded at the Udaygiri Hill near Bhubaneswar and is famous as the Hitigumpha inscription. The date of Kharavela has been debated among scholars, some of whom regard his rule in the first half of the 2nd century B.C., while others in the 1st century B. C. His achievements, however, were remarkable. He conquered many countries, gave them a good administration, and played a prominent part in religious activities. His army went as far as Mathura in the north; and in the far south, the Pandya king recognised his supremacy. Side by side with wars and conquests, the emperor involved himself with public works, such as, reconstruction of the city of Kalinganagar, laying of embankments and gardens, and repairing canals. In the thirteenth year of his reign, Kharavela retired to the Kumari Hill at Khandigiri near Bhubaneswar where one hundred and seventeen caves were constructed to serve as the resting-place for the Arhatas. Kharavela was a Jaina. The ruins of Jaina architecture of Kharavela are still to be seen on the twin hills of Udaygiri and Khandagiri, in the vicinity of modern Bhubaneswar (M. N. Das 1962). In the middle of the 4th Century A. D. when the Gupta Emperor Samudragupta undertook his military expedition to the South, Orissa was a divided territory. In the 8th Century A.D., the most remarkable feature of the Orissan history was the culmination of Orissa's overseas activities in the establishment of the Sailendra Empire in Malayasia. From ancient times, the people of Kalinga were pioneers of maritime adventure. Commercial relations continued for many centuries side by side with settlement of colonies in Bali, Java, Sumatra, Borneo and Malaya. By 7th century, the Chinese had learnt to call Java 'Ho-ling', the Chinese equivalent of the word Kalinga (M. N. Das 1962). During the 8th, 9th, and 10th centuries, a powerful dynasty known as the Bhauma-Kara ruled over Utkal. The Soma Vamsi rulers flourished during the 10th and 11th Centuries (M. N. Das 1962). A new chapter in the history of Orissa was opened with the coming of the Ganga Dynasty to power. By the end of 11th Century A.D. and in early 12th Century, they rose into prominence and brought the whole of Orissa under their sway. Vaishnavism received the royal patronage, and Vaishnavite temples were built at many places such as Mukhalingam, Srikurmam and Simhachalam. The most prominent manifestation of this new movement was the foundation of the great temple of Jagannath at Puri. Ramanuja came to Puri during the days of Chodagangadeva, which had profound religious significance. The temple was completed by the successors of Chodaganga notably, Anangabhimadeva (M.N. Das 1962). For a long time the Gangas were in control of Hindu Orissa. In 13th

Century, Orissan architecture reached its climax in the construction of the famous Sun Temple of Konark by Narasimhadeva I who ruled from 1238 to 1264 A.D. The time of Prataprudra saw the rising tide of Bhakti movement in Orissa. Sri Chaitanya came to Puri and preached there for long. The King became a devout disciple of the Master. This in consequence adversely affected the political strength of Orissa at a time of external invasions. In 1568, Orissa lost her independence – being almost the last Hindu Kingdom of India to fall to the Muslims (M. N. Das 1962).

Diverse Religious Predispositions and Syncretic Jagannatha Tradition

There are various sects within and outside Hinduism and in Orissa they provide collective identity. They are also central and unifying force in Oriya society. The overwhelmingly important Vaishnava sects have their supreme deity, Jagannatha, whose main temple is at Puri on the sea, where the famous annual festival with huge wooden chariots dragged for the regional divine triad—Jagannatha, Balabhadra, and Subhadra (goddess sister)—draws about half a million devotees. The famous Lingaraja temple of Lord Shiva at Bhubaneswar, the famous Viraja goddess temple at Jajpur, both in coastal Orissa, and Mahimagadi, the cult temple of the century-old Mahima sect of worshipers of Shunya Parama Brahma (the absolute soul void) at Joranda in central Orissa, are highly sacred for the Oriya people.

The people of Orissa profess Hinduism overwhelmingly (96.4 per cent), with Christianity (1.73 per cent), Islam (1.49 per cent), Sikhism (0.04 per cent) and Buddhism (0.04 per cent) trailing far behind. Tribes pursue their own religions even though many have declared Hinduism as their religion. Apart from supreme beings, gods, and goddesses of classical Hindu religion, the Oriyas propitiate a number of disease spirits, village deities, and revere ancestral spirits. The religious practitioners belong to numerous caregories. In the villages each Brahman priest has a number of client families of Kshatriya, Vaisya, and some Sudra castes. There are also magicians (*gunia*) practicing witchcraft and sorcery. Kalisi or shamans are consulted to discover the causes of crises and the remedies.

A large number of rituals and festivals mostly following the lunar calendar are observed. The most important rituals are: the New

Year festival (Bishuba Sankranti) in mid-April; the fertility of earth festival (Raja Parab); festival of plowing cattle (Gahma Punein); the ritual of eating the new rice (Nabanna); the festival worshiping the goddess of victory, known otherwise as Dassara (Durga Puja); the festival of the unmarried girls (Kumar Purnima); the solar-calendar harvest festival (Makar Sankranti); the fast for Lord Shiva (Shiva Ratri); the festival of colors and the agricultural New Year (Dola Purnima or Dola Jatra); and, finally, the festival worshiping Lord Krishna at the end of February. In November-December (lunar month of Margashira) every Thursday the Gurubara Osha ritual for the rice goddess Lakshmi is held in every Oriya home. The ancient name of Orissa, Utkala, literally means "the highest excellence in the arts." The Oriya are famous for folk paintings, painting on canvas (*patta-chitra*), statuary and sculptures, the Orissan style of temple architecture, and tourist and pilgrim mementos made of horn, papier-mâché, and appliqué work. Classical Odissi dance, the virile Chhow dance, colorful folk dances with indigenous musical instruments (percussion, string, and wind) and also Western instruments, dance dramas, shadow plays (Ravana-Chhaya) with puppets, folk opera (*jatra*), mimetic dances, and musical recitation of God's names are all very popular. Orissi music, largely following classical (*raga*) tunes, and folk music, are rich and varied. Illness is attributed to "hot" or "cold" food, evil spirits, disease spirits, and witches; and mental diseases to sorcery or spirit possession. Leprosy and gangrenous wounds are thought to be punishment for the commission of "great" sins, and, for general physical and mental conditions, planets and stars in the zodiac are held responsible. Cures are sought through herbal folk medicines, propitiation of supernatural beings and spirits, exorcism, counteraction by a *gunia* (sorcery and witchcraft specialist), and the services of homeopathic, allopathic, or Ayurvedic specialists.

Death is considered a transitional state in a cycle of rebirths till the soul (*atma*) merges in the absolute soul (*paramatma*). The god of justice, Yama, assigns the soul either to Heaven (*swarga*) or to Hell (*narka*). The funeral rites and consequent pollution attached to the family and lineage of the deceased last for ten days among higher castes. The dead normally are cremated.

In the first part of the seventh century A.D., Sasanka, the king of Gauda, who was the overlord of Kongoda, gave a definite turn to the ascendancy of Saivism in Orissa. His coins indicate that he was a follower of Siva and Yuan Chwang's accounts represent him as an enemy of Buddhism. The Saiva temples of Jaipur, built during this period, bear Tantrik influences. Viraja, the presiding deity of the place, has found mention in the Mahabharata and the Harivamsa and her antiquity is to be traced to a much earlier period. Tantras had become inextricably mixed up with all forms of religions in Orissa, when the Somavamsis started their rule in this country about A.D. 931. The Samovamsis were the staunch Saivas, as their surnames Mahasivagupta and Mahabhavagupta indicate. They revived the most important Vaisnava shrine of Jagannatha at Puri; the kings of this dynasty were instrumental in raising the great Saiva temple of Lingaraja at Bhubaneswar and Udyota-kesari's mother Kolavatidevi built the temple of Brahmesvara at Bhubaneswar. They thus seem to have been cosmopolitan in their religious outlook, retaining all the conventions that had acquired religious sanction through long practice in the preceding centuries (Panigrahi 1981: 319). The Gangas were originally Saivas, but after their conquest of Orissa they becamc more inclined towards Vaisnavism as represented by the Jagannatha cult.

Sacred texts suggest the prevalence of the goddess cult in the early history of Orissa.The inland part of Orissa has strong tribal roots. Many of the people here were absorbed into Hinduism within the last several hundred years. This is probably the main reason for the prevalence of the non-Brahmin style of worshipping the goddess, with its associated animal sacrifice and independence from Jagannath at Puri. By contrast, temples on the coast are located along the piligrimage corridor where there is a long history of Hinduism (Preston 1980: 20). In Orissa, only the temples of the goddess Bimala at Puri, Biraja at Jaipur and Bhubaneswari at Vhubaneswar are mentioned as *pithas* in the classical Sanskrit literature. In Orissa the appearance of Sakti cult can be traced back to the 2nd century B.C. The orthodox made up their mind and worshipped Stambhesvari, Seen Matrukas along with Virabhadra and Ganesha, and folk deities. The spread of Sakti cult was marked by the worship of diffent Durgas. The two-armed Viraja at Jaipur in the district of Cuttack is the earliest form of Mahishamardini Durga. The various images of Buddhist Tara worshiped attest to the popularity of the Sakti cult in Orissa (Panda et.al. N.D. : 48).

Etymologically, the word Jagannatha means the Lord of the universe. Lord Jagannatha epitomizes love and universal brotherhood. The cult of Jagannatha has assimilated the influence of many religious creeds, sects and has thus become unique (Khuintia 2002). Jagannath is a splendid synthesis not only of the different schools of thought in Hinduism, but it has also assimilated within it concepts and core thoughts of Buddhism, Jainism and Tantra. This spirit of integration is even apparent in the architectural style of the Jagannath temple. Jagannath has been looked upon as Krishna, Rama, Buddha, and Narayana, all in one. He has also been identified with the Mahayana Buddhism's Surya and the Brahma of Advaita Vedanta. It is wrong to characterize the religious ceremonies or philosophical ideas surrounding Jagannath worship as Jagannath cult. Since long, different theories have been propounded pertaining to the origin of the Jagannath cult. Stevenson first mooted the hypothesis of Buddhist origin of Jagannatha. General Cunningham in his Bhilsa Topes discussed the theory that Jagannatha Triad represents Buddha, Dharma and Sangha. At Puri, the Buddhist Stupa was erected with the usual carving of Triratna symbol of the Stupa in the 1st century A.D. At that time the Trinity was known as Jagannatha, the other name of Buddha. The celebrated poet Jayadeva (12th century A.D.) mentions Buddha as the ninth incarnation of the Lord. Since then, Jagannatha has been hailed by a larger number of Oriya people as the manifestation of Lord Buddha (Baba Mishra 1995: 47-48).

There is a strong tradition in Orissa, which suggests that Jagannatha had a tribal origin. At Chodaganga's time the Jagannatha cult offered both the necessary prerequisites to combine the two types of legitimation: it retained on the one hand a strong 'aboriginal' and autochthonous element. On the other hand it was no more a simple Hinduized cult, but had already enjoyed royal patronage and had thus been brahmanized. Once the identity of Jagannatha with Purusottama was well established, a further identification, namely that of Krisna almost suggested itself. The cult of Lord Jagannatha has two broad dimensions; physical and spiritual. When we look at the physical dimension of the cult, its emergence in a particular way depends on evidences from historical, the anthropological or cultural sources. The primary source of such a belief is the myth of Biswavasu, the Savara chief, his daughter Lalita, and the Brahmin son-on-law, Vidyapati. One has to believe that all his so-called tribal temple servants are nearest to him. It is only tribal Daitas who can worship him for 30 days during the Car Festival without uttering my Sanskrit or Vedic mantras. They do all the rituals in a typical tribal manner. Significantly enough, they are also treated as the lineage members of the deities, as a result of which they have to weep when old idols of the Triad are buried and have to observe all the rites of the mortuary on the occasion of Navakalevara ceremony. Though Lord Jagannatha is worshipped for the rest of the eleven months through Vedic practices, these observances of tribal rites for a period of one month are crucial and they prompt us to trace out the tribal link as well as the origin of Lord Jagannatha.

It also happens during the famous Navakalevara ceremony that only the Daitas, the tribal servants of the Lord, take a leading role in the expedition team for the procurement of the sacred "Daru" or wooden logs (of Neem tree). During this period, these Daitas live in a place near the temple of Goddess Mangala and the place is named as Savara Palli (village) of the Savaras, a tribe of Orissa. All the rites here are performed as per the tribal practices of spirit worship, ancestor-worship and the worship of village goddess (here Mangala). It is often said that the Saoras, a Mundari speaking tribe of Orissa, has some linguistic connection with the temple traditions.

Rath Yatra (or the car festival) is foremost among the twelve yatras of Lord Jagannatha, the presiding deity of Purushottama-Kshetra, i.e. Puri. It is celebrated on the 2nd lunar day (*tithi*) of the bright fortnight (*shukla dvitiya*, conjoint with Pushya Naksatra) in the month of Ashadha (June-July). In Ratha Yatra, however, the Deity himself has to be taken out in a Car in procession to a garden (*bithika*) near a tank or the riverside. The journey should be the longest among his annual peregrinations, and the stay out, for a period of 7, 9, 19, 15 or 30 days. After Snana Yatra (the bath ceremony) held on the full moon day of Jyestha, the three deities like ordinary mortals fall sick. They take rest, remaining on sick diet, i.e. pana and fruit alongwith medicine (*modaka-s*) administered by Rajavaidya for a fortnight. On the 16th day, i.e. on the eve of Ratha Yatra, they present themselves for worship after the ceremony of opening of the eyes (Netrotsava) and attainment of rejuvenation. Ratha Yatra which extends over a period of 9 days has three components, namely (a) the inward journey (Purva Yatra), (b) the halting week (Adapa) and the return journey (Bahuda Yatra). On the fifth day of the Yatra, i.e. on Shukla Shasthi Lakshmi, the consort of Jagannatha is taken in a *vimana* to spy the activities of her lord at the Gundicha temple. While on return journey, the Car of Jagannatha is detained near a small temple called Mausi-Ma's (maternal aunt's) temple. Ratha Yatra comes to an end ceremonially with Naladri Vije.

Alekha: Satya Mahima Dharma

Satya Mahima Dharma (otherwise known as Alekha Mahima Dharma or Kumbhipatia Dharma) has its origin in Orissa. Many people belonging to Scheduled Castes and Scheduled Tribes have embraced this sect. According to Mahima Dharma, Brahmo is one and only one. He is *alekha* (who cannot be written), Anadi (without any beginning), Ananta (without any end) and Anakar (without any shape). Thus Mahima Dharma preaches the theory of monotheism. Hindus believe in idolatry. Mahima Dharma preaches the theory of shapeless God. Mahimaism was originated taking a bold step against caste prejudices by proclaiming equality of mankind before God. The disciples of Satya Mahima Dharma believe that Mahima Gosain, the founder of this sect, was the incarnation of great *brahmo* who came to this world to revive Hindu religion from the state of degenaration. Several anthropologists (such as Lidia Guzy) have studied the *mahima dharma* and its ramifications. During the life time of Mahima Gasain, the sect was divided into two sections, viz., Kumbhipatias (who wear bark of Kumbhi tree) and Kanapatias (who wear red ochre dyed cloth). At that time there was conflict among these sections. Kanapatias and Kumbhipatias generally attended the annual festivals held at Mahulpada and Joranda, respectively. After the death of Mahima Gasain his followers were divided into three groups. They were known as Chappan Murtia, Tetis Murtia and Kodie Murtia according to the number of *sanyasis* in the group (TRB 1968).

The followers of Mahima Dharma may broadly be divided into two groups, Sanyasis and Gruhis or Asritas. The Sanyasis have to renounce the worldly life. It is essential for all sanyasis to devote life for realization of truth. Sanyasis lead a life of wanderings to preach ideas and thoughts of the sect. Gruhis on other hand live in their homes and enjoy worldly life, with certain restrictions. The Gruhis wear red ochre dyed cloth as uniform of Mahima Dharma. There is a common belief that red ochre dyed clothing is not polluted. The Gruhis are not allowed to rear goat, sheep, fools, as these are sacrificial animals for Hindu deities. The followers of Satya Mahima Dharma should wake up at dawn taking a purificatory bath; they salute seven times to Brahmo uder the canopy of sky. Likewise before sunset they salute five times. The followers do not take food after sun set. Except Brahmon, no other Hindu deity should be worshipped. Brahmo is one and only one. Image worship is discouraged. Intoxicants (specially drinking) are strictly prohibited. But they can chew tobacco or smoke Ganja. They should spend leisure by *Bhajana, kirtana* and *Smarana*. Western medicines are also discouraged. After Gosain's death it spread to other parts of Orissa as well as outside the State. Some centres have been established in Assam, Bengal, Bihar, Andhara Pradesh, Nepal, Burma (TRB 1968).

Tribal State Formation and patterns of Social Change

With the separation of Chhattisgarh from Madhya Pradesh recently, Orissa has emerged as the state having the largest tribal population concentrated in north western and southwestern parts of the state. Of all the tribes, the Saoras / Savaras were most intimately related to others in the ancient texts where they were mentioned both generically as any forest based group and specifically as forest dwellers in Orissa and central India. They participated in state formation, owned the land where they worshipped the early incarnation of Lord Jagannath and passed on the cult to the king and Brahmans. The Sudh Savaras are still active players in rituals.

In Orissa one encounters both endogenous and exogenous processes of state formation. The tribals had generally a two tier structure of authority, one at the level of the village chief selected by members of the village and the other at the level of a group of villages (*pidha*) inhabited by the tribe. A Rajput chief used to ritually marry a tribal girl and accord a position of honour and a significant role to the chief of the main tribe in coronation ceremony, adopt the tribal practice of naming the grandson after the grandfather, etc. Third, a distinction should be made between Kshatriyaization and Rajputization. Some tribal chiefs claimed the *varna* status of Kshatriya but would not give up the *jati* status, for example Nagvansi, the Gonds, Binjhal retained their jati status even while claiming a place in varna order. Some tribes "stole" minor Rajput scions and installed them as their rulers, for example, in Bamara, Gangpur, etc. Fourth, the tribal chiefs of Bonai, Keonjhar, Mayurbhanj, Gangapur who originally belonged to the tribal groups went through the process of Kshatriyazation and Rajputization. Thus the Bhuinya of Bonai and Keonjhar and the Bhanj of Mayurbhanj which means breaking of the eggs of the peacock claimed the status and got recognised as Rajput or later as a high status Rajput. Fifth, the tribes became peasants and Hinduised while maintaining a great deal of cultural autonomy such as Sounti, Bhuyan, Kisan, Bathudi, Mirdha, Gond and Savara. Sixth, the tribe remained a tribe among hunting-gathering groups.

Many other elements of Oriya identity emerged during the medieval period, language, literature, script, Jagannath cult, etc. The Jagannath cult is traditionally traced to the fifth century AD when the founder of Somvansi dynasty Yayati Keshari brought the wooden images from western Orissa together with Daita priests and set up the images in the new temple constructed by the ruler. However it was during the 400 year rule of the Gangas (11 to 14 century), when Orissa was territorially and politically integrated that the temple dedicated to Purshottama was constructed in 1196 AD., and Jagannath was elevated from a *rashtradevata* to an imperial god. Anangabhim in 1216 AD. called himself a deputy (*rauta*) and the son (*putra*) of the three deities, Purshottama, Rudra and Durga.

After the downfall of the Gupta Empire, the process of state formation shifted from the provincial centres to the hinterland. At this stage of state formation, there was need for legitimising the Hindu tribal rajas that ruled over relatively egalitarian tribal communities. The consolidation of state faced two sets of problems. First, the political problem of institutionalising powers over the people and translating it into authority. The new Hindu rajas, the nouveau riche among the former tribal chiefs, usually followed a long-drawn strategy. They sought the tribals' loyalty and, in exchange, patronised their powerful deities as the state deities (*rastradevata*), which helped to legitimise their rule over tribal or

Hindu-tribal frontiers. The generous patronage of these deities and their priests helped to politically bridge the gap between the new rulers and the ruled. Secondly, the economic and administrative problems relating to the newly established kingdoms were resolved by the rajas by systematically inviting new settlers, who were often drawn from the Brahmin and upper castes, as ritual and administrative specialists. The main function of Brahmins was the propagation of the new idea of Hindu kingship and the hierarchically structured caste society with the new Hindu rulers and priests at its top. They were responsible for the erection of the whole infrastructure of the New Kingdom, particularly its administration (Kulke, 1979: 24). This social consolidation of small kingdoms and principalities was a long and gradual process. The king needed their land for the gradual extension of peasant agriculture to generate sufficient surplus for sustaining the state. In Orissa, it was a continuous process of 'assimilation' and partial integration (Kulke, 1978: 32). The tribe-Hindu caste intermingling is epitomised in the Jagannatha worship, which is today at the centre of Brahminic ritual and culture, and the regional tradition of Orissa, yet tribal in origin.

Tribal people have been in continuous contact with Caste Hindus and in the process each has influenced the other in various facets of social life. Sanskritization, Aryanization and Hinduisation are widely used concepts denoting the process. In our study of culture change in western Orissa in 2004, we observed that there was a fusion of two processes of Sanskritization and tribalization, which appeared to be contrasting but complementary processes of cultural change. Karma festival is widely prevalent among the tribal people of central and eastern India. Though it is more a tribal festival, it is well within the fold of the Sambalpur Hindu folk tradition. Karma is a beautiful example of the tree worship among the tribal people in central and eastern India. The adorable deity of Karma festival is Karamsani who is represented by twig branch called Karma *dal*. The twig branch of Sal tree is worshipped as Karamsani in Sambalpur. From religious point of view, it may be suggested that the use of a twig branch of Sal tree in Sambalpur may be due to some impact of Buddhism. According to the legend, Lord Buddha died in a grove of Sal trees. Also the Sal tree is associated with his birth. It is because of these associations that Sal tree is regarded as most sacred by the Buddhists. In ancient period, tantric Buddhism flourished in Sambalpur area. Buddhist monks had set up innumerable centres in this area. Today, most of the ruins are found in the forest and hilly tops which are inaccessible and richly inhabited by tribal people. Besides, some of the Karma songs are in Malashree raga, which is reportedly used, in the tantric form of the mother goddess worship. In view of this, the possible link between the Buddhism and the uni-conical image (Sal tree) of Karamsani deity may be taken into consideration. Karamsani has been regarded as the Goddess of vegetation, fertility and destiny. Both the tribal people and caste Hindus in the village worship her. Karamsani is believed to have a dual personality. On the one hand she is a gracious mother and on the other, a ferocious power, on one side she is the savior or preserver of the tribal society, provider of their welfare and thereby merciful towards people and on the other as destroyer (C. Pasayat 1994). Karma is observed on various occasions. Bahma Karma is held at the time of crop failure and drought, which are caused by Bhama, an insect that destroys the crops. Thus, Karma puja is celebrated in times other than the day of Bhadrava Ekadasi to get blessings of Karamsani and to recover from untold sufferings or miseries. Karamsani is propitiated rather than adored. The ritual unity of the village is prominent during such festival. Karamsani is worshipped for curing diseases, well being of the children, and ensuring good crops, restoring hope and confidence among people. The annual worship in the month of Bhadrava marks an important stage in the agricultural operations and calendar in the village (Pasayat 1994). Not only Karma but in many rituals and festivals we note the participation of both tribes and caste people at village level. We observe that despite considerable influence of Hinduism and other religions such as Christianity, a large section of the tribes of Orissa continue to pursue in a traditional manner the old tribal religious practices, often with engagement of tribal priesthood. The hill tribes consider the mother earth as the supreme deity and she is to be pleased by offering sacrifices of blood of any living being, either of animal or bird. The Kandhas even used to offer human beings to propitiate earth goddess. Further their deities are usually symbolised by images of stone slabs or stocks; the trunks of the big tree. Totemism and non-recognition of Supreme Being are two other features of tribal cult.

Animism, i.e. the attribution of a soul to natural objects and phenomena and fatalism belief in charms, magic, witchcraft and ghosts are two other characteristic features of the cult of the hill tribes. In fact the majority of tribes have gradually absorbed Hindu customs and they are found to have been largely Hinduised (J. Patnaik 1998). Like the Hindus the tribal folks are polytheists. The Kondhas' pantheon, consisting of 84 deities, is broadly divided into two types of deities–the native and imported. The Earth God, the Iron God and the village deity are considered to be the chief tribal deities. The third category of deities among the Kandhas are those who have been borrowed from the Hindu pantheon. They are Mahadeo, Hara-paravati, Kali, etc. Mr. Taylor, who was the sub-divisional officer for more than 48 years during the British rule, thus writes about the Hinduised cult of the Kandhas "The Kandhas are in fact completely Hinduised". They venerate cow, set up a Hindu God, get a Hindu priest to minister to them and adopt. Some of the customs of the pure Hindus and thus become in time recognized as low class Hindus. Like every Hindu village having its own deity, every Khanda village has its own Grama Devata or Thakurani as guardian spirit (Patnaik 1978).

The Santal tribes which stand numerically next to the Kandhas, are also polytheists. Their supreme deity is Thakur Jiu who is also called Sin Bonga or Dhorom. In their theological pantheon another chief deity , Maran Buru, has taken a prominent place. They have several village deities too who are worshipped in all public festivals. The Santals like other tribes are also found to have been influenced by the Hindu pantheon. Many traditional Hindu deities (such as Rama, Hari, Paravati) have been adopted and given a place in Santal pantheon of Bongas (Patnaik 1978). The Gonds constitute the principal tribe of the Dravidian family and perhaps the most important of the non-Aryans of the forest tribes in India. They are polytheists. They worship Jangadeo, Lingadeo and Bura Deo. Bura Deo is considered as their supreme deity. Their pantheon also includes many Hindu gods and the animals and implements to which the Hindu names have been attributed. There are also households deities like Jhulan Devi, the gods of forest nymphs and crops and the goddess of Earth. They are worshipped to evade sorrows and miseries. They also worship Hindu gods like Mahadeo, Jagannath, Krishna, Rama and the goddesses like Kali and the educated among them read Oriya Bhagbat, Ramayan and Mahabharat and other Puranas. The Bhumijs who also constitute one of the major tribes worship quite a number of like clan deity, jungle deity, village deity, ancestor deities and minor mischievous deities. They also believe in magic, witchcraft and ghosts (Patnaik 1978).

As in the case of other religions, there exists priesthood in tribal society. Different tribes call their priests in different names such as the Kandhas say Jani, the Gonds, Disari, the Bhuija, Dehuri or Ojha and so on. There are priests both aboriginal and the Hindus. The Bhumijas require Brahman priests for their marriage and funeral rites. But offerings to their own deities are made through Dehuri belonging to their own tribe and not through Brahmins. Now a days with the exception of the chief God namely Bera Penu, no hereditary priesthood exists among the Kandhas. Any man who can win the belief of his neighbour by show of magical arts and incantations becomes a priest. Even on the strength of a dream or a vision a man could elevate himself from the common man and may not eat with the laymen nor partake foods prepared by them. They also possess extraordinary power like walking on burning charcoal. The presence of a priest in the Meriah sacrifice festival performed by the Kandhas to propitiate their Bera Penu was a must. When this was substituted by another festival called Kedu Jatra, the Kandhas also used to invite the priest to this festival to perform the rites. In Gond village a priest (either a male or a female) is appointed to perform this function. On the closing day a goat is killed and the priest drinks the blood of the goat and walks on the burning charcoal in a ditch specially prepared for the purpose. The followers who observe this function also join the priest. The priests are also consulted to find out the auspicious day for certain occasions like Nuakhia or first eating of the new crop. When anybody falls ill, it is believed to be the work of the evil deity, which is to be driven out by means of incantations, to be performed by the shaman priests. The Bhumijas take to magic with the help of the Shamans so as to cure their diseases. Even in case of difficult delivery, the Shamans or the Ojhas are called to perform rites so as to expel the Ghosts supposed to be creating obstacles (Patnaik 1978).

Both the tribal and non-tribal people of Sambalpur worship the major regional tribal deity, Samaleswari Devi. She is believed to be the guardian of this area and regarded as the supreme deity.

There are other deities like Pataneswari, Budhima, Mahamayi, Saramangala and Batamangala, who receive offerings of the devotees. These deities are collectively called *sat bahuni* (seven sisters). They are also feared as they may cause calamities when they are displeased. Significantly, the non-Brahmin priests worship her. The image of Samaleswari Devi is found in the form of a large head-like stone. The deity is worshipped in the form of a stone. Deity descends through spirit possessors of lower caste people. Deity was worshipped under a Semel tree in the past. Later, the deity has been enshrined in the temple. This may be a part of Sanskritisation as regular puja is performed with the Vaishnavi *mantra*. Most of her *sevakas* are tribal in origin. The practice of buffaloe sacrifice was stopped in mid-twentieth century. Nowadays, only he-goats are offered to the deity (Pasayat 2002).

Mahavira's connection with Kalinga (Orissa) is suggested by the traditions recorded in the Jaina sacred literature. The Jaina Harivamsa-Purana records that Mahavira preached his religion in Kalinga and Jaina Haribhadriya-vritti says that he went to this country as its king was a friend of his father. The early spread of Jainism in Orissa is evident from these traditions and it will not be unreasonable to conclude that Jainism made its first appearance in Orissa in sixth century B.C. when Mahavira visited it, and since then it continued to be one of its major religions at least up to the end of the first century B.C. when Kharavela's dynasty seems to have ended. Jainism was the major religion of Kalinga in the fourth century B.C. and we shall not be far from the truth, if we conclude, that it was its state religion. There was thus a period of proselytisation following the conquest and ushering in the new religion of Buddism which in conquest obtained a foothold in Orissa, but it can not be imagined that Buddhism ousted the old religion of Jainism (Panigrahi, 1981: 297). Jainism suffered an eclipse with the subsequent rise of Buddhism and Saivism in Orissa. It must be noted that Brahminism remained a major religion of Orissa throughout ages, though Jainism and Buddism had their periods of ascendancy. Several Jaina images have also been preserved in the Orissa State Museum at Bhubaneswar. Most of the images referred to above, are those of the Tirthankaras and were no doubt the objects of worship. The Saiva temple of Muktesvara at Bhubaneswar has thus a number of miniature Jaina images on the outer face to its octagonal compound wall. These short inscriptions clearly indicate that the Khandagiri again became the centre of the Jaina activities in the eleventh century A.D. in the reign of the Saiva king Udayatakesari who evidently tolerated them (Panigrahi 1981: 303).

The spread of Buddhism in Orissa started in right earnest from the third century B.C. after the Kalinga war of 261 B.C. We have already seen that Asoka conquered Kalinga after devastating this country in a terrible war and then incorporated it into his empire.The war greatly changed the mind of the great emperor and he found solace in Buddhism. Soon after the Kalinga war he became a Buddhist and started propagating Buddhism throughout India and outside. It is Kalinga, which gave him a new faith, and therefore, this country also became the region of his special propaganda and proselytisation. He introduced some new features in the admnistration of Kalinga, which did not exist in the administration of his other provinces. In his Kalinga Edicts the emperor has expressed his solicitude for the people of Kalinga, who must have received his special attention for their material and spiritual uplift. After the Kalinga war Asoka firmly believed that it was through Buddism that the uplift of the spiritual and moral conduct of people could be achieved (Panigrahi 1981: 304).

By the seventh century A.D. the Hinayanas and the Mahayanas had become sharply divided in Orissa. Yuan Chwang during his visit to Odra (Orissa) saw the temples and the monasteries of both the sects. From the beginning of the Bhauma rule in the first part of the seventh century A.D. the existence of Buddhism in Orissa is attested. The first three Bhauma rulers, bore the Buddist titles, Paramopasaka, Paramatathagata and Paramasaugata clearly showing that they were Buddhists. But the Buddhism of Mahayana form, was of a very different type. It seems that Buddhism of this period was tending to merge into Hinduism, particularly into Saivism and Saktism. It is stated in the Neulpur Plate of Subhakaradeva that Ksemankaradeva, the first member of the dynasty, placed the castes in their proper position. This evidence proves that he was a supporter of caste system, even though he was a Buddhist.

The great monastery of Ratnagiri had become in this period a centre of Buddhist religion, learning, Tantras and Yoga. In the

Tibetan work, Pag Sam Jan Zang, it is stated that Bodhisri practised Yoga at Ratnagiri in Orissa. The first part of the Bhauma rule in Orissa was thus marked by the ascendancy of Mahayana Buddhism, but the subsequent rulers of the dynasty, as their titles in their inscriptions indicate, became Brahmanical Hindus. Buddhism did not completely die out, but it became changed and it distributed its potentialities among the Brahmanical sects (Panigrahi 1981: 312). Orissa is intimately associated with the spread of Buddhism in India and abroad through the efforts of Emperor Ashoka during the 3rd century B.C. The historic Kalinga war was fought and won by Ashoka. The war transformed Chandasoka to Dharmashoka; it also made Buddhism a potent spiritual and cultural force in the Indian subcontinent. A new era of peace and goodwill began. The message of Budha, world's earliest message of peace and non-violence, inspired Tapassu and Bhallika, who became disciples of the Enlightened one. One of these two merchant brothers carried Buddha's Kesa-Asthi (hair relic) to Orissa. The sacred tooth relic of Budha was taken away to Srilanka from Dantapura, the capital of Kalinga (B. P. Samal 2002). Excavations have led to the discovery of several monasteries and stupas at different places in Orissa. It is believed that Buddha had visited South Kosala in his lifetime. Buddhism continued to prevail in Orissa till about A.D. 13th century, long after it had vanished from most of the other regions of India. The Bhaumakara rulers are believed to have patronised Buddhism. In Orissa, the Vajrayana of Indra-Bhuti and Sahajayana of Laxmikara of Oddiyan, one of the four-tantrik pithas of India, flourished during the 8th century. Lalitgiri, Ratnagiri and Udayagiri are the three great centres of Buddhism in Orissa. The Buddhist complex at Lalitgiri formed one of the important seats of Buddhism (B. P. Samal 2002).

Both Jainism and Buddhism took root and spread in Orissa after the 5th century B.C. In the 3rd century B.C., during Ashoka's time, Buddhism reigned supreme, and in the 2nd century B.C. during the rule of Kharavela, Jainism became the state religion. Then, from the 3rd country A.D., Buddhism began to flourish again and this continued for five centuries, after which Brahmanism once again gained ascendancy. Orissa became the stronghold of the Vajrayana offshoot of Buddhism, and one of the ways in which this manifested itself was through a new and vigorous school of

Buddhist art, influenced by the Gupta tradition, which came into existence and rapidly spread everywhere (P. Misra 1962).

In Orissa one encounters both endogenous and exogenous processes of state formation. The tribals had generally a two tier structure of authority, one at the level of the village chief selected by members of the village and the other at the level of a group of villages (*pidha*) inhabited by the tribe. A third tier of authority was also emerging with a *raja* selected in a peculiar way. Of all the tribes the Saoras/Savaras were most intimately related to others in the ancient texts where they were mentioned both generically as any forest based group and specifically as forest dwellers in Orissa and central India. They participated in state formation, owned the land where they worshipped the early incarnation of Lord Jagannath and passed on the cult to the king and Brahmans. The Sudh Savaras are still active players in rituals. The historical processes of Kshatriyazation or Rajputaization never operated in their standard mode. Some tribal chiefs claimed the sort of Varna status through adoption of Singh title but no clear *jati* status was accorded to them in all cases. Tribal rituals and tribal priesthood always survived. We may cite the examples of the Nagbansi, the Gonds, and the Binjhal. This author has studied the Binjhal state formation closely. K. S. Singh has observed that some tribes "stole" minor Rajput scions and installed them as their rulers, for example, in Bamara, Gangpur, etc.; in his view the tribal chiefs of Bonai, Keonjhar, Mayurbhanj, Gangapur, who originally belonged to the tribal groups, went through the process of Kshatriyazation and Rajputization. However there are scholars who feel that Kshatriyazation and Rajputization processes never operated in Orissa. This author observed that even the Jagannath trend had limited impact in western tribal areas. The tribes became Hinduised while maintaining a great deal of cultural autonomy such as Sounti, Bhuyan, Kisan, Bathudi, Mirdha, Gond and Savara. K.S. Singh has reviewed the theory whether Orissa had or did not have a viable Kshatriya Varna (Sahu, 1992). He thinks the issue deserves reconsideration in view of the presence of indigenous ruling lineages, a strong peasant warrior-caste, like in other parts of the country, the Khandayats (wielder of the swords) who emerged in the medieval period and the influx of Rajputs from other parts who toppled the tribal kingdoms or established their own. The

Kshatriya class was always of obscure origin including the Nandas. Those who managed to acquire power became Kshatriyas or Rajputs. Orissa was no exception. The Karan-Kayasthas emerged as state functionaries and masters of *sashtras*. There was a flourishing Vaishya class of traders. The Sudra consisted of peasants (*gahapati/kutumbin*) artisans, potter *(kambhakara)*, bronze-smith *(kamsyakara)*, weaver *(tantravaya)*, cowherd *(gokuta)*, distiller *(saundhika)*, blacksmith *(lauhakara)*, coppersmith *(tamrakara)*, carpenter (*patakara*), oilmen (*telikas*). There is no explicit mention of untouchables; the Domba, Pana, Hadi, Ghasi and Chandalas appear later in the medieval centuries with the consolidation of the caste system (Sahu, 1992).

People of India Project: Communities and Social Organisation

Many important conclusions can be drawn from the material available in People of India project publications. Anthropological Survey of India has studied 279 communities under the POI project in Orissa. One community, a territorial unit, Kummari/ Kummeri was added later. Most of the communities i.e., 226 constituting 81.0 per cent live in rural areas and only 13 communities (4.7 per cent) live in urban areas. About 36 communities constituting 12.9 per cent live in rural/ urban settings. The major communities of Orissa and their approximate population according to 1931 Census is: Brahman 21,01,287, Khandait 8,82,195 (including Bihar), Kayastha Karan Prabhu 5,30,185 (includes Bihar). The major tribal and scheduled caste groups (1981 census) are Khond, Kondh 9,89,342, Dom / Dumar 4,27,078, Dhoba/Dhobi 4,18,383, Gonda 4,18,956, Gond, Gondo 6,07,249 (1981), Munda 3,38,936, Sabar, Lodha 3,29,209, Saora 3,70,060, Kotha 3,26,522, Paroja 2,67,185 and so on. Of 279 communities 67 are scheduled castes and 56 belong to scheduled tribes. Scheduled castes/ include Bauri, Bhuminj, Dom/ Dumar and Ganda, while the scheduled tribes include Khond/ Kondh, Saora, Juang and Paroja, to mention a few. A large number of communities are aware of *varna* order (247 /88.53 per cent) and recognise their place in the *varna* order (217/ 77.78 per cent). One hundred sixteen communities (41.58 per cent) recognise themselves as Sudra, followed by communities which can be put under the category of Vaishya (52/18.64 per cent), Kshatriya (36/12.90 per cent)– which are relatively large – and Brahman (12/7.89per cent).

However, as mentioned above, historically, the *rajas* in Orissa have upgraded the individuals and families to higher ritual status. Orissa has reported sharing linkages with most of the communities on a larger scale than elsewhere because of the equalising influence of Jagannath cult. These linkages and sharings include acceptance of water (268/96.06 per cent), exchange of water (210/75.27 per cent), *kachcha* food (265/94.68 per cent) and *pucca* food (257/92.11 per cent), sharing of water resource (206/73.84 per cent), cremation ground (141/50.54 per cent) and religious shrines (227/81.36 per cent). Putative kinship (195/70 per cent) and symbiotic relationship (187/60.03 per cent) exist extensively in Orissa within the framework of caste system. The functional castes like Dhoba, Barika, etc., have specific roles in various phases of rite-de-passage of the castes they serve. The Ghasi and Hadi are cultural workers, drum beating musicians and scavengers. Brahmans act as priest of the people of high and middle castes. We collected data on the rise of operators of modern linkages such as entrepreneurs, white collar employees, artists, teachers, etc., and found that Orissa's position was less than the national average. The same was the picture in respect of the rise of leadership at village, regional and national levels. This reflects general backwardness and retarded progress in education and political mobilisation.

Like major cultural and linguistic regions of India, Orissa has its own cluster of communities including tribes, fisherfolk, 'dalit' castes, peasants and former 'warriors'. There are both indigenous and immigrant components of the Brahmans, Karna (like the Khatriyas), and others. Orissa has dynamic indigenous communities. The important Mundari tribes of the State are Santals, Hos, Mundas, Birhors, Bhumijs, Kharias and Juangs, constituting the northern group and the Gadabas and the Bondos forming the southern-most extension of the Mundari speakers. The Khonds (referred to as Kandhas by the Oriya), Gonds, Bhumias, Kisans, Oraons and Koya are the more important among the Dravidian tribes found in Orissa. A good proportion of the Khonds has given up the Kui language and speaks only Oriya. The process of transformation of rich tribals into Kshatriyahood as observable in the past is not observable now. In Keonjhar, a Kond priest performs, as a relic of the past, "certain religious rites to a rough-hewn stone inside the chief's house, though the ruling family has long since been converted to Vaishnavism." The Gonds have thoroughly Hinduized and retain very few of the traits of tribal culture; they claim to be treated as Kshatriya! Tribal pattern of life can still be seen in the hill sections of the Konds, Juangs, and the Bhuiyas, though it is rapidly changing (Aiyappan *et al.* 1962). In Orissa, many village godlings worshipped by the villagers are tribal in origin. Priests of these godlings are invariably men of the lower castes. The Karans (the writer caste) closely correspond to the Kayasthas of Bengal. The Khandayat mostly recruited from the farming castes constitute the militia and claim Kshatriya rank. Castes such as the Bauri, Dom, Hari, Sundhi, Teli, and others are closely analogous to those of Bengal. The Brahmins of Orissa constituting the Utkala branch of Pancha Goudas show considerable regional variation in their organisation (Aiyappan et.al. 1962). The high status groups referred to as Sasan Brahmins are later immigrants. They perform the highest rituals while the temple Brahmins (Panda Sevaks) perform the pujas, etc. The agriculturist Brahmins who work with the plough and the forest Brahmans are among the most backward among the Brahmins. The service castes such as the barber and washerman do not live in a Sasan village but a little away from it. Risley reported the rise of a caste consisting of ex-communicated persons out of the famine of 1866. This caste came to be known as Charar-khai.There exists now in Orissa a caste, called Charar-khai, recorded in the lists of 1881, which is made up of people who lost their caste in 1866 for eating in relief-kitchens (*chatras*). The caste is divided into an upper and a lower sub-caste–the former comprising Brahmans, Karana, Khandaits and Gop-Goalas, the latter consisting of the castes ranking below these in the social scale. Members of each sub-caste marry within that group, irrespective of the caste to which they originally belonged; but no intermarriage is possible between members of the two sub-castes (Risley 1891, p. viii).

The villages are still fairly well knit; the service castes and their patrons are still bound by several ties of mutuality. The horizontal extension of caste through well-organised caste assemblies is another interesting feature in the social scene. Several castes (such as Oilman, Fisherman, Barber and Sudra) have caste councils which sit regularly once or twice a year to discuss matters relating to social reforms. The textiles of Orissa have been famous over the centuries. The Chola kings of Southern India settled weavers from Kalinga in the imperial capital at Tanjore; the best fabrics known to the Tanjore court was named after Kalinga. There exist a large number of weaver castes each with its own special techniques and monopolies.

The most remarkable symbolic feature of the socio-religious life of the communities of Orissa is the relationship with the Jagannath temple. Not so well known feature however, is the practice of exchange of the Mahaprasad (food offered to Lord Jagannath) to establish bond friendship. Two persons intending to enter into strong, unbreakable bond friendship get Mahaprasasd from Puri and put a morsel of it into each other's mouth. The institution of bond friendship of the above type and various other types is widely prevalent in Orissa and is an important device to establish intimate personal ties beyond caste, factions and the narrow bounds of the religion. There are bond friendships known as *sahi, sangata,* and *maitra*. Two persons engaged in the same or similar business or occupation enter into the *sahi* form of bond friendship; if they have some physical resemblance to each other, they become *sangata*; if they have the same given names, they become *maitra*. To establish these relationships, there is usually a ceremonial exchange of clothes. To this class of institution belongs the common practice of establishing ritual kinship i.e. "ritual brother," "ritual son" (*dharam bhai, dharam pua*) (Mishra 1995).

Of particular interest are the weavers and metal workers of Orissa who have been for centuries engaged in exploiting natural resources and pursuing traditional crafts. Tanti or weaver is a term commonly used in Orissa for a person engaged in handloom. The Weaver castes of Sambalpur and Bolangir are divided into seven groups. These seven groups, in spite of their common caste occupations, function as seven distinct castes. These castes are – Bhulia, Krushna, Dhera, Patra, Rangini, Kuli, and Ganda (TRB 1972). The first four castes weave superior type of clothes. Kuli and Ganda weave inferior and coarse type of clothes. The Ganda are equivalent to the Pano caste and are regarded as one of the lowest among the Scheduled Castes. They also have matrimonial relationship with the Pano caste. Patra and Rangini specialise in the weaving of "Pata" or silk clothing. Krushna are specialised in the weaving of "Matha" clothing, which is a type of handspun silk different from that of "Pata". The Kulis have been more hard hit because they specialise in coarse and inferior type of clothing, which is generally used, by the poorer section of the people (TRB 1972). Bhulia are famous for tie and dye designs mostly on silk commonly known as Sambalpuri design. The bell-metal ware occupies a pride place in Orissa's casting history. The bell metal and brass utensils of Orissa are remarkable for the beauty of their shape and exquisiteness. They blend a striking harmony of beauty and utility. Even during the era of stainless steel and synthetics, rural folks in Orissa still prefer to sue the bell-metal pots be it is for their watered rice "Pakhala" during lunch break or be fuffed rice or "Mudi" during breakfast or evening tiffin. Traditional method of manufacture of bell-metal wares was however purely casting method. The brass and bell-metal utensils were produced in Cuttack. Sambalpur, Puri and few places in Balasore and Mayurbhanj districts do have high reputation. Not just bell-metal, but the fancy brassware of Orissa is totally different than that produced elsewhere. The flexible brass fish of Belguntha in Ganjam district is one such unique product. The metal casings (Dhokras) of the Sithulians are typical example of tribal metal ware of Orissa, though it has now spread into nontribal belt also. These products are cast in brass by lost-wax-process and display an intriguing wire work finish. The wax-work done with great skill form wires of bees-wax. These pieces with their antique look go well with interior décor. Basically a 'tribal technology', it was subsequently adopted by others and now is being produced in several places of Orissa. In past, it was produced out of base elements like brass and bell-metals, mixing at liquid stage after heating. Although this method continues in some pockets, in many places it is produced out of broken brass and bell-metals mixing molten tin at appropriate proportion. There are a couple of Dhokra producing villages in Mahurbhanj district which thrived with Royal patronage during earlier year. In Cuttack district Dhokra is being produced in Badamba and Narsingpur belt otherwise known for weaving too. In the districts of Sambalpur, Phulbani, Bolangir and Kalahandi, there are a number of villages known for the production of Dhokra. While during British rule, these art flourished only in the areas ruled by feudal chiefs, the independence completely changed the complexion. The artisans could get appropriate support from State Handicraft Development Corporation with backward and forward linkages upto certain extent (Ghosh G. K. 1993).

Filigree work in gold was also introduced upto certain extent utilising the talent of the same group of artisans. The silver ornaments produced around Berhampur in Ganjam district is unique. They are different from the designs of Cuttack and are close to South Indian designs. The artisans of Berhampur are known also for manufacture of silver utensils. The "Banias" of Orissa are also known for production of gold ornaments. They adopt various designs to attract the customers. Traditionally three type of designs are adopted in Orissa according to area. The first is adopted by coastal Orissa usually having influence of Muslim art and Bengal design, second by Southern Orissa with influence of South India and the last by Western Orissa with influence of Marhatta and tribal designs. The migration of goldsmiths from other States primarily Bengal, Gujarat and Andhra Pradesh during past few decades has also changed the complexion of the designs. The brass ornament produced in Sambalpur is also unique. (Ghosh, G.K. 1993: 124).

Development and Social Change

Orissa is predominantly an agricultural state. The per centage of people dependent upon agriculture in the state is as high as eighty. The total cropped area in the State is 79,34,000 hectares. The principal crops grown in Orissa are cereals, pulses, condiments and spices, oil-seeds, fibres, vegetables and fruits and cash crops like sugarcane, jute, cotton and tobacco (Dash 1997: 33). Rice, jowar, bajra, maize, ragi, millets, wheat and barley are the cereals grown in the State. Of these, rice is by far the most important crop and is grown all over the state. There are local varieties of forest crops and seed traditions, which are part of the traditional knowledge systems.

The existence of the Central Rice Research Institute at Cuttack carries on valuable research for the development and improvement of paddy cultivation. The State produces pulses or Rabi crops like mung, gram, biri or black gram, Kulthi or horse-gram and arhar. The people of Orissa being predominantly rice eating need these pulses for the preparation of dal, which is an essential ingredient of a good rice meal. Mung is the most common pulse used for dal; poor sections also use biri and kulthi for preparing dal and other subsidiary food (Dash 1997: 34). Except the coastal belt rest of the districts are partially or fully declared as scheduled area out of which the districts of Mayurbhanj, Sundargarh and undivided Koraput are fully declared as scheduled districts. Of the total 314 C.D. Blocks of Orissa 128 (37.3%) are tribal block (Panigrahi 1996). Around 2200 sq. kms. i.e., 36.6% of the total land area of Orissa, is declared as Scheduled Area, which constitutes nearly 31% of the total scheduled area of the country.

Orissa has an average of 150 cm rainfall and the rainy season is of only four months' duration but different crops grow in different seasons for which regular flow of water is very necessary. Orissa's rivers are in high flood during the rains but they dry up in other seasons. The Government of Orissa paid serious attention to the expansion of irrigation facilities in the State and it resulted in building up of water reservoirs under the Hirakud Dam Project, the Rushikulya Project, the Delta Irrigation Project and the Ghodahad Project; the total irrigated area through perennial canals is now about 11 lakhs hectares constituting about twenty-two per cent of the total cropped area (Dash 1997 : 38). By the end of 1992-93 we notice that 32,682 villages had been electrified. This constitutes 69.6 per cent of the total number of villages in the state. The energy generation in the state is inadequate as the supply is much less than its requirement.

As discussed above Orissa is famous for its filigree works, bell-metal industries, stone, wood and Chalk carving, basket making and horn works. Besides these, applique work, tassar, eri and other materials also excel in artistic quality. Orissa has always been a leading producer of handicrafts and products of cottage industries. Cloth is woven in handlooms with artistic borders and pictures in the districts of Sambalpur, Bargarh, Cuttack and Ganjam whereas tassar and matha are woven in Mayurbhanj, Sambalpur and Balasore. Bell-metal industry has flourished in Bhatimunda in Cuttack, Remuna in Balasore, Balakati, Bhainchuan and Kantilo in Khurda, Jagmohan, Boirani, Purushottampur and Belluguntha in Ganjam, Paralakhemundi in Gajapati and Bhuban in Sdhenkanal districts. Fish made of brass and bell-metal at Belluguntha in Ganjam has a world market. Utensils are made of stone in Nilgiri, Bhubaneswar, Soro, Remuna and Baripada. The silver filigree works with similar artistic ornaments in gold are produced at Cuttack which has earned worldwide fame. The Government of

India purchases these products for presentation to foreign dignitaries visiting India. In horn works, Cuttack and Paralakhemundi are equally famous (Dash 1997: 41). The Orissa Textiles Marketing Organisation has taken up the responsibility of marketing the cotton, Matha, tassar and other varieties of textile goods.

There are industrial estates in Barbil, Rajgangpur, Rourkella, Jharsuguda, Sambalpur, Bargarh, Balasore, Rupsa, Baripada, Jajpur, Aska, Berhamour, Sumandi, Nawapara, Mancheswar and Cuttack. Government give loans to the artisans directly or guarantees loans taken by them from the State Finance Corporation. The Orissa Small Industries Corporation has also undertaken to construct buildings, purchase machinery and supply raw materials and marketing facilities to the industries. The All India Khadi and Village Industries Board has a State unit in Orissa. The Government of Orissa with a view to revitalising the handicrafts has encouraged the establishment of the Orissa Cooperative Handicrafts Corporation Limited. It has its branches at Puri, Bhubaneshwar and New Delhi. A Handicraft Training and Design Centre has been established at Bhubaneshwar and craft institutions are established at Bhubaneswar and craft institutions are imparting training in different crafts, namely, golden grass weaving, cane bamboo and Lalia grass and ornate weaving (Dash 1997: 44).

A cement factory at Rajgangpur in Sundargarh, a match factory in Talcher, a soap factory in Khariar in Kalahandi district and a few ice factories in Cuttack and Sambalpur districts were all the industries that Orissa could boast of in 1947. There is a glass factory at Barang and a textile mill at Chauduar in Cuttack district. Sugar mills are at Rayagada in Koraput, Aska in Ganjam and Banki in Cuttack district.

The Orissa Industrial Development Corporation, set up in 1962, is in direct charge of the aforesaid undertakings. The Government of India has also set up large scale industries in the public sector. These include Rourkela Steel Plant under the Steel Authority of India, the MIG Aero-engine factory under the Hindustan Aeronautics Ltd. at Sunabeda in Koraput district, a fertilizer unit under the Fertilizer Corporation of India at Talcher, the Paradeep Phosphates Ltd. at Paradeep for production of phosphatic fertilizer, and the National Aluminium Company Ltd. (NALCO) – the biggest integrated bauxite/ alumina/aluminium project in Asia. A heavy water plant is in operation at Talcher.

Orissa is a larger producer of high-grade iron and manganese ores. Iron ore deposits are found in the districts of Sundargarh, Keonjhar and Mayurbhanj. Orissa is one of the largest producers of manganese and its deposits are found in Jeonjhar, Sundargarh, Bolangir and Kalahandi districts. Orissa accounts for twenty per cent of the total output of manganese in India. Coal is mined in Talcher in Angul district and Sambalpur. Other important minerals found in Orissa are limestone, dolomite, graphite, China clay, fire clay, white clay and soapstone. India is an exporter of iron ore and manganese, and Orissa has a major share in this export trade. The port at Paradeep is important on account of iron ore exports to Japan. The State Government has established the Orissa Mining Corporation for exporting the mineral wealth of the State. Orissa produces 5.2 per cent of the minerals produced in India (Dash 1997 : 47-48). There are 1,624 kilometers of national highways in Orissa. National highways nos. 5 and 6 which pass through Orissa, are now linked with many laces through assistance given by the World Bank. There are 5,007 kilometres of State highways. Major district roads and other roads are of 29,435 km.There are 2,322 kilometres of railways in Orissa. The railway line of the South Eastern Railway which links Howrah with Chennai passes through the coastal districts. (Dash 1997 : 50).

There is a modern airport at Bhubaneswar. There are regular flights from here to Delhi. Plane services also link Bhubaneswar with Calcutta, Bombay, Chennai, Hyderabad and Nagpur. The State is served by 8,048 post offices, 2,409 post and telegraph offices and 538 telephone exchanges. Electronic mass media plays a vital role in entertaining and informing people throughout the State. Doordarshan network comprises three high power transmitters at Bhubaneswar, Sambalpur and Bhawanipatna, 27 low power transmitters and one programme production centre at Bhubaneswar. All India Radio with four full fledged MW radio stations at Cuttack, Sambalpur, Jeypore and Bhawanipatna; four local radio stations at Keonjhar, Baripada, Berhampur and Bolangir and one commercial broadcasting service at Cuttack covers about 86 per cent of State's population (Dash 1997 : 50).

Review of the developmental planning and investment over decades in different regions shows that the human resource development in five districts, viz. Cuttack, Balasore, Puri, Ganjam and Mayurbhanj appears to be relatively higher than the state average, whereas in Bolangir, Kalahandi, Phulbani and Koraput area remain highly backward (Parida, 1987). Similarly as regard to infra-structural facilities the districts like Cuttack, Balasore, Puri, Ganjam, Sundergarh and Sambalpur are seen to be relatively developed as per the state average and the remaining districts like Koraput, Kalahandi, Mayurbhanj and Dhenkanal are more backward. In area of economic activities which include both farm and non-farm operations Sundergarh, Puri, Cuttack, Sambalpur and Ganjam are relatively advanced whereas Koraput, Kalahandi, Mayurbhanj and Keonjhar are found backward. It can be said that the underdevelopment of the state is highly related to the low level of economic activities, human resource development and infrastructure facilities on one hand and positive correlation between human resource development, infra-structural facilities and economic activities on the other (Panigrahi 1996).

The situation of industrial development in Orissa largely related to the agriculture expansion, and agricultural development, basically dependent on industrial development. The large-scale application of agricultural inputs viz., fertilizer, pesticides, pumps, sprayers, tractors, power tillers, etc., are the product of industrial development. In spite of limitations prevailed with the people, the state and the market the state could bring a land mark achievement by establishing units like Rourkela Steel Plant in later part of fifties, and Sunabeda Mig Factory in early part of sixties. In 1980 the industrial policy of the state promoted joint ventures, established IPICOL in 1973 Industrial Development corporation in 1956, liberalising term loans through Orissa Financial Corporation and implementing other financial subsidy based schemes. In the later period during Sixth Five Year plan aluminium complex of NALCO at Angul and Damanjodi, Phospetic Fertiliser Plant at Paradeed and Defence Ordinance factory in Bolangir were established. The thrust of revised industrial policy of 1986 was to generate employment in general and for women in particular, to spread industrial establishment in backward areas, to adopt antipollution measures, to introduce appropriate turnover package of incentives for rehabilitation of sick industries, etc. (Panigrahi 1996).

From 75% of the total cultivated land of Orissa, only 22% have irrigation facility. Due to the lack of irrigational facilities and poor use of fertilizer the yield is low and income of the farmers is low, resulting constraints in industrial development (Sahoo, 1987). The facts, as stated above, seem that the state has failed to coordinate the integrated development of agriculture and industry. As a result, the expectations desired out of such development to meet the basic needs of the people become a mystery. The solution lies with the combined efforts to be made jointly by planners, implementors, politicians and NGO workers while adopting a well coordinated and integrated strategy for agro-based development commensurating with the need of the people as people defined for themselves. People oriented and resource oriented developing strategies are equally important (Panigrahi 1996).

The gradual increase in their population and rapid loss of their means of production pushed the tribals as landless labourers who earn their living either as wage earners or as agricultural labourers. The creation of scheduled areas and restriction imposed in post independent era on their traditional practices of cultivation and use of forest not only brought a huge tribal population to penury but encouraged the capital to grow using the cheap tribal labour. Moreover, the restrictions imposed on their rights to land, forest and its resources have threatened their very survival since the British period has been encountered by many tribal groups in a militant way (Panigrahi 1996).

As regard the shifting cultivation, as the major mode of production and economy of the tribals, various legal prohibitions have been imposed on them which have forcibly brought many to the level of labour. Since independence till date Orissa is one of the states to have few major developmental units as irrigation dams, industries, minings located in inland areas largely dominated by minority groups. Some of such project units are multi-purpose hydro-electric units, viz : Hirakud Dam Project, Upper Kolab Dam Project, Machakund Dam Project, Indravati Dam Project, Rengali Dam Project, Subarnarekha Dam Project, located in the districts of Sambalpur, Koraput, Dhenkanal and Mayurbhanj respectively; the major industrial units are Rourkela Steel Plant (SAIL), Hindustan

Aeronautic Limited, Ordinance Factory, Aluminium Factory; Mining of iron, coal, bauxite, limestone, etc., in the districts of Mayurbhanja, Kenojhar, Sundargarh, Sambalpur and Koraput. Through some of such units started since 1950s, the Government of Orissa did not emphasise on their displacement, rehabilitation and resettlement till 1975. The ad hoc approach in the form of cash compensation for displacement was largely adopted. Though a few colonies have been made for the displaced in case of Mahanadi hydro-election project, Rourkela Steel Plant, provision of civic amenities to such settlement colonies were not given much importance. The need of enlarging the scope of previous rehabilitation strategy becomes a necessity to settle the displaced of Rengali multi-purpose project. However, the Government of Orissa adopted policy resolutions in 1975, 1977 and 1978 for rehabilitation of the displaced in a more liberal way (Panigrahi 1996).

Orissa has 49.1 per cent literacy. The rate of literacy in Orissa is lower than the national rate because the Scheduled Castes and Scheduled Tribes constitute more than forty per cent of the State's population and the literacy rate among the Scheduled Tribes and Castes is less than fifty per cent. There are several universities in Orissa. They are the Utkala University founded in 1943, the Orissa University of Agriculture and technology founded in 1962 and the Berhampur and the Sambalpur Universities established in January 1967 and Sri Jagannath Sanskrit Vishwavidyalay, Puri started in 1982. The Utkala university has at present a faculty of Engineering with a private Orissa College of Engineering at Bhubaneswar and the Indira Gandhi Institute of Engineering at Saranga in Angul district. Berhampur University has no engineering faculty at present. There are 615 degree colleges affiliated to Utkal, Berhampur and Sambalpur universities. In Orissa, there are five engineering colleges, three medical colleges, ten teachers' training colleges, one agriculture college, one college of veterinary science and animal husbandry and one college of agricultural engineering. There are departments of Hindi literature and language in some of the major colleges of the state. Two colleges in Orissa–the Ravenshaw College at Cuttack and the Khallikote College at Berhampur in the district of Ganjam–are over a century old. The number of students on the rolls of the Ravenshaw College is about four thousand (Dash 1997 : 53).

From the period of the Second Five Year Plan, considerable attention has been given to the training of teachers. The Government of Orissa has proliferated certified post-matric teachers' training and elementary pre-matric teachers' training institutions throughout the state. There is a Sainik School, and the Regional College of Education for the eastern region is also located at Bhubaneswar. Education has been very popular in Orissa from time immemorial and the system of *pathshalas* is continuing from the past. The institution of Bhagabatgadi, which is a collection of palm-leaf manuscripts worshipped by the people, reminds one of Oriyas' love of learning, and the Bhagabatghar, a common reading-room where the Pandit reads Puranas and scriptures for the benefit of an audience consisting of men and women from a number of adjoining villages, has been a popular institution which operates in most of the villages of coastal Orissa (Dash 1997: 55). The Adivasis in Koraput district were described as excluded under the Government of India Act, 1935 and kept under the direct administration of the Governor. The district of Sambalpur was called a partially excluded area and was in the special charge of the Governor. The Adivasi-inhabited areas of Ganjam were known as Agency areas and they had also been parts of the excluded areas of the Province to be administered by the Government at its discretion (Dash 1997: 79). Rice has become the staple food of Adivasis. Certain cereals growing naturally on the hillsides are also used as food. Country wines called Mahula and Salapa are in use among them. The drinking of wine is so much a part of their social and religious life that the Government of Orissa while introducing prohibition had excluded the districts with a large Adivasi population out of its purview. They were advised to use rice, pulses and *ragi* as their food for which they have recently taken to cultivation. In rocky areas, hardly a plain field was available for the purpose of cultivation; they were clearing the jungle on the mountain sides and practicing shifting cultivation. As there was no alluvium in the soil, they were shifting from one place to another in search of land on account of which they had no permanence in habitation. Because of this mobility, they have been responsible for a good deal of deforestation. They also cultivate Haldi and Kandula, a kind of rabi crop and sell them in the market (Dash 1997: 81).

The Government has established Sevashram Schools where education up to the primary standard is imparted. The higher institutions are called Ashram Schools, which impart education up to the middle school standard. There are 100 Ashram and about 2,300 Sevashram schools in the State and the number of students on the rolls are eight lakhs. The Government also provides free tuitions and reading materials to Adivasi boys and girls pursuing studies in the ordinary schools and colleges, and in many places Adivasi hostels have been built. Besides, women workers are being trained in the Gopabandhu Seva Sadan at Sakhigopal, the training centre in Angul and Harijan Udyogsala in Delhi. These trained women workers are to work in the tribal areas for their development. Steps have been taken to set up mobile dispensaries and distribute free medicines.

Adivasis are being settled on free land and assistance in diverse ways is being rendered to them for their agricultural and other forms of economic development. Law has prohibited alienation of agricultural lands from the tribal people to the non-tribals. This may be more of an ideal position. Reality is that whether the tribes or the scheduled castes, both have suffered enormously in recent years. Multi-purpose cooperative societies have been formed to grant them credit and also provide them with improved marketing facilities for their agricultural and industrial produce and forest items collected by them. They are also being taught the art of bee keeping, poultry farming and wood shearing. The Government has a Department of Harijan and Tribal Welfare. This is in charge of a Minister. There are district welfare committees to look after the administration of welfare measures. There is a Harijan and Tribal Research-cum-Training Institute in Bhubaneswar through which data about the tribes are collected. Useful information collected through them helps the Government in formulating plans and schemes for improving the condition of the Adivasis (Dash 1997: 83-84).

Acknowledgement

This paper is based on a review of vast and scattered literature on Orissa. The works, which are of anthropological nature, are given priority. Works available in the Anthropological Survey of India and particularly the People of India findings as contained in the writings of Dr. K.S. Singh, and are refereed to, in length. The author is thankful to Dr. V.R. Rao, Director-in-charge, for his kind support and encouragement in writing this paper. The views expressed are those of the author alone. The author is also grateful to Professor Sachchidananda for inviting him to contribute the earlier version of this paper in a seminar on "The state of the art of social anthropology in eastern India" March 2007 at Patna. Critical suggestions received from Professor Sachchidananda in finalising the paper are gratefully acknowledged.

References

Aiyappan, A., N. Patnaik, and P.D. Prasad Rao (1962), *The People of Orissa,* Souvenir of Indian Science Congress, Cuttack.

Ayengar, N. S. R. and N. D. Jayadeva. At the Cross-roads: A Socio-cultural Perspective. In *Jayadeva and Gita Govinda.* Mishra T and B. Mohanty (Eds.). Bhubaneswar: Utkal University of Culture.

Bailey, F. G. 1957 (1959), *Caste and the Economic Frontier: A Village in Highland Orissa.* Manchester: University of Manchester.

Bailey, F. G. (1960), *Tribe, Caste and Nation.* Manchester: Manchester University Press.

Bailey, F. G. (1963), *Politics and Social Change.* Manchester: Manchester University Press.

Basa, K. K. (1999), Neolithic and Post–Neolithic Cultures of Orissa. In *Reconstructing Indian History and Culture.* Vol. 16 Ed. S.Pradhan. New Delhi: D. K. Printworld.

Behura, N. K. (1989), Religious Rites and Festivals of the Tribes of Orissa. In *Tribes of Orissa: The Changing Socio-economic Profile.* B.C. Ray. Ed. New Delhi: Gian Publishing House.

Bose, N. K. (1929), Juang Associations. *Man in India*: 47-53.

Bose N. K. and D. Sen (1948), *Excavations in Mayurbhanj*: Calcutta: Calcutta University.

Census of Mayurbhanj state (1931), Mohammad Laeequddin Compiler. Calcutta: Caledonian Printing Co.

Choudhary, S. (1979), *Economic History of Colonialism : A Study of British Salt Policy in Orissa.* Inter-India Publication, New Delhi.

E. T. (1872), *Descriptive Ethnology of Bengal.* Calcutta: Office of the Superintendent of Government Press.

Danda, Dhapa and Karma. *Orissa Review.* May-June 2002.

Das, Anirudhdha (1968), Impact of Christianity on the Tribals or Orissa. *Adibasi* Vol. X. 1968-69-No. 1. April 1968.

Das, B. S. (ed.) (1978), *Life and Culture in Orissa.* New Delhi: S. Publishers

Das, B. S. (1984), *Life and Culture in Orissa* Calcutta: Minerva Associates.

Das, Binod, S. (1984), *Life and Culture of Orissa,* IIT, Kharagpur, India.

Das, Biswarupa (1985), *Orissa*. Delhi: Sundeep Prakashan.

Das, C. R. (ed.) *Folk Culture and Literature*. Vol. I Cuttack: Institute of Oriental and Orissan Studies.

Das C. R. (ed.) (1978), Folk Culture and Literature. Vol. III. Bhubaneswar: IOOS.

Das, C. R. (1978), Folk Culture. Vol. II. *Folkways in Religion Gods, Spirits and Men*. Bhubaneswar: Institute of Oriental and Orrisan Studies.

Das, Chiranjiv (1966), *Gita-Govinda* (Verses in Hindi. Translated by Chiranjiv Das). Raigarh: Basanti Prakashan.

Das, H. C. (1962), The Traditional Occupation of Saora of Sripur: *Orissa History Research Journal*, Vol. XI, No. 3 (PP. 178-89), Bhubaneswar, Orissa.

Das, H. C. (Ed.) (1978), *Folk Music and Dances*. Vol. IV. Bhubaneswar: IOOS.

Das, Harish Chandra (ed.) N. D. Shri Jayadeva's Gitagovinda and the Sculpture Tradition of Orissa. In *Jayadeva and Gitagovinda*. Misra T. and B.Mohanty (Eds.) Bhubaneswar: Utkal University of Culture.

Das, M. N. (1962), History of Orissa. Souvenir of Indian Science Congress, Cuttack.

Das, N. (1965-66), The Birinda of Lanjia Saora. *Adivasi*, Vol. VIII/No. 2 (PP. 5-12).

Das, N.K. (1973), Three Dimensional study of Oriya Novel Amrutar Santana. Dissertation for Master's Degree in Anthropology.Deparatment of Anthropology, Ravishankar University. Raipur.

Das, N. K. (1990), The Simko Movement. *J. Anthrop. Surv. India*, 39: 06-112.

Das, N. K. (1997), Some Aspects of Tribal Ethnicity in Western Orissa. In *Ethnicity, Politics and Political Systems in Tribal India*. B.Goswami et al. (Eds.). Calcutta: ASI.

Das, Sibir, R. (1989), Effects of industries and urban centre on the tribal culture: A Case-study from Koraput, Orissa. In *Acculturation and Social Change in India*. Eds. S.C. Panchbhai and M.K.A. Siddiqui. Calcutta: ASI.

Dash, Dhiren. (1978), "Jatra": The Theatre of the People of Orissa. In *Folk Music and Dances*. Vol. IV. Ed. H.C. Das.

Dash, Durgamadhab (2002), Darubrahma and the cult of Jagannatha. Orissa Review. July 2002.

Dash, J. (2000), Tribal Origin of Jagannatha. *Orissa Review*. July 2000.

Dash, S. C. (1970), *"Orissa, States of our Union,"* Publication Division, Govt. of India, New Delhi.

Eschmann, A. H. Kulke and G. C. Tripathy (1978, 1986), *The Cult of Jagannatha and the Regional Tradition of Orissa*. New Delhi: Manohar.

Fabri, Charles (1962), Introduction to Orissi Dance. 49th Indian Science Congress Souvenir. Cuttack.

Fabri, Charles, L. (1974), *History of the Art of Orissa*. New Delhi: Publications Wing.

Ghosh, G. K. (ed.) (1993), *The Dazzle from Within*. New Delhi: Ashish Publishing House.

Hunter, W. W. (1872), Orissa or the vicissitudes of an Indian Province under Native and British Rule. In *The Annals of Rural Bengal*. Calcutta: Government Press.

Jena, S. C. (2002), Guru Nanak's Pilgrimage to Puri. *Orissa Review*. July 2002.

Kanungo, Sidhdhartha (2002), Tantricism and the Jagannatha Cult. *Orissa Review*. July 2002.

Kanungo Pralay. Hindutva's Entry into a 'Hindu Province': Early Years of RSS, in Orissa. *EPW* August 2, 2003.

Kar, I. B. (1978), The Musical tradition of Pala and Dasakathia. In *Folk Music and Dances*, Vol. IV H.C. Das (Ed.)

Khokar, Mohan (1962), Myths, Legends and Historical Facts about Orissi Dance. 49th Indian Science Congress Souvenir. Cuttack.

Khuintia, Rekharani (2002), Lord Jagannatha and the Chilika Lake. *Orissa Review*. July 2002.

Mahapatra, K. (1998), Linguistic Landscape and Literary Cultivation. *Adibasi*. Vol. XXXVIII. No. 1 and 2. Jan.-June 1998.

Mahapatra, S. C. (2002), Car Festival, *Orissa Review*. July 2002.

Mahapatra, Sitakanta, *Modernization and Ritual*. New Delhi. Oxford University Press.

Mahapatra, S. K. (1978), The Ecstasy of Love and Communitas: A Note on Jagannath Culture. In *Life and Culture in Orissa*. Ed. B.S. Das. New Delhi: S. Publicashers.

Mahapatra, Sitakanta (1978), Folkways in Religion, Gods, Spirits and Men. Ed. S. Mahapatra. *Folk Culture* Vol. II. Bhubaneswar : IOOS.

Mahtab, Harekrushna (1959), *The History of Orissa*. Vol. I, Cuttack : Prajatantra

Miller, Barbara, Stoler (ed.) (1984), *The Gitagovinda of Jayadeva*. Delhi : Motilal

Misra, P. (1962), Dance Sculptures from Orissan Temples, 49th Indian Science Congress Souvenir. Cuttack.

Misra, T. and B. Mohanty (ed.) *Jayadeva and Gita Govinda*, Bhubaneshwar: Utkal University of Culture.

Misra, T. N. D. "Jayadeva and Gitagovinda: The Issues and Problems" in *Jayadeva and Gitagovinda*. Eds. T. Misra and B. Mohanty N.D. Bhubaneshwar: Utkal University of Culture.

Misra, Trilochan (2002), Ratha Yatra, *Orissa Review*. July 2002.

Ratha Yatra, *Orissa Review*. July 2002.

Mishra, Baba (1995), *Medieval Orissa and Cult of Jagannath*. New Delhi: Navaranga Publications.

Mishra, Biranchi (2002), Sambalpur. *Orissa Review*. May-June 2002

Mishra, Rajkishore (2002), Not merely a God. *Orissa Review*. July 2002.

Mohanty, T. (2002), The Lord of the universe. *Orissa Review*. July 2002.

Mohapatra, R.C. (2002), The Applique Craft of Piplai. *Orissa Review*. November 2002.

Mukherjee, S. (1978), Mystical Lord Jagannatha, in *Life and Culture in Orissa*. Ed. B.S. Das. New Delhi: S. Publishers.

Nanda, Bikram Narayan (1994), *Contours of Continuity and Change*. New Delhi: Sage.

Nanda, P. K. (2002), Vedic Symbolism and Lord Jagannatha. *Orissa Review*. July 2002.

Nayak, Durga Charan (2002), The Birth Anniversary of Jayadeva, *Orissa Review*. May-June 2002.

Nayak, P. K. (1989), *Blood, Women and Territory: An Analysis of Clan Feuds among the Dongaria Konds*. New Delhi: Reliance Publications.

Nayak, P. K. (1996), Jagannath and Adivasi. *Man in Society*, Vol. 10.

Panda, P. C., D. Pathy and B. K. Rath (eds.) N. D. *The Heritage of Orissa*. Bhubaneshwar: Orissa Tourism Development Corporation.

Padhi, Sakti (1999), *Land Relations and Agrarian Development in India*. Thiruvananthapuram: Centre for Development Studies.

Panda, S. C. (1986), *Naga Cult in Orissa*. Delhi: B.R.Publishing Corporation.

Panigrahi, K. C. (1981), *History of Orissa*. Cuttack: Kitab Mahal.

Panigrahi, Nilakanta (1996), *Development and Displacement in Tribal Orissa*. Bhubaneshwar: NKC Centre for Development Studies.

Parija, H. K. (1989), Aryanization of Tribal Deity : The Jagannatha, in B.C. Ray (Ed.) *Tribals of Orissa*, New Delhi: Gyan Publications.

Patel, C. B. (2002), The Jagannatha Triad. *Orissa Review*. July 2002.

Pasayat (2002), Goddess Samaleswari in Sambalpur. *Orissa Review*. August 2002.

Patnaik, H. S. (2002) Contributions of Orissa to the National Culture. *Orissa Review*. July 2002.

Patnaik, J. (1978), Folk Cults in the Feudatory States of Orissa. In Folk Culture, Vol. II. *Folkways in Religion, Gods, Spirits and Men*. Bhubaneswar. Institute of Oriental and Orrisan Studies.

Patnaik, N. (1963), From tribe to caste: The Juangs of Orissa. *The Economic Weekly*, 15 (18) 741-742.

Patnaik, N. (1969), *Caste and Social Change: An Anthropological Study of Three Orissa Village*.

Patnaik, N. (1977), *Cultural Tradition in Puri: Structure and Organization of Pilgrim Centra*. Simla Indian Institute of Advanced Study.

Patnaik, N. (1972), *Tribes and their Development: A Study of two Tribal Development Blocks in Orissa*.

Patnaik, N. & S. Bose (1976), *An Integrated Tribal Development Plan for Keonjhar District*, Orissa. Hyderabad: National Institute of Community Development.

Patnaik, Nihar Ranjan (1992), *History and Culture of Khond Tribes*. New Delhi: Commonwealth Publishers.

Patnaik, Nihar Ranjan (1989), *Social History of Nineteenth Century Orissa*. Allahabad: Vohra Publishers and Distributers.

Patnaik, Nityananda (2002), *Folklore of tribal Communities Oral Literature of the Santals, Kharias, Oraons and the Mundas of Orissa*. New Delhi: Gyan Publishing.

Pattnaik, Prafulla (2002), The Origin of Jagannatha Worship. *Orissa Review*. July 2002.

Prachar Samity. Souvenir (1962), Indian Science Congress Souvenir. 49th Session Indian Science–Congress. Held at Cuttack. Orissa.

Pasayat, C. (1993), Tribe-Caste integration in Orissa : A study of Naukhai Festival. *Adibasi, The Journal of the Tribal and Harijan Research-cum-training Institute*. Vol. XXXIII, No. 2, June 1993.

Preston, James J. (1980), *Cult of the Goddess*. New Delhi: Vikas Publications.

Rath, Jayanti: (2002), Sun-God in the Art and Literature of Orissa. *Orissa Review*. November 2002.

Ray, B. C. (1989), *Tribes of Orissa*. New Delhi : Gian Publishing House.

Razeq, K. A. (1989), Acculturation among the hill Saoras. In *Acculturation and Social Change in India*. Eds. S.C. Panchbhai and MKA Siddiqui. Calcutta: ASI

Roy, S. C. (1935), *The Hill Bhuiyas of Orissa, with Comparatives notes on the Plain Bhuiyas*. Ranchi. Man in India office.

Samal, B.P. (2002), Bhuddhism in Orissa. *Orissa Review*. May-June 2002.

Schnepel, Burkhard (1993-94), Goddess, Kings and Tribals: Remarks on the Ritual Policy of South Orissan Jungle Kingdom. *Man and Society*. Vol. 8.1993-1994.

Singh, R. L. (ed.). (1971), *India: A Regional Geography*. Varanasi: National Geographical Society.

Singh, K. S. (In Press) *People of India: State Volume on Orissa*. Anthropological Survey of India.

T. R. B. (1968), Impact of Satya Mahima Dharma on Schedule Castes and Scheduled Tribes in Orissa. *Adibasi* Vol. X. 1968-69-No. 1. April 1968. Published by Tribal Research Bureau. Bhubaneswar.

T. R. B. (1972), *Status of the Kuli Caste in the District of Bolangir and Sambalpur.*

Adibasi. Vol. XIV. (1972-73), Number One. Tribal Research Bureau. April 1972.Nanda, P.M. 1987.Bond friendship among tribes of Orissa. *Adibasi*. Vol. XXVII No. 4 Dec. 1987.

Tondon, J. S. (1970), *Social process in the industrialisation of Rourkela.Census of India*. 1961 1Part XIE 1970.

J. P. Frye. (1860), On the Uriya and Khond Population of Orissa, in *Journal of the Royal Asiatic Society of Great Britain and Ireland*. 17. 1- 38.

J. A. May (1873), Notes on the Bondos of Jaypur. *Indian Antiquary*. 2. 236-238.

Verrier Elwin (1948), Notes on the Juang. *Man in India*. 28 (1) 1-46.

Verrier Elwin (1945), Zevo Bondo Murderers. *Man in India*. 25 (1).

Verrier Elwin (1955), *Bondo Highlanders*. Bombay. Oxford University Press.

Elwin, Verrier (1955), *Religion of an Indian Tribe*, London: Oxford University Press.

Hunter, W. W. (1976), A Statistical Account of Bengal. Vol. XIX, Concept Publishing Co., New Delhi (Reprint).

Mohanty, H. B. (1957), *An Industrial Survey of Orissa*, Orissa Govt. Press: Cuttack.

Mohanty, U. (1978), "Muthadari System in Orissa" Paper presented in International Congress of Anthropology & Ethnological Sciences. New Delhi. Mimeographed.

O' Malley, L. S. S. (1808), *Bengal District Gazetter of Cuttack, Puri, Balasore.* Calcutta: Govt. Press.

Pati, Biswamoy (2004), *Identity, Hegemony, Resistance: Towards a Social History of Conversions in Orissa, 1800-2000*. Gurgaon: Three Essays Collective

Parida, J. K. (1987), Inter-District variations in the level of Development and causes in Orissa state, in *Orissa in Perspective*, (Ed.) B.Sahoo, Satanetra Publications, Bhubaneswar.

Pathy, J. (1987), "Ethnic Minorities and Processes of their Development", UGC Report.

Pathy. J. (1987), Land Problems of Tribes, *The Times of India*, Sep. 9th New Delhi. P. 6.

Randall, A. (1983), The Problem of Market Failures. *Natural Resource Journal*, 23(1).

Roy Burman, B.K. (1980), "Integrated Development of Tribals Incorporating Forest Resources", paper presented in seminar on "Development Aspects of Tribal areas", Bhubaneswar.

Sahoo, B. (1987), "Agriculture Industry Syndrome: A Case Study of Orissa", In Orissa in Perspective (ed) B. Sahoo, Satanetra Publication, Bhubaneswar.

Kulke, H. (1978), Jagannatha as the State Deity under the Gajapatis of Orissa. In *The cult of Jagannath and the Regional Tradition of Orissa*, Eschmaan. A et.al. New Delhi, Manohar.

Kulke, H. (1979), Early State Formation and Royal Legitimation in Tribal Areas of Eastern India. In *Aspects of Tribal Life in South Asia*. R. Moser nd M.K. Gautam (Eds.) Bern: Studio Ethnological Bemensia.

Kulke, H. (1978), Jagannatha as the State Deity under the Gajapatis of Orissa. In *The Cult of Jagannath and the Regional Tradition of Orissa*, Eschmaan. A *et al*. New Delhi, Manohar.

Kulke, H. (1979), Early State Formation and Royal Legitimation in Tribal Areas of Eastern India. In *Aspects of Tribal Life in South Asia*. R. Moser nd M.K. Gautam (eds.) Bern: Studio Ethnological Bemensia.

Mazumdar K. (1984), "British Baptist Missionaries in Orissa" in Life and Culture in Orissa, B.S. Das Ed. Calcutta: Minerva Associates.

Mahapatra, G. (1983), The Saora View of Good life and Development: *Adivasi*; Vol. XXIII, No. 2, (pp. 30-40).

Miller, Barbara Stoler (1984), Ed. *The Gita Govinda of Jayadeva*. Delhi. Motilal Banarasi Das P. 139.

Mahapatra, L. K. (1976), Gods, Kings and the Caste System in India. In *The Realm of the Extra-Human : Agents and Audiences*. A. Bharati (Ed.) Paris: IUAES.

Patnaik, U. N. (1955), Saoras of Ganjam Scheduled areas: *Orissa Tribal Research Journal*, Vol.1 (Introduction), Bhubaneshwar, Orissa.

Patnaik, U. N. (1989), *The Saora*; Bholanath Press, Bapuji Nagar, Bhubaneshwar, Orissa.

Sahu, L. N. (1946), *History of Orissa*. Poona: Calcutta: Servants of India Society.

Singh, Bhupinder (1984), Level of Leadership in Saora Society; Souvenir of Adivasi Exhibition (1984) (PP. 20-28), TRHTI, Bhubaneswar, Orissa.

7

SITUATING NGOs IN TRIBAL DEVELOPMENT OF ORISSA

S. M. Patnaik

In recent times, the issues pertaining to the role of NGOs in development have assumed greater significance. The growing role of the NGOs in the task of social development has been widely discussed and debated at various levels. Experiences across the country testify to the importance of collective action initiated by the NGOs in achieving success in different fields of human living (Venkateswaran 1995).

The present work explores the scenario of tribal development in Orissa with special reference to the role of the NGOs taking an anthropological perspective on their structures, strategies, the kind of issues they take up and the problems faced by them in their work. The study was carried out through ethnographic field work over 1995-2001. The study was conducted at two different levels: (i) at the level of the organizational set up of non-government agencies; and (ii) at the level of local communities to assess the actual impact of NGOs on tribal societies. Fifteen non-government organization were selected for a detailed study of their work culture with special reference to the background and motivation of the staff, leadership style and decision making processes. Few pockets of tribal concentration with operation NGOs were covered from (i) Kashipur (Rayagada), (ii) Mudulipada (Malkangiri), (iii) Pallahara (Angul); and (iv) Phulbani (Phulbani).

Understanding Voluntary Action and NGO Movement

The NGOs have established a viable and meaningful link between the grassroots organizations and the international agencies through the intermediate state or national level organizations. The linkage is sensitive to any change at the local, regional, national or international level. Such a link is composed of several strands dyed with multiple hues. Understanding the history and genesis of the NGOs, their contemporary relevance and future implications cannot be ignored in any attempt to comprehend the changing development scenario. Even the state has finally recognized the role of NGOs as copartners in the area of social development.

Most of the literature on NGOs does not distinguish between "voluntary association", "NGO", and "people's organization". Rather they use these terms interchangeably. However, the present study intendes to distinguish these three types of social action as such a distinction carries great analytical and empirical significance.

In the early part of the twentieth century, a large number of voluntary organizations came into existence in response to Gandhiji's call for constructive work (Sachchidananda and Prasad, 1994). The term 'voluntarism' derives its origin from the Latin word 'volunteers' meaning 'will'. It refers to a group of persons coming together purely on their own will, desiring to carry out certain activities at the grassroots level with commitment, dedication and sincerity for social amelioration and other good causes. They adopt a flexible working strategy and believe in an effective communication system, human touch and closer personal care in mobilizing community resources. Mutual accountability, devotion, personal rapport with local people and greater flexibility are the essence of voluntary action.

Several authors have attempted a classification of voluntary action on the basis of its quality, ideology and motivation. The voluntary action could either be indifferent or neutral towards the state. It is neither pro nor anti establishment and, therefore, it explores the local idioms, resources, both human and natural, and local knowledge for realization of its objective. This voluntarism rests on the commitment and dedication of a small group of people guided by the ideology of 'service to mankind is service to God'. They demonstrate a missionary spirit, but not necessarily Christian, in accomplishing their task. In their ideological scheme, state is taken neither as a promoter nor as an oppressor of social justice. The voluntary associations formed during the freedom struggle were mainly of this type and derived inspiration from the ideology of social justice. With passage of time, another type of voluntary association emerged which Sharma (1996) has called "Social Action Group". These groups have anti-state ideology, the state is regarded as oppressive and, therefore, social transformation should be carried out by devising an alternative strategy for development. They are 'non-party', 'non-institutional' and 'non-professional' groups (Sharma, 1996; Dhanagare, 1993). Sharma (1996) distinguished social action groups from that of development NGO's' which mainly carry out state sponsored development programmes and gradually operate as a proxy for the government. On the other hand, the social action groups declare the state as anti-people agency of centralized power and authority. The emergence of such groups was attributed to state directed development programmes and hiatus between the existing structures/institutions and growing demands/expectations of the people (Dhanagare, 1993).

The emergence of social action groups has been viewed as a positive phenomenon in the modern democratic system. These groups are non-violent, critical and constructive in nature. It is critical of persisting structure of exploitation and oppression. They operate at grassroots level by involving sensitized or radicalized middle class youth (Sethi, 1984), who involve themselves due to deep strings of consciousness (Kothari 1984). (Thus, their grassroots level operations, adherence to non-violence and participation mainly by youth make them different from organized movements.)

Vohra (1990) distinguished between 'development NGOs' and 'organisation NGOs', not on the basis of their relationship with the state, as done by Sharma, but on the basis of its emphasis or focus of activity. The development NGOs focus mainly on economic programmes, often large ones, which will lead to alleviation of poverty and rise in the standard of living. The organizational NGOs, on the other hand, emphasize on creating grassroots organizations that can stand up for the rights of the deprived. Vohra further admits that to maintain a water-tight dichotomy of organizational and developmental categories would be unrealistic, since no NGO can totally neglect organizational work while organizational NGOs have implemented economic programmes.

In a nutshell, the voluntary organization comprises like minded people who willingly and selflessly contribute a part of their labour, time or resources for social welfare so that the idea of social justice can be realized. For them voluntary work was never their profession but a means to attain a broader goal.

But in case of non-government organizations, the spirit of voluntarism is not fully manifested. Social service is taken as a job or career which grows over time. Individuals always wait for a good bargain; social service spirit needs to match with adequate compensation in terms of lucrative pay packages. This has a direct relationship with the socio-economic background of the workers of the voluntary organization and non-government organizations. In the case of former, the people mainly come from elite and rich economic class whereas in case of latter, it attracts people from poor and middle class.

The NGOs carry out activities, implement programmes which were hitherto being carried out by the government machinery. And, therefore, to avoid the possibility of confusing them, a prefix of "non-government" became a necessity. The non-government organizations have their own staff, administrative machinery and infrastructure such as its campus, building, vehicles, etc. A voluntary organization might also have these resources but they are more pronounced in case of former. However, in both cases, the volunteers or workers come from a socio-cultural background different from that of the local people with whom they work.

In case of people's organization, as the name suggests, the group comprises of local people who themselves take initiative and manage their affairs. Usually, there are some outside organizations who act as catalytic agents but the task of taking decisions and managing resources lies with people themselves. In fact most of the NGOs believe that creating such grass-roots or people's organizations, before withdrawing from their area of operation, is their final goal. It refers to a social order where the people are able to manage their own resources, handle their own problems and achieve their goals without the help of an outside organization.

Besides the concepts of voluntary and non-government organizations, the present study has used the concept of development. The term 'development' *per se* envisages a battery of changes, changes for betterment of the community. It involves the notion of progress, growth, upliftment and welfare of the collectivity. This multifaceted term carries different meanings for the economists, political leaders, bureaucrats, administrators and social anthropologists. For the economists, it is an increase in growth rate or per capita income, for politicians it is an acquisition of some symbols of modernization and progress, for administrators it is achieving the targets and for social anthropologists it is the enhancement of quality of life or standard of living or satisfaction of basic need aspiration level and happiness. There is a growing realization that development can no longer be understood in terms of statistical indices, political symbols or economic parameters and the present study shares its concern with this emerging trend. For an integral development of a community, the developmental strategies should be formulated in accordance with the locally felt, culturally conditioned individual and group needs. And NGOs are seen to be effective catalysts and facilitators at the grassroots level mediating between the people and the state.

In the next section, I dwell on the ethnographic background within which the NGO activities in Orissa are situated, i.e. the tribes and their social-cultural set up.

Tribes in Orissa: Population and Distribution

In India the term 'tribe' refers to the indigenous *jana*. They are commonly designated as *adivasi* (original settler), *girijan* (hill dwellers), *vanyajati* (forest dwellers) and *adim jati* (primitive caste), *janjati* (fold communities), *anusuchit janjati* (Scheduled Tribe). In Orissa, the term *adivasi* is commonly used for tribes.

Orissa is one of the States which has remained a source of unending fascination for ethnographers. It has as many as 62 different tribal communities, numbering 5, 915, 067 people which form 22.43% of the State's population as per 1981 census. Next to Madhya Pradesh, the state comprises the largest tribal population in the country. Barring the tribal states of north-eastern hill areas, it ranks first in the percentage of tribal population among the other states of the country. The distribution of tribal population in different districts of the state is uneven; however, it is noteworthy that in Orissa more than 50% of the total tribal population is found in six districts, namely Koraput, Sundergarh, Mayurbhanj, Nowrangpur, Malkangiri and Rayagada. The distribution of Scheduled Tribe population over the thirty districts of Orissa is given in Table 1.

Table 1
Distribution of Scheduled Tribe Population Over the 30 Districts of Orissa

S. No.	*Districts*	*Tribal Concentration in Percentage*	*Total Tribal Population*
1.	Mayurbhanj	57.87	10,90,626
2.	Makkangiri	57.67	2,46,799
3.	Nowrangpur	55.26	4,67,919
4.	Rayagada	54.99	4,01,501
5.	Sundergarh	50.74	7,98,481
6.	Koraput	50.35	5,19,719
7.	Gajapati	47.86	2,17,538
8.	Keonjhar	44.51	5,95,184
9.	Phulbani	50.13	2,81,595
10.	Boudh	13.51	40,813
11.	Sambalpur	42.11	97,958
12.	Deogarh	41.88	1,23,243
13.	Jharsuguda	36.48	1,98,176
14.	Nowapara	32.82	2,55,582
15.	Kalahandi	29.04	3,28,448
16.	Bolangir	22.04	2,71,677
17.	Bargarh	16.98	1,47,774
18.	Dhenkanal	13.66	1,20,226
19.	Angul	12.34	1,16,520
20.	Balasore	11.52	1,81,941
21.	Sonepur	9.50	1,45,286
22.	Jajpur	7.41	1,02,741
23.	Nayagarh	5.81	46,624
24.	Khurda	5.13	77,242
25.	Cuttak	3.49	69,437
26.	Ganjam	3.16	79,120
27.	Bhadrak	1.60	18,805
28.	Jagatisinghpur	0.61	6,157
29.	Kendrapara	0.40	4,534
30.	Puri	0.23	3,016

Language

The entire bulk of Orissa tribals is ethno-linguistically classifiable into three groups: Munda (Austric), Dravidian and Indo-Aryan. Each group has its inter-community language affinities. The languages of each group have a common source, common ancestry and cultural heritage. On the other hand, above the group level or inter-group level, they share certain basic features in their verbal behaviour regardless of their own linguistic ethnicity. Thus, Santhali and Sora of the same Munda family and Bonda, Parji and Desia of Munda, Dravidian and Indo-Aryan families show certain remarkable common features in nature and structure of tribal language. The demo-linguistic picture of the tribal languages and dialects of Orissa is as follows:

Munda: Bhumij, Birhor, Bonda, Didayi, Gadaba, Ho, Juang, Kharia, Korku, Koda, Mundari, Parenga, Santali, Saora.

Dravidian: Gondi, Konda, Kul, Kuvi-Kondh, Kisan, Koya, Kolami, Naiki, Oraon, Ollar (Gadaba), Parji, Pengo.

Indo-Aryan: Bathudi, Patri, Bhumia, Bhuiyan, Desia, Halbi, Jharia, Kurmali, Sadri, Sounti.

Among all these languages, writing systems (or scripts) have been invented in recent past for four languages only, namely, Santali, Saora, Ho and Kui.

Economy

The tribes of Orissa are at various stages of socio-economic formation. At one extreme, we come across groups which lead relatively isolated life while at the other extreme are groups which are indistinguishable from the agricultural communities. The tribes of Orissa can broadly be divided into the following six categories on the basis of their economic position: (1) hunters and food gatherers, (2) cattle rearers, (3) shifting cultivators, (4) settled cultivators, (5) artisan communities, and (6) industrial and agricultural workers.

The tribes pursuing hunting and food gathering are very small in number. They do not produce any food and depend upon natural resources for their subsistence. The examples of such communities are the Hill Kharia, the Mankirdia and the Birhor of Similipal forest region of Mayurbhanj district. Among such people, the notion of private property is poorly developed. These people have almost an egalitarian type of society. Some of these tribes have highly developed skills with respect to hunting and food gathering. For example, these communities are expert in spotting a nest of wild bees and getting honey from bee-hives, in trailing and killing birds on the wing, in lurking in the bush for some hiding animals and for shooting at them and in watching the fish for the chance of spear.

Some of the tribal communities (such as the Bonda, the Saora, the Kandh, the Bhuimya and the Juang) are primarily shifting cultivators. Traditionally the shifting cultivators were in harmony with natural environment. But with changing times and with the unleashing of several modern forces, the equation has changed.

The pastoral tribes comprise a small section of the total tribal population. The Koya of Malkangiri, a Dravidian speaker, is perhaps the only example. The Mahali and Kol-Lohara practice crafts like basketry and blacksmithy respectively. But recently these artisan tribes are facing a tough competition in the local market from their modern counterparts.

There are many tribes (usually the large ones, such as the Santhal, Munda, Ho, Bhumij, Oraon, Gond and Paraja) practising settled agriculture. The agrarian structure of tribal Orissa is characterized by crude technology, unproductive holdings, land alienation, indebtedness and lack of irrigation facilities resulting in low yield and economic hardship.

A considerable section of tribal population in Orissa has moved to mining, industrial and urban areas and tea gardens of Assam and West Bengal for earning a secured living through wage-labour.

Social Structure

The social organization of Orissan tribes generates an ethos different from that of the mainstream Oriya society. Most of the tribes are divided into a number of sub-tribes which are further divided into clans. For example, among the Kondha, which is a large tribe, there are about 20 sub-divisions and among the Saoras more than 25 sub-divisions are found. The sub-tribes with sizable population function as independent tribes. Among Kondha, there are three sub-tribes namely, the Kutia Kondh, the Desia Kondh and the Dongria Kondh. The Paraja of Koraput are divided into Bodo or Sodia Paraja, Sana or Jhadia Paraja and Parengi Paraja. Among the small tribal communities (like the Bonda and Birhors) the divisions are small in number. The Bonda are divided into two groups, namely the plain Bonda and the Hill Bonda.

The sub-tribes are divided into various exogamous and totemic clans with territorial cohesion and strong corporate identity. The clan is the pivot of all socio-economic activities. The number of clans a tribe may have varies from one tribe to another. The clan organization is very prominent among the Kondh, the Gadaba, the Paraja, the Juang and the Santhal. Among the Juang, as many as twenty four clans have been reported. The members of a clan, believed to have descended from a common ancestor, observe certain totemic taboos and worship the common totem with great reverence. The clan organization is, however, absent among the Saora where the main exogamous unit is the extended family called *birinda.*

Every clan is divided into several lineages which in turn are divided into several families. Among the tribes of Orissa, simple or nuclear family consisting of married couple and their unmarried children is the usual form. Joint families are very rarely met with. A son after marriage establishes a neo-local residence. The family is patrilineal, patrilocal and patriarchal.

Marriage is an important institution. It has an important bearing in the social life through which alliance between two clans is established. Among the tribes of Orissa, mostly adult marriage, is in vogue. Among all the tribes, with the exception of the Bonda, the boy is always older than his marrying partner. But among the Bonda, it is just the opposite. Although monogamous marriages are held ideal yet polygynons marriages are found among certain tribal groups. Payment of bride-price forms an integral part in tribal marriage. Although this custom is present among almost all the tribal groups, the amount of bride-price prescribed differs from tribe to tribe. Bride-price in the form of either cash or kind or both is paid to the bride's family by the bride-groom's parent at the time of marriage. Among the various ways of acquiring mate, the important ones which are now in practice among the tribes are marriage by negotiation, marriage by capture, marriage by service and marriage by elopement, besides levirate, sororate and cross-cousin marriages are some of the preferential forms of marriage found among the tribes of Orissa. Divorce remarriage (of widows and widowers) on reasonable grounds are also permitted.

Village Organisation

The tribal communities have a village organization headed by a traditional chief who arbitrates the village disputes. He is assisted by other officials of differential power and the village council. The extent of his power responsibilities are culturally defined in case of different tribes. The tribes also have the institution of youth dormitories where unmarried boys and girls assemble at night, sing, dance and engage in merry making. This provides them with an opportunity to know each other and select life partners. Dormitory also plays an important role in imparting basic training to youngsters in traditional skills of their culture (such as hunting, fishing, singing and dancing, etc.) The dormitory is known by various names in different tribes such as *majang* (Juang), *dindaghara* (Kondh), *basaghar* (Paraja).

Issue in Tribal Development

In successive UN reports, Orissa has been notorious in terms of extremely poor indicators of human development index. In the whole state, 74.6 per cent of all workers are engaged in agriculture either as cultivators or agricultural labourers (Registrar General and Census Commissioner, 1981). Large section of agriculturalists are landless and depend on *podu* (shifting) cultivation as their primary source of livelihood and rest others, who have land holding, supplement their produce with *podu*. Shifting cultivation is marked with low productivity and leads to depletion of forest cover. Orissa has 7.36 per cent of forest cover and forms 20-33 per cent of total geographical area (The State of Forest Report, 1989, Forest Survey of India) which is less than the stipulated extent of forest cover. Several causes have been attributed for extensive deforestation in Orissa and all over India, such as construction of dams, mining, encroachment for agricultural purposes, and population pressure. Large scale displacements have become order of the day, uprooting thousands of tribals from their traditional habitats. Illiteracy, ignorance and poverty are also seen as the root causes of backwardness of the tribals. Tribal habitats even till date remain cut off from mainstream, due to poor rail and road connectivity. Many districts are malaria prone. Due to lack of awareness and inaccessibility of medicines, the tribals face serious health problems. Health is recognized as a social issue which is integrated into the strategy of social development. Public distribution system has failed to deliver in tribal areas where the inhabitants are reeling under abject poverty, curse of alcoholism and land alienation. Tribal development in Orissa suffers largely from official apathy and political indifference.

The NGOs in Orissa

History of Growth

The voluntary activism in Orissa dates back to 1928 when the Servants of Indian Society (SIB) was floated in the undivided districts of Cuttack and Koraput (now Rayagada). With their multi-pronged approach, they handled a variety of issues like education, awareness, health, environment, income generation for women and general welfare programmes for tribals. For almost two decades, there was no other registered voluntary organization working in the field of social welfare. In 1984, two more organizations were founded, namely Jayanti Pathagar at Ganjam and Sakhigopal Mahila Indu Co-operative Society at Puri. The former aimed at building and improving the community potential by focusing on non-formal education, dissemination of relevant information and creating awareness through community organization. While the Jayati Pathagar had the total community as its target group, the Sakshigopal Mahilla Indu Cooperative Society chose to focus on a particular section of society, i.e. women. It made every effort to build up the female potential by focusing on various income generation programmes like matting and coir work.

After 1960s, there was a gradual development but till 1975 the process of establishment of voluntary organizations has remained rather slow. Towards the late 1970s a spur in this field was observed; by mid 1980s a large number of NGOs became active in the field of rural and tribal development. Since then, the mushrooming of the NGOs has been countinuing as evident from table 2.

The contemporary pattern of distribution of NGOs in various districts of Orissa is worth mentioning here. Most of the NGOs are found to be working not in backward and tribal areas, but in relatively well connected and better off areas. The districts of Khurda (237), Dhenkanal (94), Puri (84) and Cuttack (63) have the highest number of NGOs whereas less number of NGOs are found in the districts of Deogarh (3), Jharsuguda (9), Nuapada (8), Sonepur (4), Malkangiri (7) and Boudh (10). The last two districts are predominantly inhabited by the tribal population. Other districts with concentration of tribal population do not have many NGOs working for them.

Table 2
Growth of NGOs in Orissa

S. No.	Year of Establishment	No. of NGOs
1.	Before 1950	4
2.	1951–1955	2
3.	1956–1960	3
4.	1961–1965	10
5.	1966–1970	10
6.	1971–1975	30
7.	1976–1980	79
8.	1981–1985	138
9.	1986–1990	359
10.	1991–1995	435
11.	Total	1,066

Distribution of NGOs in Orissa

S. No.	Name of the District	No. of NGOs
1.	Angul	40
2.	Balasore	56
3.	Baragarh	12
4.	Bhadrak	37
5.	Bolangir	28
6.	Boudh	10
7.	Cuttack	63
8.	Deogarh	03
9.	Dhenkanal	94
10.	Gajapati	25
11.	Ganjam	74
12.	Jajpur	35
13.	Jagatsinghpur	20
14.	Jharsuguda	09
15.	Kalahandi	24
16.	Kendrapara	43
17.	Keonjhar	44
18.	Khurda	237
19.	Koraput	23
20.	Malkangiri	07
21.	Mayurbhanj	45
22.	Nayagarh	58
23.	Nowrangpur	10
24.	Nuapada	08
25.	Phulbani	67
26.	Puri	84
27.	Rayagada	25
28.	Sambalpur	29
29.	Sonepur	04
30.	Sundargarh	23
31.	Total	1,066

Mapping NGOs in Orissa

Location of different NGOs in the field areas:

S. No.	Name of the NGO	Field	Station District
1.	Agragamee	Kashipur	Rayagada
2.	Gram Vikas	Mohuda	Ganjam
3.	SEDP	Pallahara	Angul
4.	NIPDIT	Phulbani	Phulbani
5.	ASRA	Mudulipada	Malkangiri

Information collected from the above five field stations was compared and cross-checked with each other. Besides these five organizations, fieldwork was also conducted among other NGOs located in at different places. They are:

1.	Centre for Youth and Social Development (CYSD)	1. Bhubaneswar
2.	Council of Professional Social Workers (CPSW)	2. Bhubaneswar
3.	Jana Bikas Kendra (JBK)	3. Pallahara (Angul)
4.	People's Rural Education Movement (PREM)	4. Mandiapalli (Berhampur)
5.	Regional Centre for Development Co-operation (RCDC)	5. Bhubaneswar
6.	LIPICA	6. Berhampur
7.	Phulbani Rural Developments & Technology Agency (PRDATA)	7. G. Udayagiri (Phulbani)
8.	Anu Santi	8. Berhampur
9.	Village Reconstruction Organisation (VRO) (Keonjhar)	9. Baya Kumutia
10.	Malyagiri Unnayan Mahilla Udyoga (MUMU)	10. Pallahara (Angul)

Agragamee

Agragamee was established on 19 April 1987. It was initiated in 1981 by a group of young men who were deeply moved by the poor living conditions of the tribes in Kashipur block of Rayagada district. The team was supported by a group of tribal youth who joined them in 1982. The organization was in search of an alternative strategy for the awakening of tribals to come up in order to bring about a change in their socio-economic condition. The attempt was to create alternative leadership. At present, the organization is working with various communities like Soura, Kolha, Ho, Santhal, Munda, Juang, Kandha, Mankadi, Kondha and Paraja.

Agragamee's area of operation is spread in Kashipur Block (Rayagada), Dasmantpur (Koraput), Thuamul Rampur (Kalahandi), Tentulikhunti (Nowrangpur), Phiringia (Kandhamal), Thakurmunda (Mayurbhanj), Sukruli (Mayurbhanj) and Pallahara (Angul).

The problems faced by local people are of starvation, hunger, diseases, malnutrition, problem of money lending, bondage, payment of low wages, landlessness, low literacy rate, non-functioning of the primary schools and also lack of political will and local leadership among the tribals.

The organization has concentrated in three broad areas– (1) Food security for the marginalized and deprived sections; (2) Educational and political literacy through village level organization; (3) Protection against over-exploitation of natural resources. The organization has promoted a number of Youth Clubs and *Mahila Mandals* and other informal local organizations to reduce its scale of involvement in a phase manner. For the growth of individuals and for a feeling of team spirit, decentralization has been emphasized. Natural resources and human resource development are considered to be two primary aspects of development by Agragamee.

Village committees are formed and training is imparted to various sections like landless agricultural labourers, small and marginal farmers, women groups and progressive minded youth groups. They are kept up with the current issues and programmes initiated by the government. They are taught the management of village funds and activate public distribution system. They are made aware of the forest protection and forest laws, common property resources and their utilization, soil and water management, bio-farming, etc. They also train animators who organize and mobilize people for community development and people obtain information from them.

The organization is being supported by CAPART, Ministry of Rural Development, for programmes like implementation of JRY, providing safe drinking water facility, construction of WHS under

Water Technology Mision (WTM), Training on Watershed Management, etc. Collaboration with Ministry of Human Resource Development, Department of Education, has resulted in promotion of literacy through Non-formal and Experimental Innovative Education Centres and establishment of District Resource Unit (DRU). The Orissa Household Food Security (OHFS) project is being implemented in Kashipur and Dasmantpur block of Rayagada and Koraput district respectively with the collaboration of UNICEF, Field Office, Bhubaneswar as well as the Panchayati Raj Department, Government of Orissa. In the implementation of Watershed Management Project, Agriculture Department, Orissa University of Agriculture and Technology (OUAT) and Krishi Vigyan Kendra, Koraput, have been involved.

Gram Vikas

Gram Vikas is a voluntary organization registered in 1978. The organization has its origin in the Young Students' Movement for Development (YSMD), a Madras based student organization. They had moved to Orissa to undertake relief and rehabilitation efforts after a devastating cyclone and tidal wave hit the state's coast. And then settled down with head office at Mahuda, near Berhampur, and branch office at Bhubaneswar (Orissa). The organization mainly works for the tribals and in Orissa many tribal communities are benefited by their service. The economic status of the tribals has improved who were earlier caught in vicious web of moneylenders and were exploited.

The major activities of Gram Vikas include field projects, networking, training, action, research, etc. Funding comes from West Germany, Australia and CAPART. In India, the Governing Bodies of the organization are at Delhi, Bangalore, Madras and Calcutta. The funding comes to the head office at Orissa through Delhi. The grants are project based. The different aspects of networking are (i) ITDP– Integrated Tribal Development Programme, which looks after programmes of housing, saving, education, working development, land development, social forestry and medicine; (ii) water sanitation, septic tanks, bathroom and tube-well construction; (iii) bio-gas; and (iv) cane project.

The organization has clear cut hierarchy in its structure with the Director as the executive head of the organization. The Assistant

Executive Director assists him in his work and takes charge in his absence. The four Programme Managers prepare and select different programmes according to the place and problem. While preparing a programme, expenditure, duration of work, and numbers of workers reqired are taken care of. There are 20 Project Co-ordinators and 40 Assistant Project Co-ordinators. The Project Co-ordinator looks after the project and takes charge of the project. He decides the place, type of construction required, and how a project should perform.

The 260 animators or supervisors work in the field. Every field has one or two supervisors. They look after the field workers and take care of the raw material. Till the end of the project, they remain in the field. Large number of field workers are not appointed because the organization believes in involving local people in various projects. In Orissa, the Gram Vikas is working in many districts. The programme of ITDP emphasizes on housing, education, saving, land development, social forestry and medical. In housing, they provide *pacca* houses; this brings people living in jungle to a common settlement. The people are encouraged to save money and workers tell them its benefit. And they regularly collect money (in whatever amount) and deposit it on behalf of the villagers. Literacy programmes are also conducted.

Gram Vikas allots them the unused government land to encourage forestry and agriculture. Beneficiary plants are grown in plantation and thus giving opportunity for better economic status. In health programme, every month a doctor and some workers visit the villages and supply free check up and free medicines. Cane project and other handicraft work are encouraged so that people can become independent. Special attention and training is given to women, so that they can utilize their leisure time. Gram Vikas has always ensured that the organization incorporates a perspective which views people and their activities as an integral part of the eco-system. Conservation was integrated into the development philosophy, alternative energy in the form of biogas was promoted, and maintaining an ecological balance and the necessity of integrated development initiatives was highlighted by Gram Vikas.

NIPDIT

The National Institute for People's Development Investigation and Training (NIPDIT) has been working since 1983 in Phulbani. Here it has been working since 1979 and is popularly known as Research Team, and later the area of operation expanded to other districts, i.e. Bolangir, Kalahandi, Keonjhar, Mayurbhanj and Nayagarh. NIPDIT focuses its activities on Scheduled Castes, Scheduled Tribes, women, children, landless labourers and rural artisans and other weaker sections of the society. NIPDIT tries to involve the community at all stages from planning to monitoring and evaluation of its activities. It also enters into collaboration and maintains a network with like minded national NGOs and government departments, particularly in study, research and campaigning a common action programme.

The action plan takes into account a few essential aspects such as eliciting community participation, finding out the developmental requirements of operational areas, reorientation of organization at cluster ievel, reorganization of resource support system, improving the implementation of existing programme, and designing new schemes to plug the groups and implement more effective programmes.

The other primary aspect of NIPDIT developmental strategy is environment building. In 1985–86 it was awarded with the *Prakuti Mitra* (Friend of Nature) by the Government of Orissa. Since 1987, NIPDIT has been observing 'National Environmental Awareness Campaign', sponsored by the Ministry of Forest and Environment, Government of India. The basic aim behind this environment building is to create a sense of urgency about community development activities and enthusiasm to take part in the programme, and identification of volunteers, activists and mobilisers.

According to NIPDIT sources, the success of the programme/ project depends upon the participation of the community in all stages of planning, implementation and evaluation. There are various models of community participation.

The cluster level committees are the planning and executive bodies of the project in the village. They mobilize the community for various development activities according to the targets set by it. They are given thorough training and exposed to the field situation so that they can perform their work at grass-roots level, can organize various activities to ensure maximum participation, and establish a dialogue between the local level administration and the community. Special emphasis was given to bringing women into the fold of development process by creating women CLO(s) and *Mahila Sangha.*

A process of environment building has been established in operational areas of NIPDIT by training a few village youth who are enthusiastic and committed to play an animator's role in their community. These animators are helping CLOs at all operational levels, i.e. helping in survey, environment building, campaigning, persuading parents to send their children to school and ensure effective participation of the community in all sectors of development.

SEDP

The Socio-Economic Development Programme (SEDP) got registered under the Societies Registration Act in 1975 in West Bengal. Thc SEDP Pallahara Project (Orissa) started its activities in 1985. Dominant development ideology is Alternative Development Paradigm and it requires people's collaboration and co-operative intervention at all levels of all the action programmes. SEDP felt the need of people's organization at the village and area level and the need of marcro linkage of such organization for sustenance. Most common and basic issue was drought. Orissa Drought Action Forum was established just then and SEDP entered it as a member. ODAF was formed in 1988 with the common mission to combat drought hazards through research, reflection and analysis. In 1991, the SEDP Pallahara Project launched the preparatory phase of People's Participatory Process (PPP) in 20% villages of its operational area. The success of this programme led them to implement at all the 62 villages of its operational area in Pallahara Block. The alternative drought action is based on community's and people's multi-directional and multi-dimensional action directed to the most marginalized societal groups, the marginal and small farmers, the landless, the women and the children contributing to socio-economic transformation of the weaker and deprived ones.

Monitoring of the activities is done continuously at all levels by the unit staff, zonal co-ordinator and the cluster co-ordinator appraise the "Workers Forum". Meetings are held at regular intervals to discuss the progress and problems. Members of Village Committees also participate in the on-going monitoring process. Besides, staff from SEDP Head Office also visits the project area and interacts with the project staff as well as the target people.

Consultancy services are extended from cluster office to field office and to the villages, from SEDP to departments of the State Government and vice-versa. Experiences as well as consultancy during this period were also shared with like-minded NGOs and resources were also made available. Consultancy services as well as resources were extended to other NGOs seeking for such services and to government departments in various disciplines like agriculture, animal resources development, tribal welfare, waste land development, etc.

Anu Santi

Anu Santi is a small voluntary organization registered in 1985. The funding countries are Germany and Switzerland. Other supporting international organizations helping it are ILEP (International Leprosy Federation Programme), NLEP, NACO, UNICEF, DWCRA, UBSB, WATSAN, and NPIC. Their first project was in G. Uday Giri on health and leprosy. Now, it is working in Gosani Block (Andhra Pradesh), the village in Garabandha which is at the border of Andhra Pradesh and Orissa. The tribal community is of Saora. The founder of this organization is a paramedical doctor.

Since the organization is very small, the funding is also less. Each staff is paid nominally. The staff members visit different villages and organize camps and give free medical services. If necessary, they bring emergency and serious cases to government medical hospital. Indian government also provides instruments and essential medicines to them. In other matters they provide help.

LIPICA

LIPICA is Lower Income People's Involvement for Community Action. It was registered on 13 October, 1989. The objectives of the organization were initially health and education. But, at present, the organization works on the issues of health and education, agriculture, literacy, non-formal education and *balbadi*. The working area is tribal and rural.

The director regulates the organization, brings projects funding. She appoints people and prepares programmes and plans. Co-ordinator helps in this. The co-ordinator visits the areas and selects the location where the work should be done. The plans are made to suit the locality. Fieldworkers work at the grassroots level. They approach the local people and find out their problems. They make them understand different programmes and give them training for the work.

In Jarada, they are running a project on health and education. The programme gives special attention to women, educating them to take care of themselves and their children. They also organize medical and literacy camps. The basic objective is to involve local people in the development process. The villagers are provided training in handicraft and tailoring and better agricultural operation.

LIPICA works in Patrapur Block under which a *panchayat* comes. In other blocks also (like Bhanjanagar and Chikati) they work. Tomba comes under Patrapur Block which is completely tribal. The funding comes from the Ministry of Human Resource Development, Government of India.

CPSW

The Council of Professional Social Worker (CPSW) was established in 1989 by a group of young social workers, who had passed out from the National Institute of Social Work (NISWASS), Bhubaneswar. The dominant ideology of this organization has been of social welfare and social work. CPSW has focused on rural and tribal communities with special reference to women and children. Its head office is located in Phulbani with a branch office at Bhubaneswar. It operates in the villages of Bamnigaon and Khajuriput of Kalahandi district and a few villages of Nua Pada district. The major activities include (i) documentation; (ii) advocacy; (iii) empowering people's organization; (iv) women's development; (v) tribal development; (vi) action project; (vii) development issues; and (viii) child labour.

There are animators, community organizers, supervisors, and programme officers, looking after the planning and execution of various programmes.

An animator is a part time worker and not a full-fledged staff of the organization. The animator (locally called *Gramya Sahayak)* is entrusted with the preliminary work of mobilizing and training people. A community organizer is locally known as *Gosthi Sangathak* and is a full-time staff of the organization. His primary task is to identify, employ and motivate the animators, through whom he enters into the community. The *Gosthi Sangathak* is usually from the same region, but not necessarily from those villages where the programmes are to be implemented. The supervisor assesses the activities of several community organizers and provides the link between them and the regional/head office. He is also responsible for organizing the meeting of various community organizers where the issues and problems emerging from a particular programme are discussed. The programme officer is solely responsible for implementing and monitoring the programme.

The co-ordinator is the chief of the organization. He looks after the day-to-day activities of the organization, the policy matters and the financial position. However, there is a finance co-ordinator who is exclusively looking after the financial matters of the organization. The working body meets at least once in two months and takes decision regarding policy matters. The members of CPSW claim that there is no hierarchy among the members of the working body. It takes collective decisions and functions in an informal family-like atmosphere.

CYSD

The Centre for Youth and Social Development (CYSD) was established in 1981. It mainly works among disadvantaged poor sections of rural and tribal areas. The headquarter is in Bhubaneswar. Their dominant ideology is of the development professional. Its main activities include community health, non-formal and adult education, development of watershed areas, watershed management, rural credit schemes, small saving schemes and business enterprises for women. They were earlier associated with organizations, like Nehru Yuva Kendra, Oxfam, etc. Now, it is mainly supported by the Plan International, an international funding organization. The Ministry of Human Resource Development provides some funds and 20% is generated by CYSD itself.

Training primary groups forms an important part of their activities. They train these groups, motivate individuals and middlemen, sensitize them and professionally equip them to work as catalysts. They also train chief functionaries of various NGOs for specific purposes, like women's development, self-help group formation, etc.

CYSD has been initiating various action programmes at the field which is sponsored by a number of government and international donor services. Major activities in action programme and training include sustainable agriculture, community health, non-formal and alternative education, micro-enterprise and income generating programmes and community organization with a view to strengthening community action.

Social research (being another important activity) is directed towards purely academic exercise based on data emerging from the grass-roots level. At present they are pursuing research on developing a model for watershed management.

At macro level, CYSD works as a support system, where it collaborates with other agencies at regional level working on development issues, collaborating in areas of action research and innovative action and also intervencs in public policy issues.

Community social health programme includes drug addiction, AIDS awareness and family counseling, though there is no specific focus on family planning. Action in legal research aid is also being carried out by them.

Every programme has a co-ordinator, programme officer and field staff. CYSD has recruited specialists for different activities, for administration and research purposes.

The Centre for Youth and Social Development (CYSD) created Development Resource and Training Centre (DRTC) for taking care of training people-centred learning activities. It is designed and dedicated to offer need-based training programme to development organizations. It was established in 1992.

DRTC offers professional development workshops and programmes for educators. HRD personnel, community development activists, rural development functionaries, change agents and development managers. The courses are offered in areas of self development, effective communication, team building and facilitation, project management, strategic planning, human resource development, participatory techniques for planning and decision making, gender sensitization and emergent issues relating to contemporary happenings in the development sector.

VRO

Village Reconstruction Organisation (VRO) is a part of chain of organizations working for the upliftment of the village, through reconstruction measures, in the rural area of Andhra Pradesh. It is located at Baya Kumutia village of Keonjhar District. It mainly focuses on the promotion of cottage industries, such as manufacture of table clothes and bed-sheets with embroidery work, preparation of sweaters and table-covers through knitting. The volunteers of the organization believe that local resources, both human as well as natural, should be tapped for better living conditions.

The major objectives of the organization are 1. improving the existing health condition through nutrition; 2. reliance on kitchen garden; 3. providing an atmosphere of learning to children, both at home and school; and 4. achieving community involvement and participation in all walks of village life with special reference to development activities.

The VRO has three centres in Orissa, Baya Kumutia, Gonasika and Bir Govinda Pur. All the centres of Village Reconstruction Organisation have a mobile unit which continuously monitors the programme initiated in distant villages mainly in the field of health. The argument which the organizers provide is that it is very difficult to look after such programmes unless there is constant monitoring. Therefore, a jeep carries one or two volunteers, trainers and health workers who visit different villages motivating the people, imparting the necessary training and supplying the medicines whenever the need arises.

It may be mentioned here that the Baya Kumutia Centre has a girls' hostel where tribal girls from Munda and Ho communities reside. The Centre admits girls of twelve years of age and above to the hostel. The Baya Kumutia Centre imparts training only to boys. The latter also has a boys' hostel. The Bayakumtia and Gonasika deal with tribals whereas Vir Govinda Pur deals with the rural section. In Baya Kumutia Centre, the staff includes an administrator, mobile unit in-charge, centre superintendent, teachers and accountant. The Gonasika Centre has an administrator, two teachers and an accountant.

PREM

The origin of People Rural Education Movement (PREM) dates back to 1980 when the Mohana Block of Ganjam District initiated the challenging activity of spreading education and its values in rural and economically backward areas. Therefore, in 1982, 40 Adult Education Centres were opened for awareness and organization. In 1983 this education based policy was further strengthened and restructured.

Government policies for betterment of these people did not benefit them. Under the organizational network of PREM, aspects of family planning, saving, regeneration of forest, preservation of plantation, health care, sanitation, immunization, child care and education, were cultivated among tribals and fisherpersons.

They began from 40 neglected villages in Mohand Block and now are spread over 1800 centres; 183 non-formal schools are operating for children; 3 vocational training centrs have also been opened. It has installed 22 watershed projects, 240 dug wells for drinking water and cultivation. Besides, it has constructed 100 community centres. It has developed fish cultivation and for food security, 1100 grain banks have been opened and for agriculture purpose, 400 seed banks through the village committees and centres.

This Society was formally registered in 1984; it opened 20 more Adult Education Centres in Mohana Block and moved on to other Blocks with 30 more Centres. PREM can be termed as a facilitator of people's organization. Its multifarious development activities include literacy programme to the income-generating scheme and schemes of providing houses to those who have been rendered homeless in flood and other natural calamities.

PREM gave primary emphasis to education and took a pioneering role in bringing about 100% literacy in the areas where it spread its operational network together with welfare of women, introduction of saving as a measure of individual safety, opening up of co-operative seed banks, grain banks, etc. It has expanded its activities and programmes. Therefore, it became essential for it to extend financial and technical guidance to other similar people's organizations. The Managing Committee of PREM has unanimously decided to make 34 volunteer organizations independent in all respects so that they can discharge their responsibilities in terms of their services to the people more conveniently. On them PREM will have no direct or indirect control. Also, by 31 March 1994, these voluntary organizations would enjoy full freedom and would decide on their work plan independently. This historic policy decision taken by PREM is indicative of its belief in work-culture. It has been further resolved that when other voluntary organizations would seek technical assistance, PREM would willingly extend its support to them. The purpose of Vocational Training Centres and Correspondence Education Programme would be to impart necessary training to the volunteers of other organizations. PREM would remain an organization to impart developmental advocacy and consultancy to the associate members of other organizations.

VDCIO

Village Development and Cottage Industrial Organisation (VDCIO) is located at Gonasika in Keonjhar District, and was registered on 26 March 1993, under the Society's Registration Act. It was founded by a former lower division clerk of the state government. He took voluntary retirement to take up some development activities in his region. At present, the organization is running several programmes with its limited resources. The programmes are community child care programme, plantation and nursery, environment, health and sanitation survey, herbal medicine, plantation, handicraft training programme and women's development.

VDCIO is also organizing training camps, health camps in different villages. Under health programme, the volunteers visit the operation area every month and distribute medicine. The president of this organization has studied upto tenth class, but could not complete matriculation. He found out that villagers of his locality were basically lethargic, most of the time sitting idle or wasting time in gossip. Even the women folk were not used to work during the afternoon. So to keep them engaged in some creative and constructive work, he started this organization in his area. He is optimistic that given the financial assistance, he would definitely be able to make use of locally available human resources through the formation of cottage industry which will lead to an overall development of the village. According to him, the

Government must identify and encourage such small organizations which might not have visibility in the state, but be quite active in a local situation.

MUMU

The Malyagiri Unnayan Mahila Udyoga (MUMU) started functioning in 1987 with tribal women in Dhenkanal and Angul districts of Orissa. It seeks to build a self-reliant society through awareness building and development activities. Its main objective is to organize tribal women to experience group activities so as to improve their quality of life through programmes like formal and non-formal education, training for income generation, social forestry and community health.

MUMU is still in infancy and is guided and helped by SEDP whenever necessary. Its activities are more of experimentation and exploration. The secretary (the Project Director) of MUMU co-ordinates the programmes and is assisted by one programme co-ordinator who is usually on constant tour for meeting co-workers and the participating people at the unit and the village levels. Generally all the workers of MUMU meet at a central place (in most cases at Pallahara Complex) once a month to review the activities of the previous month while planning for the next. Discussions are often held on the action plans for implementation in fulfilling the objectives giving particular emphasis on the process analysis. Efforts are made to create transparency in activities and they cover all level workers through intensive sharing of documents and information, so that the members may be motivated to take appropriate decision in a decentralized fashion.

In the existing area of operation, the organization has been proceeding with its activities systematized by effective co-ordinating efforts with a staff strength of thirteen. The secretary at the apex is responsible for the overall activities, while the co-ordinator holds the charge of selecting the places and the relevant programmes and obviously with the responsibility of getting them executed. Each of the two unit incharges looks after the overall affairs of the allotted unit (of 12 villages). The animator and the three community workers are engaged in motivating, training and implementing tasks mostly of the field level. Two homeopathic physicians are rendering the necessary health service. The financial work is looked after by account assistant. One office peon is there for relevant assistance. The animator and the three community workers meet at village levels involving the beneficiaries as and when required for planning and deciding about different action programmes. The secretary, the co-ordinator and programme co-ordinator are on frequent tours to cover such village and unit level meeting for making communication and networking faster and effective.

With its commitment to serve the remote areas hitherto unexplored by any NGO or government agency, the organization is on the move to adopt a set of 36 new villages in phases after its planned withdrawal from the existing area of 24 villages. Preliminary survey, rapport-building, discussions and negotiations with the proposed beneficiaries and the key persons of the community are going on in this newly adopted area.

RCDA

The Regional Centre for Development Co-operation (RCDC) is a forum of NGOs and individuals working at a regional level on issues pertaining to management of natural resources and is designed to act as a regional applied resource centre. The organization is located in Bhubaneswar and was registered on 17 March 1993 by a group of young people working in different NGOs. They were unanimous about the fact that a change was required in the structure and function of NGOs for meaningful contribution and for bringing about the desired change in the management practices of natural resources.

The mandate of RCDC is protection and management of local natural resources with direct participating of local people at all levels. Dominant ideology of the organization is involving development professionals for the task. The infrastructure consists of a team of twelve professional staff-members and three administrative associates. It is an inter-disciplinary team drawn from specializations like ecology and environment, social work, women's studies, economics, forestry, law, mass communication, people's movement, etc. The infrastructural funding is provided by Oxfam and they also mobilize the partner organization for rest of the funding.

The objective of RCDC is to reduce poverty and hunger through sustainable management of local resources in community participation and development of the rural environment and natural resource base and also, to enable men and women to develop their institutional and human resources, plan and implement environmentally sustainable rural development models and improve policies. It also aims to facilitate and support community based systems for management resources and establish rights of the community on local natural resources.

Primary target groups of the activities of RCDC are tribals and women, and secondary target groups are grass-root level development organizations. Areas of operation are in three different geographical regions of Orissa: (1) The Central Orissa (Angul and Dhenkanal district), the organization is documenting and lobbying on the issue of population displacement and rural unorganized labour. (II) In coastal Orissa (Balasore, Cuttak, Puri and Ganjam districts), RCDC is networking with other NGOs on coastal ecological issues. The organization is also documenting indigenous knowledge for water resource management and flood control mechanisms. (III) In South-West Orissa (Balangir, Sambalpur and Koraput district), the organization is organizing community institutions and primary groups to establish sustainable models for community based forest management. It is facilitating the forest protection communities to evolve forums at regional and district levels.

Through these micro-level efforts, RCDC (along with its collaborating agencies) endeavors to propagate the concept of 'Community Forest Management' and it also undertakes researches on legal issues, dependency of people on forest, issues in management of non-wood forest produces, institutional arrangement for community based resource management systems.

JBK

The Jan Bikas Kendra (JBK) was formalized in 1989 and their primary concern was the tribals and the underprivileged people. They started their work in Pallahara Block of Angul and Banspal Block. Jana Bikas Kendra (JBK) Project Banspal has laid stress on the issues of (i) education and awareness among the tribal and other backward people; (ii) sustainable agriculture by utilizing the streamwater; (iii) youth mobilization for village development; (iv) awareness campaign for preservation and promoting forests.

These are not rigid categories; they might overlap with each other. Emphasis is on sharing of work and importance is given to the person's skill, ability and expertise.

The JBK people are convinced that planned social change for people can only begin from within the natives themselves. And so JBK works to enable people to see their own situation critically This is done through training, camps, workshops for men and women. These programmes are combined with community funds, irrigation, multipurpose tank, etc. Thus the people are encouraged to work out solutions on their own.

JBK believes in participation and involvement of the people prior to the taking up of any programme. Gradually, through close association with the people, the approach for people's development has been identified. JBK intervenes in the socio-economic and socio-political aspects of tribal society in an attempt to initiate a self sustaining process of social change. The efforts are directed towards building up the information for local tribals, irrigation potentials and creating wage employment and environmental conservation.

ASRA

Association of Social Research Action (ASRA) is a voluntary organization at Mudulipada, a highland Bonda village in the Khairiput Block of Malkangiri district, mainly working on issues relating to education, health and income generation. ASRA organizes the village level meeting, conducts regular health checkups and records the body weight of pregnant mothers and new born children; and creates health awareness among the villagers by telling them the basic principles of health, hygiene and cleanliness. Among other programmes, ASRA runs two weaving centres and two night schools for the Bonda tribe. The weaving centres are located at Andarahal and Mudulipada. Each weaving centre has 30-40 looms and a trainer. The Bonda women are given a daily stipend of Rs. 12 each for learning the skills of hand weaving. The products are marketed by ASRA through the network of local co-operatives. The basic purpoe of this programme is to provide employment opportunities to local women during the off season, thereby harnessing the human resources to its optimum.

The two night schools are situated in the villages of Tulagurum and Patrapur. The former is mainly a Bonda village and the latter contains a mixed population. In Tulagurum the school is run by Husi Udam, who is a Bonda himself. He has studied up to class seventh. And has been teaching there for the last three years. In Patrapur school, the teacher is a Gauda by caste. He is a matriculate from Navrangpur and has been employed by ASRA for at least three years. ASRA is funded by several funding agencies of India and abroad. The two major funding agencies are Oxfam and IDPI.

Pradata

Phulbani Rural Development and Technology Agency (PRADATA) was registered in 1986 with its headquarter at G. Udayagiri. The agency's approach is to improve the condition of the socio-economic life, rural and tribal health, rural water sanitation and development of appropriate rural technology and non-conventional energy sources in the district of Phulbani. Even though the term 'rural' appears in its name, the agency also works among the tribal population. Presently, it is working mainly in the Balliguda sub-division of Phulbani district, especially in the blocks of G. Udayagiri, Raikia, K.Nuagaon, Tikabali, Chakapada and Daringbadi.

Dynamics of NGOs of Orissa: A Synoptic View

NGO movement in India began with a belief and conviction that bureaucracy breeds redtapism and corruption and only through democratic process and decentralization, one can involve people of all sections in the decision making process. Emergence of NGOs occurred as an alternative to the governmental bureaucratic structure which, they believed, largely failed to serve people. It was held by people involved in voluntary sector that small collectives can only be effective at the grassroots level as they would try to democratically initiate participatory process for the people in question. So the stress on informal democratic and participatory processes became the guiding force of organization of any voluntary association. In light of this fact, it was interesting to note that a majority of the big organizations like PREM, Agragamee and Gram Vikas, have been initiated by people who believe in this stream of thought and still claim to believe in the democratic participatory process.

It is significant to note that organizations over a period of time have become so big, both in terms of money, power and human resource, that their organization itself needs a large bureaucratic structure. For example, beginning from a collective organization, the Gram Vikas has matured into a very rigid bureaucratic structure. Some people call it an empire and for others, it is not an NGO but an industry. In Gram Vikas, the executive director and his close associates have total hold on the organization. In theory, they do talk of participatory decision making process. Their internal structure, nevertheless, belies it. Decision making is completely centralized mainly in the hands of selected few, the lower level of staff does not have any access to his superiors and an overt power structure is manifest in the organization.

In some NGOs (like Jan Bikas, CPSW and RCDC), we found an existence of team work and a collective spirit. These organizations consist mainly of younger people and there is a great deal of enthusiasm and zeal for work among these people. Many of these workers attributed this fact to the informal structure of the organization itself. In many organizations, like NIPDIT, there is a great deal of freedom given to the co-ordinators who work at different field stations. This helps these people to improvise strategies according to the field situation, so they may not have an access to major decision making. However, they are given some free hand to deal with the local situation. In the field stations of Jan Bikas and NIPDIT, we found a great deal of informality and rapport between the co-ordinators and village level workers. This good relationship also percolates down to influence the villagers and many of these workers are very popular in the village circle.

The pay structure was surprisingly found to be rather low for major categories of workers in these organizations. This low pay structure is one of the factors due to which workers do not seem to stick to an organization for a long time. Bureaucratic principles of seniority and educational qualifications loom large in fixing up a pay package for grassroots worker, whereas qualities such as the level of commitment, sincerity, and dedication of a worker is of secondary importance in pay fixation.

The NGOs work entails staying in remote field stations far from their families which makes it less attractive. In the Pallahara centre of SEDP the co-ordinators were allowed to have their families along with them, however, in other places like Agragamee, the emphasis was on communal living, they shared a common mess and common sleeping arrangements. In Agragamee, we found few women workers too who were finding hard to adjust to this kind of life. Many young women, who generally join in the beginning, often have to leave due to their marriage and for others, marriage prospects become rather dim because they are not able to leave the job due to economic pressure at home.

Most of these NGOs seem to revolve around a certain personality. The graph of these NGOs indicates the emergence of one or two persons becoming all powerful and he or she gradually gains control over the organization. This centralization of power in one person has led to rigidification and bureaucratization of the NGO like any other formal organization.

The field of tribal development involves both the government machinery and the non-government agencies which are playing crucial roles in bringing out change in the life styles of tribal communities. It was noted that there is a difference in the manner in which a single issue, such as agriculture or forest, has been approached and handled by two or several NGOs. Further, different NGOs give priority to different issues which also change over time. The issues handled by the NGOs are many and complex.

Most of the NGOs are facing the problem of getting the right kind of people who can make their goals or dreams a reality. It is very difficult to get technical staff such as doctors, agricultural engineers, environmentalists and veterinary doctors. Persons with professional and technical qualifications are not willing to go to the field and stay in remote areas, cut off from the mainstream.

Sometimes the genuine NGOs face problems in obtaining FCR license, as their interests clash with that of the government. When the local people do not like an administrative or political decision, they stage protest march and carry out mass agitation. In most cases, the NGOs working in the area either initiate or catalyze or support such movement. As a result, they are perceived, in the government eye, as trouble makers. Most of the NGOs are also facing severe problems due to the interference of local politicians.

This study identified several trends of change among the tribals of Orissa due to the NGO activities. One of the most important findings suggests that NGOs have won greater support of local people than the state. This is mainly due to their close rapport, sympathetic and helping attitude of workers. State machinery still has a patronizing attitude towards the NGOs and they do not treat them at par. Government needs to simplify rules for granting funds to NGOs and also facilitate the process of disbursing the money spent since this is one of the most common complaints in government sponsored programmes by NGOs. Among the Desia Kondhs of Ganjam district, the NGO activity has led to abolition of child marriage and prohibition of liquor on some ritual and ceremonial occasions. The local NGOs of Keonjhar district have been quite successful in empowering the tribal communities, especially the Munda and Juang. In Kashipur area, tribals were found to be aware of their rights and they have been holding protest against the L&T aluminum factory. NGOs are seen to be important tools of dissemination of information. The government policies at the level of practice still remain distant from people's lives. Shortsighted planning has led to disastrous implications such as large scale migration, land alienation, consumerism, disenchantment and even, at times, prostitution. Though the NGOs are closer to ground nevertheless they are also limited in understanding the cultural nuances, therefore unwittingly become carriers of unforeseen changes.

References

Cernea, Michael (1988), *Non-governmental Organisations and Local Development*, Washington DC, World Bank Discussion Papers, No. 40.

CPSW (1992), *Women and Environment. Impact of Environmental Degradation on Rural Women: Case Studies from Selected Villages of Orissa.* Bhubaneswar: Women Development Council, Council of Professional Social Workers.

Dhanagare, D.N. (1993), "Action Groups and Social Transformation in India: Some Sociological Issues". *Themes and Perspectives in Indian Sociology*, Jaipur, Rawat Publications.

Dwivedi, O.P. (1994), *Development Administration: From Underdevelopment to Sustainable Development*, New York: St. Marlina Press.

Fernandes, Walter and Geeta Menon (1987), *Tribal Women and Forest Economy*, New Delhi: Indian Social Institute.

FSI (1989), *The State of Forest Report. Forest Survey of India.* Dehra Dun: Ministry of Environment and Forests.

Fowler, Alan (1991), *The Role of NGOs in Changing State–Society Relations: Perspectives from Eastern and Southern Africa.* Development Policy Review.

Francis, C. 1993. "Rural Development, People's Participation and the Role of NGOs". *Journal of Rural Development*, Vol. 12.

Kothari, Rajni (1984), "The Non-Party Political Process". *Economic and Political Weekly*, Vol. No. XIX, No. 5.

Mehrotra, Nilika. 1997. Grass Roots Women Activism: A Case Study from Delhi. *Indian Anthropologist*. 27, (2) 19-38.

Mehrotra, Nilika (2004), Situating Tribal Women *The Eastern Anthropologist*. 57 (1) 61-73.

Menon, Geeta (1995), 'The Impact of Migration on the Work and Status of Tribal Women in Orissa' In *Women and Seasonal Labour Migration*. University of Amsterdam: Indo-Dutch Programme on Alternatives in Development, New Delhi: Sage Publications.

Oommen, T.K. (1995), The Theory of Voluntary Associations in a Cross-Cultural Perspective, In *Alien Concepts and South Asian Reality, Responses and Reformulations*. New Delhi: Sage Publications.

Patnaik, S.M. (1996), *Displacement, Rehabilitation and Social Change: A Case of the Paraja Highlanders of Orissa*. Inter-India Publications, New Delhi.

Patnaik, S.M. (2001), "Culture and Displacement: Continuity, Protest and Change". In V. Bhasin and V. K. Srivastava (eds.) *Human Ecology in the New Millennium*. Delhi: Kamla-Raj Enterprises.

Patnaik, S.M. (2004), "Tribes, State Policies and NGOs," *Indian Anthropologist*. Vol. 34, No.1

Sachchidananda and R.R. Prasad (1994), *Tribal Development and Voluntary Action–A Case Study of the Badlao Foundation*. Tribal Studies of Indian Series T- 168, Inter-India Publications.

Sethi, Harsh, 1984. "Groups in a New Politics of Transformation" *Economic and Political Weekly*. Vol. XX, No. 9.

Sharma K.L. (1996), The Indian State and the NGOs. *Social Action*, Vol. 46.

Tribes of Orissa, (1990), *Harijan and Tribal Welfare Department*. Government of Orissa.

Venkateswaran, Sandhya (1995), *Environment, Development and the Gender Gap*. New Delhi: Sage Publications.

Vohra, Gautam (1990), *Altering Structures–Innovative Experiments at the Grassroots*, TISS, Series No. B–68.

World Bank (1991), *Gender and Poverty in India. A World Bank Country Study*. Washington D.C: World Bank.

8

SARAT CHANDRA ROY

Sachchidananda

The pursuit of the science of man cannot be perfect and fruitful without love and sympathy for people. Bereft of these it may degenerate into a mere recording of specimens or a collection of curiosities. Sarat Chandra Roy, the father of Indian ethnology, was drawn to anthropology through sheer love of the poor tribal people with whom he came into close contact in the everyday business of life as a lawyer. Roy's love of the poor led him not only to study them but also to fight for their cause.

Sarat Chandra Roy was born on 4 November 1871 in a well known Kayasth family of landed aristocrats in village Karapara of Khulna district (now in Bangladesh). One of his ancestors, Parmanand Roy, was regarded as one of the twelve big landlords in East Bengal. His family was closely related to Raja Basant Roy, a big landlord of that area. Sarat Chandra's father, Purna Chandra Roy, was a member of the Bengal Judicial Service. Young Sarat Chandra moved along with his father wherever he was posted. It was when his father was posted in Purulia that he had his first contact with the tribal people. His father died in 1885 when Sarat Chandra was only fourteen years old. For the next few years his life was one of adversity as the family was involved in litigation relating to property. Sarat Chandra, however, continued his studies under the guardianship of his maternal uncle at Calcutta. He passed his matriculation examination in 1888 and graduated with honours in England in 1892 from the General Assembly Institute (now Scottish Church College) in Calcutta. He passed his M.A.

examination in English from the same college and took his law degree in 1895 from the Rippon College, Calcutta. He then worked as Headmaster of the Mymensingh High School and was later invited to work as the Principal of the GEL Mission High School, Ranchi. It was during this sojourn at Ranchi that he was intimately drawn towards the sad plight of the tribals. He, however, left teaching to set up practice as a lawyer. He became a pleader in the district court of 24-Pargana at Alipur, Calcutta, in 1897. The call of the tribals, however, proved irresistible for him and in 1898 he transferred his practice to Ranchi. In a short period he built up a lucrative practice in the court of the Judicial Commissioner, Ranchi.

As a lawyer, Sarat Chandra used to visit the interior areas of Chotanagpur on commission from courts and could observe the tribals from close quarters. He was moved by the oppressions and hardships of the Munda and other tribes at the hands of the aliens who were placed over the heads of the Munda and other tribal communities through the ignorance and apathy of the government authorities. He was distressed by the way the tribals were treated in the courts of law. He saw that the courts of law could not give them justice as their cases were not pursued with sympathy by the lawyers the tribals engaged. This could not be done as the lawyers had no knowledge of the tribal languages, culture, and customary laws. He, therefore, made it a point to study tribal culture in depth and also to master their language. His interest in the tribals and the publication of his book on the Munda in 1912 attracted the attention of Sir Edward Gait who was at that time the Lieutenant-Governor of Bihar. Gait saw merit in Roy's work and gave him financial assistance for his further research on the Oraon. Thus, Sarat Chandra was launched as an anthropologist and in course of time produced a number of monographs on the Birhor, Hill Bhuiya, and Kharia.

Since Roy was devoted to Indological researches, he took keen interest in the activities of the Bihar and Orissa Research Society which was started in January 1915 and of which he became the General Secretary. Anthropology and folklore were included in the scope of research for this organization and Sarat Chandra was also placed in charge of the Anthropology and Folklore Section, with Sir Edward Gait and Mahamahopadhyay Har Prasad Shastri as members. He regularly contributed to the journal of the society and also enriched the Anthropology and Prehistoric Gallery of the Patna Museum with his personal collections.

His deep concern for the poor and the downtrodden tribals of Chotanagpur and devoted labour for their uplift led to his election as a member of the Bihar Legislative Council for several terms from 1921 to 1937. He was also elected as a member of the Provincial Committee that sat with the Simon Commission in 1928. He also served as a member of the Indian Franchise Committee headed by Lord Lothian. His interest in anthropological studies began to take most of his time and he gave up his legal practice in September 1933. From then on till his death he devoted himself entirely to his own researches and to editing of *Man in India*, the first anthropological journal in the country which he founded in 1921.

Sarat Chandra Roy was deeply interested in social work. He served the Ranchi District Board as a Vice-Chairman for many years. He was the President of the Governing Body of the Bengali Boys' School and also of the Bengali Girls' School at Ranchi. He was at the same time President of the Harijan Sewak Samiti, the Anti-Drink Society, the Oraon-Munda Siksha Sabha, and the Brahmacharya Sangh. These wide ranging interests kept him extremely busy and one wonders how he could combine his professional work as a lawyer and scholarly interest as an anthropologist along with the huge burden of social work.

In fullness of time, the services of Sarat Chandra Roy in the field of anthropology and in that of social service received due recognition. He was awarded a Kaiser-i-Hind-Silver Medal in 1913 and the title of Rai Bahadur in 1919 besides two certificates of honour and two other medals. In 1920, he was elected an honorary member of the Folklore Society of London, the only Indian to be honoured with this distinction. The same year he was elected President of the Anthropological Section in the Indian Science Congress. In two successive years, 1932 and 1933, he was elected President of the Anthropology and Folklore Section of the All-India Oriental Conference. Later, he was elected a member of the Council d' Honour of the International Congress of Ethnological Sciences. He was a Foundation Fellow of the National Institute of Sciences in India and also of the Patna University. In 1941, on the occasion of his seventieth birthday, the Indian Science Congress decided to present him with a commemorative volume, *Essays in Anthropology*, written in his honour by some eminent anthropologists of the day. Unfortunately the volume was published one week after his death. The list of contributors to this volume shows the high esteem in which Sarat Chandra Roy was held by his colleagues at home and abroad.

Sarat Chandra Roy breathed his last on the morning of the Buddha Purnima, 30 April 1942, after a prolonged illness of several months. His death was widely mourned not only at Ranchi but by anthropologists in different parts of India. The eminent scientific journal *Nature* in an editorial observed. "The dry light of pure science and the disinterested research was kept aflame (in India) by a small band of devoted enthusiasts among whom the veteran anthropologist Sarat Chandra Roy will ever be held in honour."

Although anthropology was more a labour of love than a profession for Sarat Chandra Roy, his devotion to the subject was unbounded and he kept the flame of the new social science burning. He not only added to the existing knowledge in the discipline by his unceasing efforts, but left no stone unturned to stress its importance and usefulness in quarters where it mattered most. He was the first person to deliver a University Readership Lecture in Anthropology at Patna University in 1920. The topic he spoke on was "Principles and Methods of Physical Anthropology". This was one year before the first full fledged university department of anthropology was started at Calcutta through the efforts of Sir Asutosh Mukherjee. From time to time, he delivered lectures in the new department at Calcutta and enthused its members to make it an important centre of anthropological research in the country.

In the different presidential addresses he delivered to the Indian Science Congress, Oriental Conference, and other learned bodies, he dwelt upon the current status of research in the various branches of anthropology. He thus raised the status of the subject at national, scientific gatherings. He also demanded the opening of departments of anthropology in different universities of the country. India, being a veritable ethnological museum, offered ample scope for researches in this field. He made a strong plea for giving training in anthropology to executive, judicial, forest and excise officers serving in tribal areas.

It is in furtherance of his aim to promote anthropological research that Sarat Chandra Roy started the journal *Man in India* in

1921. This journal attracted important contributions from scholars at home and abroad. Besides original papers, it carried book reviews, notes and queries and also notices of anthropological interest in current Indian literature. It continue to be published even now under the distinguished editorship of Dr. R. M. Sarkar.

Sarat Chandra Roy was a source of inspiration and a tower of strength to many budding anthropologists. Nirmal Kumar Bose and D.N. Majumdar received active encouragement and guidance from him in their early years. In fact, Roy gave some of his own notes on the Ho to Majumdar. It was at his behest that S.S. Sarkar studied the Maler of Rajmahal Hills in 1935. He also encouraged Charulal Mukherjee, an advocate like him at Dumka, to undertake researches on the Santal of Mayurbhanj in Orissa. The study was later published as a monograph. In this way, Roy not only helped train and guide professional anthropologists but built up and nourished all through his life a vigorous tradition of anthropological research in the country.

He was a voluminous writer. He wrote with equal ease in such diverse topics as physical anthropology, prehistoric sites, racial migration, tribal social system, various aspects of religion and magic, caste and folklore. Even the sheer volume of his work would have done credit to any scholar. But much more than this was the encyclopedic nature of his scholarship and the depth which he attained in his analytical appraisal of religion and philosophy of either the tribal communities or of the Hindu social system by which they were in one way or another affected.

Roy was a deeply religious man and he looked upon the highest values of a culture as the central substance of a religion. It is with this substance that he tried to identify himself in spirit. This does not, however, imply that Roy was rigid or orthodox in his approach. Even while discussing Birsa movement or Oraon revitalizations movements and the religious or cultural forms that they took, he did not fail to appreciate that the movements arose from distressing economic troubles that pressed hard upon these tribes from all around. It is in fact these sorrows and sufferings of the tribals that had drawn him to anthropology. But he was convinced that without a deep insight into their lifeways and thoughtways any effort to solve their problems would miscarry.

Studies of Tribal Cultures

During his long innings as a student of tribal life and culture, Sarat Chandra's writings reflected the changing orientations in the discipline of anthropology. Roy did not have any formal training in anthropology, as when he began his work, anthropology was not taught anywhere in India as a distinct discipline. However, Roy once he developed keen interest in the tribals, kept himself abreast with the latest developments in anthropology throughout his life.

He was first drawn to the study of the Munda of Chotanagpur and wrote some articles in journals on some aspects of their life before his first monograph appeared in 1912. At that time most of the anthropologists even in the west, were still engaged in evolutionary and diffusionist studies. They thought that anthropology was a branch of history dealing with tribals. This history was partly valid and partly conjectural or its reconstruction was based on scanty evidence drawn from myths, legends and folklore. Roy believed that a knowledge of history of a tribe would help us appreciate its culture better. It is thus no surprise that Roy's monograph on the Munda contains only one chapter on ethnography against five chapters on history. In the only chapters, Roy makes an effort to trace the origin of the tribe from cues drawn from folklore, linguistics, and prehistoric evidences. He then proceeds to reconstruct the long history of the tribe from the time of the Vedas to the beginning of Christian era. It is only in the early medieval and modern period that some historical evidence on the tribe is available. In the modern period he brings the narrative down to the Birsa revolt. In this chapter of the modern history of the Munda, he traces in detail the various socio-economic movements that raged in the Munda country in the nineteenth century.

The section on ethnography deals with the physical appearance, dress, ornaments, weapons, material culture, the description of a Munda village, details of tribal agricultural operations, social and political organization of the Munda, religion, festivals, superstition, etc. Roy also gives some details of the Mundari language, folktales, proverbs, folksongs, etc. The book gives a short and generalised account of Munda life and culture and does not take into consideration regional differences of customs and practices among the Munda.

His next book dealt with the Oraon, another major tribe of Chotanagpur. In this book, he made amends for his earlier excessive obsession with history. Out of the six chapters only one has been devoted to history and migrations of the tribe, while the rest are devoted to a detailed ethnographic description of Oraon life and culture. The material collected on the Oraon was so voluminous that the bulk of the data on religion was left to be dealt with in another volume which was published many years later. Roy throws a flood of light on the social organization of the Oraon community. He was the first person to draw our attention to the existence of the *dhumkuria* (or the youth dormitory). He detailed its functions and explained its role in the socio-economic life of the tribe. He also gives a detailed description of the village organization, the village *panchayat* and the *parha* system. Roy realized that his account underrated territorial or regional differentiation, and, as Bose (1966a:iii) pointed out, presented "a composite picture of Oraon culture which did not actually apply to any particular section of the tribe which lived as a community and was readily identifiable either in space or time." In his preface, Roy noted that "The Oraons are spread over such a vast tract of Chotanagpur plateau that local variations of customs and usages described here can hardly be found together in any one village" (1915:i).

In a study of culture change among the Oraon, the greatest difficulty that the present writer faced was in regard to these regional variations, even for some of the most important institutions of the Oraon. It is, therefore, difficult to treat Sarat Chandra Roy's book as bench-mark data for future comparison. Since pioneers have to labour under limitations and as at that time anthropology had not developed the sophistication, precision or objectivity as now, the book was ranked among the very best monographs of an Indian tribe published by that time. Sir James Frazer congratulated Roy for collecting so much rich anthropological information and setting forth facts carefully distinguishing them from the inferences which Roy drew from them. A.C. Haddon, who wrote the introduction to this first book on the Oraon, tried to relate some of Roy's findings to the current thinking in British ethnography.

The second volume on the Oraon by Sarat Chandra Roy is devoted to a description of religious and magical beliefs, the cycle of socio-religious rites and ceremonies, feasts and festivals, and the magical practices of the Oraon. This is the first monograph in India which is completely devoted to the study of one particular aspect of tribal culture. Roy does not only deal with a description of rituals, but shows how some of these feasts and festivals intensify the feeling of social solidarity in a village. In this idea we get an echo of Durkheim's concept. Towards the end of the book we find a detailed description of the various nativistic and reform movements among the Oraon. All this reflected the impact of Hinduism. Not only have the origin and growth of the Tana Bhagat movement been traced, but some of their important hymns have been translated into English in this book. Roy came to the conclusion that these puritanical movements among the Oraon were not just religious in character but had strong social and economic undertones. The movements offered them an escape from the general dissatisfaction with their current economic condition and social status. He believed that the movements were more or less based on the Oraon's traditional way of thought and belief. Roy, however, did not elaborate the political implications of the Tana Bhagat movement and he also underplayed the very important role played by the Oraon in the national non-cooperation movement in 1921 as well as in the national freedom struggle in the years that followed. Even though Roy's good-will and sympathy for the Oraon in their period of trouble show through the narrative, he took care to avoid any reference which smacks of confrontation between the Oraon and the government of the day.

Sarat Chandra did not confine his attention to a study of the larger tribes alone. One of his monographs is on the Birhor, a small tribe which only numbered around two thousand in his day. The study of this nomadic tribe took more than fifteen years. He took help of an intelligent Birhor who acted as the primary informant and guided Roy to the *uthlu tandas* (temporary settlements) spread throughout Chotanagpur. The arrangement of data in this book follows the traditional pattern of a tribal monograph. He has succeeded in giving a description of Birhor life from which nomadism emerges as a style of life. He makes an occasional distinction between the patterns of living of settled (*jaghi*) and nomadic (*uthlu*) Bihor. At the end of the book he appended sixteen folktales and gives details of games, proverbs, riddles, and other means of recreation of the Bihor.

His next book was on the Hill Bhuiya of Orissa. In this work, his son, Ramesh Chandra Roy, who was a trained anthropologist, helped him in the collection and analysis of anthropometric data. This book gives a comparative description of plains and Hill Bhuiyas. Roy does not tell us the villages from which the data were gathered, although he takes care to describe the regional and local variations in the culture of the Bhuiyas.

The last monograph which Roy wrote in collaboration with his son was on Kharia who live in the south-western corner of the Ranchi district. Researches on the Kharia were carried out for twelve years. It was possible for Roy to give a comparative description of all the three divisions of the Kharia: the Dudh Kharia, the Dhelki Kharia, and the Hill Kharia. Roy held that the three sections of the tribe represent three successive layers in the development of a primitive culture. Since the bulk of this tribe has been converted to Christianity, it was possible for Roy to take the help of some educated informants. He was helped in his efforts by Christian missionaries. The monograph was published in two volumes and may be ranked as the most scientific and elaborate among the books written by Roy. In this book, he does not attempt any reconstruction of the history of the immigration as well as the origin of the tribe as revealed by its myths. Roy describes the various aspects of the social, economic, political and religious life of the community. Anthropometric measurements of a number of persons taken from each of the sub-tribes have also been given.

Besides the monographs that he wrote, Sarat Chandra Roy contributed a number of papers in research journals on some aspects of the life and culture of other tribes and communities both in and out of Bihar. He wrote on totemism among the Asur, the Ho of Singhbhum, and the Pahira of Chotanagpur. He also published articles on the Lepcha funeral, kinship among the Margar of Sikkim, the Khasi kinship terms, the Khond human sacrifice, the Korku memorial tablets, the Black Bhils of Jaisamand lake in Rajputana, and on the peoples of Burma. In addition to these, he put in *Man in India* ethnographic notes and notices of anthropological interest in current Indian literature as a regular feature.

Here and there in his different monographs we find Roy using the comparative method. He compared certain features of the social organization of the Munda and the Oraon, the two tribes he knew intimately. He showed how the Oraon like the Munda follow a patrilineal social system and the same type of village and *parha* organization. But unlike the Munda, the Oraon do not have an elaborate ancestor cult, although the spirits and the supernatural powers that they believe in and strive to appease are generally of the same kind and in a few instances common with those of the Munda. The one remarkable difference is that the Munda attribute all misfortunes to the wrath of the spirits, while the Oraon at the first instance attribute them to the influence of witchcraft or the evil eye.

In the monograph on the Kharia he attempts a comparison of the tribal character of the three communities as follows: "In fact, the Kharia is not as reserved as his Munda kinsmen but as candid and open as his Oraon neighbour. In fact, the Kharia tribe would appear to represent the golden mean. Though cheerful in disposition and genial in temperament and on occasions gay and jolly, the Kharia is, in general, less light-hearted and easy going but more restrained, sober and serious than the average Oraon. Yet he is not sober and unsocial, nor proud and uncommunicative before strangers as the average Munda appears to be."

As mentioned above, with the passing of years, Sarat Chandra developed his own distinct approach to anthropology. He realized the defects of the evolutionary and diffusionist approaches to the study of culture but he also criticized the functionalists for their inability to recognize the importance of evolution and diffusion. He wrote: "To picture a group at work is a worthy aim. To picture it without drawing attention to evidences within or borrowings from without may lead to misconceptions" (quoted in Madan 1952: 51). He, however, had praise for the functional approach for the integrated outlook on culture that it provides. He had faith in the organic unity and dynamic nature of culture. The vital function that each item and aspect of the culture fulfils in the entire scheme of it and the bond that unites them into a whole is to him extremely important. He however, feels that all items of a culture whether borrowed or acquired through evolution are integrated in it and none of them is without purpose. He held that since functionalists study only certain institutions in relation to other institutions and the culture as a whole, functional studies can only supplement and not replace the old monographic studies. Most contemporary functionalists would fall in line with Roy's view. He paid a homage to the functional school by his confession to N. K. Bose a few months before his death that 'if he were given the chance of living his life over again, he would disregard all the ethnographic accounts which he had written in the past. Instead, he would bury himself in a single village of a small region and study in microscopic detail how the life of the community was built up as well as its culture. This desire to engage in a new adventure of intensive microscopic study was proof of his superb intellectual resilience" (Bose 1966a: iii).

Having mastered the languages of the tribes among whom he worked, Roy felt that knowledge of the tribal languages is indispensable for students of tribal culture. He also underlined the need for creating effective rapport with the people to be studied. Sympathy and understanding as well as identification or empathy with the people were pre-requisites for anthropologists. "Concentrated contemplation of facts, scenes and incidents as well as outstanding of Dharma or spiritual nexus of a people that integrates, sustains and nourishes their culture–thus may illumination be gained' (quoted in Madan 1952: 57). He emphasized the quality of intuition for the true understanding of a people. Roy was essentially a humanist and an anthropologist by accident.

Anthropology of Caste

Sarat Chandra Roy was of the opinion that our ancient books, namely the *Puranas, Samhitas, Dharmashastras,* and *Grihasutras* as well as the great epics held a rich treasure house of data for social anthropology. The *Puranas* attempt to present a crude picture of the origin of man and of the gradual development of society and culture from very early time. The *Puranas* and the *Shastras* form the storehouse of the social customs, usages, rites and ceremonies, ethics and politics and law. They furnish picture of contemporary Indian society with its ideals and different types and levels of culture. According to Roy, the *Puranas* combine in them history, cultural anthropology, and ethics. The *Samhitas* and the *Grihasutras* describe the various social regulations and customs prevalent in various localities and communities in India and by arranging, classifying and correlating them, delineated contemporaneous

Hindu society as it was governed by a system of socio-religious and religion-legal rules suited to different levels of culture in the land. Of the eight kinds of Hindu marriage enumerated in the *Samhitas*, we find many which are still in practice in tribal areas. Of these only the first four were considered good while others were tolerated but not recommended.

The *Puranic* literature has been styled on *Itihasa-Puranas* or history and tradition. Tradition is in itself an important subject matter for anthropologists and as such it could not be neglected by them. Since history in Roy's days only dealt with the activities of kings and courts, he believed that it could not reveal a complete picture of the life of the society. The style of daily life of men and women organized in society and their economic and social aspirations and activities form the real life of community which the anthropologist seeks to understand. This could easily be accomplished by a study of the *Puranas* and *Samhitas*. It is for this reason that Roy commended to anthropologists the study of our ancient books.

There was yet another reason for including these fact in our purview. He realized that anthropology is not a study of the quaint and exotic manners and customs of the primitive tribes. Anthropology did not only study primitive man, the broad subject matter of anthropology is the entire life of mankind. The only reason why much attention is devoted to "primitive society by anthropology is that primitive society exhibits the ground plan on which the more complex structure that we call civilization has been built up" (Roy 1966 : 65).

In India the task of anthropologists must include the study of complex civilizations. It is in this context that he made a detailed study of caste, race, religion in India. He tried to explore the origin of the caste and for this reason included in his sweep not ancient Hindu literature but also the vast amount of ethnographic literature on castes and tribes in parts of the country. He began with a detailed coiticisms of the different theories put forward by scholars for the origin of caste system. This was followed up by an assessment of the contributions of various ethnic element to the evolution of Indian culture with special reference to caste system. Caste systems, as it operates, is unique. Although certain elements of caste may be seen outside the Indian sub-continent, the complex as such is a peculiarly Indian phenomenon. The constant between people belonging to diverse ethnic elements and culture areas must have had a bearing on the functioning of the caste system. Sarat Chandra Roy examined the caste systems as it affected the life of the people.

Sarat Chandra delved deep into the many theories propounded for the origin of caste system. He held that these theories may be valuable at explaining one or the other features of the caste system but they cannot take us far enough in our search for the root causes of the emergence of this institution. A brief account of his critique of the different theories may be useful in assessing his own contributions to the understanding of the origin of caste. One of the early authorities who wrote on the subject, Ibbetson, held that the diversity of caste may be derived from the diversity of occupations. These occupations, in course of time, developed into functional guilds, membership of which was hereditary in principle. All these guilds recognized the superiority of the Brahmanas and accepted the Brahmanical rules of purity relating to food and marriage. Roy points out that nowhere else in the world have trade guilds and other similar associations been metamorphosed into absolutely closed corporations within which alone marriage is permitted. In addition to this, if the commonness of function had been the original binding force of caste, all Hindus following the same occupation in a local area would form only one caste. This is not so. Moreover, had the Brahmanas denigrated all occupations except their own, it is not known how they could secure the unquestioning obedience of the bulk of the population which was formed by the Vaisyas and Sudras.

Roy also discovered that Nesfield's theory that function or occupation is the only basis of caste is not supported by actual fact. Clear differences of physical type may be found within the limits of the caste system. Nesfield's view that there is only one Indian race and only one Indian caste and that the only origin of the present division of the people into castes is community of function or occupation could not be accepted as it lacks support of proved facts.

Risley's theory of hypergamy and origin of caste was also rejected by Roy as hypergamy either by itself or in conjunction with race prejudice can hardly be an effective factor in the evolution of caste and its taboos. Anthropometric investigations have shown that although a correlation between caste and race does exist in many cases, the correspondence does not go far enough to support the ethnological basis of caste to the extent that Risley supposed. Roy further rebuts Risley's conjecture that caste system was derived from Persia.

Senart believed that the caste system was a natural extension of the ancient Aryan dission of tribes into gens. He also traced the pollution with regard to food, to the exclusion of strangers from family meal and family worship. The analogy of the Roman gens however, appeared to Roy to be fallacious. The Roman gens was based on a common ancestry and the Indian caste which does not in all cases make such a claim cannot be regarded as similar. Some castes contained *gotras* of their own, while different castes may have *gotras* which go by the same name.

Roy commends Ketkar's view that caste system rests on the purity-pollution concept. His complaint, however, is that Ketkar does not carry his analysis further. The principle of purity, which Ketkar calls *saucham*, is not just ceremonial purity. Roy tried to show that differences in psychic taboos, the varying degrees of dominance of soul over the senses, the dominance of the real man or the God-in-man over the animal-in-man, namely, *sattava guna* over other *gunas* had something to do with the evolution of caste.

Slater held that caste is a pre-Aryan institution and tried to show that in Dravidian society the priestly caste enjoyed dominance over the warrior class. He also held that the present day Brahmanas were the representatives of the priest-magician class which was found among the Dravidians of South India. Slater also attributes the theory of the transmigration of soul to the Dravidian. Roy does not agree with these hypotheses as they are not supported by facts. While there may have been certain functional groups in pre-Aryan Dravidian society based on social stratification, accompanied by the principle of exogamy and certain taboos on food and drink, there is no evidence to show that it possessed all the characteristics of the Hindu caste system.

Hutton advanced a theory that the essential elements of the caste system were derived from the pre-Aryan societies, viz. Proto-australoid, Dravidian, and Mongolian. He referred to the system of endogamy prevailing among the Brahui of Baluchistan who spoke a Dravidian language as proof of the existence of caste among the Dravidians. But rules of endogamy and exogamy are a worldwide phenomenon. Also, the existence of some stratification among the Dravidians could not be taken as an evidence of the existence of caste system. Hutton added that among the Mongolians there is a great fear of supernatural danger from associating with strangers engaged in strange arts and crafts. He believed that this led to the segregation of different occupational groups. He also believed that caste may have its foundation in the concept of *mana* which came to strengthen the caste taboos on food, drink, marriage, and physical contact. Roy examined in great detail the conception of *mana* among various religious and other groups in India and abroad. Roy believed that in the case of Indian psyche, the Indian student has better opportunity of probing the consciousness of his own society and coming a little closer to the right solutions of the origin of the Varna or caste system which cannot be adequately explained as the stigmatization of a pre-Aryan taboo system.

Ghurye's theory of the orgin of caste does not go deep enough into the Aryan ideal of purity which he treated merely as ceremonial purity. Roy also does not agree with Ghurye's contention that lack of rigid and unitary control of state and its recognition of the varying customs of different groups might have encouraged separatism.

Roy agrees with Ambedkar's account of the social process by which caste developed, but Ambedkar does not point out how caste originated. His contention that caste is a parceling of an already homogeneous unit is not accepted by Roy. Ambedkar does not refer to any factor in the social conditions of time which motivated the change except the Brahmana's arrogant assumption of superiority.

Roy believed that the origin of a social institution (like caste) has to be sought primarily in terms of group ideal or ideas and sentiments behind it and only secondarily in terms of environment-racial admixture and culture contact or intercommunication or interaction of ideas between human groups. The Hindu caste system is an outcome of the interaction between Indo-Dravidian *Varna* system on the one hand and the tribal system of pre-Dravidian and the occupational class system of pre-Dravidian on the other. The religious element that worked as an adhesive force in bringing them together was besides the Indo-Aryan concept of *Karma*, certain purity-pollution or taboo holiness idea that came to be attached to the Brahmanas on account of the fact that they were credited with the possession of special spiritual energy or *Brahmashakti*. This spiritual energy flowed from the *sativa guna* and was sustained and stabilized through well disciplined continence. In course of time this concept of *Brahmashakti* and *Vaisyashakti* came to be regarded as a manifestation of pre-Dravidian concept of soul substance with its associated taboos and of the psychic power attributed by the Dravidians to the priest-magicians. This facilitated the acceptance by the Dravidians of the Aryan theories of spiritual values of the different *Varnas* or functions. The result was the formation of a four-grade system which was largely based on occupations, ethnic composition, and other distinctions. Thus the Aryan caste system was readily accepted by the Dravidians as the socio-economic conditions prevailing among them were conducive to it.

Caste as distinguished from *Varna* developed gradually and imperceptibly. Aryan social and religious leaders had to recognise what came about independently of them and fit it into their own *Varna* system so as to give it higher orientation. Flexible *Varna* system based on *gunas* was the essence of the Aryan social system. Rigidity of caste system was a later phenomenon. The differences on which the Varnas were based, represented the innate differences in mental capabilities and spiritual tendencies which may be traced to the inexorable law of variation and inequality in nature. These have been found from the early stages of civilization to divide individuals, families, and communities from one another into natural classes.

The conflict between the Indo-Aryan ideal of one universal family with four branches graded on the basis of comparative purity of the soul on the one hand and the non-Aryan spirit of tribalism and separatism on the other produced three forms of social groupings as a measure of compromise. The first was the fourfold *Varna* division based on innate *gunas*. The second was the three thousand or more castes formed on the basis of tribes or ethnic admixtures and occupations or special cults and usages, or by outcasting from well recognized castes. The third was the formation of sub-castes formed on the basis of habitat or local distribution or specialized modes of the same profession by splits through feuds, etc. Thus the social order recognized the three factors of social progress, viz. heredity, environment, and cultural ideal. However, the central idea of purity was superimposed on this system. Roy denied that the matrimonial taboos that form the basis of caste system were devised by Brahmanas for their own benefit. These were solely dictated by the need for social and economic well being of the community.

In course of time, the elasticity of the *Varna* system was impaired and the concept of *Karma* coupled with the idea of transmigration of souls which had been evolved independently by Aryans and pre-Aryans was brought up as a justification for the inequalities perpetrated by caste system. The old Hindu ideal of the purity of soul was overshadowed by a concern for ceremonial purity which emanated from the concept of *mana* borrowed from tribal sources.

Sarat Chandra Roy (1966:70) hoped that "India would once more rise through spiritual consciousness to common human consciousness and that the Hindu's consciousness of kind will not be confined to caste, community or race or religion but will comprise the whole of mankind and the social order of humanity will be regulated by moral and spiritual values as the composer of the Purushsukta had visualized it."

Roy's contribution to our understanding of caste was deeply influenced by his awareness of the debt the country owes to the diverse ethnic elements, his own intense religions convictions, and an anxiety to view it in a humanistic perspective. However, the association between the *gunas* and the *Varnas* which he sought to establish could not be operationalised and would always remain utopian. It would be more helpful to treat the *Varna* and caste as two distinct phenomena.

Study of Folklore

In his presidential address to the Anthropological Section of the Sixth Oriental Congress held at Patna in 1930, Sarat Chandra Roy made a strong plea for the study of folklore by anthropologists. It is not difficult to observe, record and study the traditional customs, rites and beliefs including stories and myths. Such customs, rites, and beliefs may belong either to individuals or to families, clans or other groups. They may stand on a lower intellectual level and are often inconsistent with orthodox or officially recognized customs, rites, and beliefs of people wherever they occur. The term folklore is no longer restricted to traditional customs, rites, and beliefs of the past lingering among backward people in complex civilizations but now extends to include folk-arts, crafts and other manifestations of the spirit of folklore both among people with civilization and among primitive communities. Roy (1966:7) believed that folklore throws a flood of light on the early intellectual evolution of human society and for this reason he regarded folklore as "pre-history of the human mind."

Indian students are in the most advantageous position to collect and study folklore but they should do so before much of such lore is lost or forgotten. Folk-rites form an important element at every step of our journey in life such as birth and childhood, puberty and marriage, disease and death. We come across folk-customs, talk about folk-beliefs and look at folk-arts in our homes, in our neighbouring houses, in lanes and streets, and in the market places. Our female folk are the repositories of the bulk of such knowledge. Roy drew attention to the observance of omens, good and bad, traditional beliefs associated with dreams and superstitions, folk-proverbs, folktales and ballads, and also folk-arts and crafts handed down to us from generation to generation. He pleaded for a systematic collection of these folklore material district by district, *taluk* by *taluk*, and even going to smaller territorial segments.

He, however, did not end there. He believed that we should apply curselves to trace the life history of each item of folk-rite, folk-custom and folk-belief and then make a careful analysis of each item of folklore into its component elements. Such an investigation would reveal how an item of folklore has been altered, attenuated, transformed, or amalgamated with other customs in course of history. The subject of folklore may point out different levels of culture. He illustrated this with a detailed description of the folk-rites performed by women in a Bengali Hindu marriage. Some of these are meant to symbolize and cement the marriage bond. Some customs are based on the principle of sympathetic magic to make the union happy, prosperous, and fruitful. Some of them are intended to ward off supernatural evil influence, some are in the nature of love charms, while some others which are very important may be of religious nature. These may have different origins and may belong to different levels of culture. Some may be a borrowing from customs of primitive people. The meaning of the different rites is not known to the women who practice them. They, however, do not dare skip them as it might bring ill luck to the newly married couple. We can only understand them if we examine them side by side with analogous rituals in more primitive neighbouring societies. It is through comparative study that we can see the primitive basis of such beliefs and practices. Roy shows how in Bihari, Bengali, and Munda marriage rituals there is provision for mixing the blood of the bride and the bridegroom in customs which differ only slightly in detail. A deeper probe into the folk rituals would reveal a pre-Aryan core over which the *Shastric* ritual has been superimposed. Under the influence of change only some of the rustic rituals are retained by the women folk or the conservative and non-progressive sections of the community.

To know conclusively about the origin of any item of folklore the student will have to make a deep analysis and distributional study of such folklore items by plotting it out on a map determining its focal centre and training its diffusion to marginal areas. Roy did not refute the possibility of independent origin of a custom at different places. He, however, advised students to study different items in the context of the culture complex in which they figured. The search for origins of folk customs was referred to by Roy as tracing the genealogy of folklore. To engage in this task the student must not only acquire full knowledge of the present culture and mentality and the past history of the peopie whose folklore he studies, but also equip himself with the knowledge of life and culture of the neighbouring communities with whom they have been in contact. The folklorist must draw upon the resources of comparative ethnology, social psychology, pre-history, philology, as well as literature.

References

Archer, W. G. (1942), "A Bibliography of Sarat Chandra Roy". *Man in India.*

Bose, N. K., (ed) (1966a), "Introduction". *Studies in Indian Anthropology.* Calcutta.

——(1966b), Sarat Chandra Roy. *Man in India,* 46:3.

——(1971), "Sarat Chandra Roy". *Man in India,* 51:4.

Elwin, V. (1942), "Sarat Chandra Roy". (comment). *Man in India,* 22:4.

Madan, T. N. (1952), "Sarat Chandra Roy". *Man in India,* 32:2.

Majumdar, D. N. (1942), "On the Life and Work of Sarat Chandra Roy." *Essays in Anthropology presented to Rai Bahadur Sarat Chandra Roy.* Edited by J.P. Mills *et al.,* Lucknow: Maxwell & Co.

——(1939-40), "Late Rai Bahadur Sarat Chandra Roy." *Journal of the Indian Anthropological Institute,* 2:3.

Roy S. C. (1912), *The Munda and their Country.* Ranchi.

——(1915), *The Oraon of Chotanagpur.* Calcutta.

——(1937), *The Kharia.* Ranchi.

——(1966), *Studies in Indian Anthropology.* N. K. Bose (ed.) Calcutta.

Sen Gupta, S. (1972), "S. C. Roy's Contribution to Anthropo-folk-lorology." *Human Events,* 6. No. 8-12.

A Bibliography of Sarat Chandra Roy's Books

Books

1912 *The Mundas and Their Country.* Ranchi. (Second edition 1970) Bombay: Asia Publishing House.

1915 *The Oraon of Chotanagpur.* Ranchi.

1920 *Principals and Methods of Physical Anthropology.* Patna: Government Printing Press.

1925 *The Birhors: A Little Known Jungle Tribe of Chotanagpur.* Ranchi: Man in India Office.

1928 *Oraon Religion and Customs.* Ranchi: Man in India Office.

1935 *The Hill Bhuiya of Orissa.* Ranchi: Man in India Office.

1936 *The Kharias.* 2 volumes. Ranchi: Man in India Office (jointly with Ramesh Chandra Roy).

n.d. *Caste, Race and Religion in India.* Ranchi (Reprinted from Man in India, Vols. 14, 18).

1966 *Studies in Indian Anthropology.* A Collection of Four Papers edited with an introduction by N. K. Bose, Calcutta.

9

ANTHROPOLOGY OF NIRMAL KUMAR BOSE

Surajit Sinha

The Gurus

Boas

When I enquired of Professor Nirmal Kumar Bose to which 'school' of anthropology he belonged, he replied that he would feel uncomfortable about any strait-jacket label and would rather like to place his identity as a 'social historian'. Among his *gurus* in anthropology, he first mentioned the name of Franz Boas. He liked Boas' critical mind and his emphasis on precision. What impressed Bose most about Boas was his inductive natural history approach which kept the mind open to unexpected discovery. Once he said to me : "Boas started with observations and then moved towards classification and generalization rather than starting with a deductive hypothetical model." Professor Bose was greatly influenced by reading *The Mind of the Primitive Man* (1911) and accepted Boas' position that language, race and culture are independent and yet historically linked variables (Boas, 1940).

Kroeber

Professor Bose read Kroeber's germane article on "The Superorganic" (1917) with great deal of interest and reacted that the over-riding role of 'culture' on the lives of men does not cover the full story of man's behaviour. At critical points of history, creative deviant individuals may be the starting point of change:

> There is no doubt that most men generally play a passive role. But they can behave in a different way also. There have been moments in history when the active element has asserted itself in individuals, as well as in large masses of mankind and given culture, including the course of economic events, an unexpected turn. That such occasions have been rare is due to the fact that men like to avoid the sufferings consequent upon every change, and thus conserve their nervous energy. And it is this inner acquiescence, born out of conservatism, which gives culture its apparent power to rule over the lives of men (Bose, 1940 : 6).

The American Diffusionists

Bose was fascinated by Kroeber and Wissler's trait-distribution studies and by the chronological implication of the distribution of cultural traits. He applied this approach in the study of diffusion of Spring Festival Culture Complex (Bose, 1927), elements of temple architecture (Bose, 1949b) and of basic material traits in rural India (Bose, 1961). The imprint of the American Diffusionist School is also very much there in his fascinating book titled *Cultural Anthropology* (Bose, 1929) written when he was just twenty-eight years old. This little book from an unknown young Indian scholar attracted the attention of Kroeber who reviewed it favourably in the *American Anthropologist* (Kroeber, 1929). Later on, Kroeber and Kluckhohn in their compendium *Culture: a Critical Review of Concept and Definitions* (1952) included as many as ten citations from Bose's *Cultural Anthropology* (1929).

Sigmund Freud

Among the masters in the social science, Freud left a deep impression on Bose. Although he did not expressedly utilize Freudian theories in most of his writings, Freud's ideas stimulated in him a great deal of interest on the behaviour of individuals under a situation of cultural stress (Bose, 1953:266-269 and Bose, 1954a). He felt that the Freudian concept of sublimation helped him to understand the apparently paradoxical behaviour of Mahatma Gandhi in the critical situation of Noakhali pilgrimage in 1946-47 (Bose, 1953: Chap, VIII).

Karl Marx

Professor Bose read Marx, Lenin and Marxist literature with great interest and reacted to them in the same manner as he did to Kroeber's theory of super-organic. He takes the position that human behaviour is much more random, individualistic and purposive than the theory of economic determinism would make it to be (Bose, 1940: 4-7). Yet he accepted from Marx the critical significance of the social organization of production in the study of persistence and change in the caste system in India (Bose, 1951).

Anarchists

Among the other social thinkers to influence Bose are 'anarchists', like Kropotkin and Gandhi. I will discuss Bose's contributions in Gandhian studies later.

Bronislaw Malinowski

Like his senior colleague, Tarak Chandra Das, Bose responded very favourably to Malinowski's functional approach to anthropology. In his book on *Cultural Anthropology*, he has independently taken a functional approach in defining the nature of culture as an adaptive device organized around what Bose figuratively calls 'the soul of culture'. But he rejected the ahistoricism of the functionalists and has taken a consistent position that the proper domain of cultural anthropology is a functional study of the process of culture change.

Men of Literature and Classical Texts

As a college student, Bose was a voracious reader of novels and short stories. Dostovesky, Turgeneve, Tolstoy, Bojer, Materlink, Rolland, Hampson and Ibsen were his favourite writers. He also read Rabindranath Tagore very thoroughly. Bose was not a Sanskrit scholar but he had read the Geeta, Upanishads and Buddhist literature in translation with great care. According to Bose, these readings must have had an impact on shaping his approach to human problems. In a letter to me dated October 15, 1971, Bose writes: "When you asked me about the books which had inflenced me, I forgot to mention one very important series namely, Conan Dolyle's *Sherlock Holmes* series. This is the source from which I learnt a lot about accurate observation and minimum inferences drawn on the basis of that." Another of his favourate authors was the famous biologist and town planner Patric Geddes, whose idea of "construction through conservation" appealed to Bose.

Besides *gurus*, Bose had a wide circle of admirers and friends. Among the illustrious ones may be mentioned J.B.S. Haldane,

Gordon Childe, T. Dobzhansky, Suniti Kumar Chatterjee, Satyen Bose, Nandalal Bose, Jamini Roy, Benodbehari Mukhopadhyaya, Stella Kramrisch, Girdindra Sekhar Bose, Robert Redfield and Erik Erikson.

Learning From Social Involvement

Although Professor Bose readily admits his intellectual indebtedness to a wide range of scholars and writers he also insists that his main learning in the social sciences has been through involvement in the problems of regeneration of a tired ancient society groaning under the shackles of colonial rule.

Famine Relief in Bankura

At the young age of 17 in 1917, Bose participated in a famine relief operation in Bankura district organized by Sadharan Brahma Samaj. He used this opportunity to conduct a systematic survey of economic conditions of a large number of rural families. This was his self-styled initiation to field studies before he had any knowledge of the disciplines of anthropology and sociology.

Repatriation of Indentured Labourers From FIJI

In 1921, at the suggestion of C.F. Andrews, Bose and two of his associates organized the repatriation of indentured Indian labourers from Fiji. Here again his passion for rigorous survey of social facts found expression in the collection of detailed census on the social background of 1050 persons belonging to about 450 families. The census provides a wealth of information on how Indian rural society placed numerous obstacles in the process of re-absorption and rehabilitation of indentured labourers who had migrated to the Indies from the Indian mainland and wanted to come back home.

Gandhian Constructive Work at Bolpur

In 1922, Bose left Presidency College of Calcutta in response to the Non-co-operation Movement under the leadership of Gandhi. From then on Gandhi's ideas and action programmes has been one of the major subjects of his intellectual interest. During 1930-36, he was engaged in a Gandhian village reconstruction programme with his Centre in a slum in the outskirts of Bolpur town. Many of his co-workers belonged to the untouchable Hari, Muchi and Bauri castes. Bose has often stated that his basic understanding of the rots of rural Indian society, particularly of the caste system, developed in the course of organizing social reconstruction programme. He learnt through close observation that peoples' loyalty could not be weaned away from the archaic and unjust caste system as long as the economic base of the traditional system remained viable and no alternative economic opportunity was brought within the social control of the masses.

Learning from the Silpis of Orissa

Bose received his formal training in anthropology as an M.Sc. student in Calcutta University during 1923-24. He came to the discipline of anthropology by accident. In 1921 after obtaining his B.Sc. (Hons.) degree in geology, he was preparing himself for a career as a geologist. In geology his special interests were palaeontology and petrology. He was acclaimed by all of his professors as an outstanding graduate student in the subject. But, as has already been said, when the Non-cooperation Movement came, he decided to leave the Government College forever. He left Calcutta and settled down at Puri.

In Puri he came across a master *silpi* (temple architect) named Ram Maharana, who initiated Bose to the traditional canons of Orissan architecture. He edited an Oriya manuscript on *Silpa Sastra* which was later published in 1932. Thus he learnt from the field that a student of civilization will have to integrate information from various levels: the texts, the material products and the learned specialists' interpretation of the texts as well as the products of arts. The elegance of ancient Orissan temples fascinated Bose so much that he started giving lectures on these temples to the visitors to Puri. It was in this connection that he came in contact with Sir Ashutosh Mukherjee, the then Vice-Chancellor of Calcutta University. Sir Ashutosh persuaded Bose to join the University as an M.Sc. student in the new department of anthropology.

Bose passed the M.Sc. examination in anthropology in 1925 with brilliant records. His M.Sc. dissertation was a diffusionist study of 'Spring Festival in India'. Since 1923, Bose has so for published 37 books, 23 in English and 14 in Bengali, and more than 700 articles. Of these about half belong to the domain of anthropology proper; the rest cover a wide range of interests like politics, travelogue, art, architecture, literature, social work, etc. Many of his important articles have been written in Bengali. As the Editor of *Man in India* since 1951, he has played a very constructive role in encouraging young scholars to publish the results of their research.

His Intellectual Interests: The Range and Foci

Scholars have sometimes been critical of the prolific productions of Bose and felt that he should have concentrated on a few themes and built up deeply and adequately. Professor Bose has been somewhat indifferent about these conventional demands of the profession. Many ideas and observations have stimulated him over the last fifty years and he has felt that his creative and critical responses should be quickly communicated to colleagues and friends, and particularly to the younger scholars.

As one patiently goes through the numerous publications of Bose, a consistent series of themes and foci do emerge. First of all, he has been interested in knowing the roots of Indian society, particularly of the caste system. Another of his consistent concern has been the nature of unity in diversity in the structure of Indian civilization and the problem in transforming an old civilization into a revitalized new nation. His preference for Gandhian ideology *vis-à-vis* Marxist socialism and capitalism grew out of his intellectual search for the appropriate perspective for transformation of a traditional society into a modern nation. Bose, however, did not have any illusion that social analysis alone would generate the spiritual steam needed for vigorous involvement in social transformation. As early as 1929 (p. 1-2) he wrote:

> Anthropology, for example, tells us how our present society and civilization came into being, how they change, what things should be taken account of in social reconstruction and so on. It is not capable of building up the hope in man, nor does it bring faith where there is none; which things are, as a matter of fact, the most vital forces in human organization. Although the social sciences are thus of limited value, yet they are of as much significance as a knowledge of physiology and anatomy are to a physician, without which he will not really know what is happening in the body of his patient. If a social worker ventures on reform before being equipped with the necessary information regarding human nature and civilization, his

efforts are more likely to fail than to succeed, however, greatly he may be inspired by idealism".

Phases of Research in Anthropological Survey of India

Bose's grand plan for developing a home base anthropological research in India was partly worked out through his imaginative phasing of research in the Anthropological Survey of India during 1959-1964, when he was the Director of the Survey:

Phase I : Study of distribution of material traits all over India and mapping out the pattern of their distribution *vis-à-vis* linguistic areas.

Phase II : Study of a few important ancient craft techniques–pottery and metal craft.

Phase III : Study of social organization of crafts and of caste organization in different regions of India.

Phase IV : Study of the superstructure of Indian society–through the study of temples, *muths* and kingship.

Phase V : Study of the process of modernization in caste and occupation, urbanization, tribal movements and social movements in different regions of India.

(Sinha, 1971 : 10–11 ; see also Saraswati 1970 : X-XI).

In the planning of research activities of the Survey he took great interest in researches in physical anthropology. He inspired a group of devoted young scholars to take up an all-India anthropometric survey and complete the reports on the important skeletal remains from Harappa and Brahmagiri.

Bose was very much interested that young scholars should collect a wealth of basic data on the peoples of India from all over the country so that fruitful generalizations may later on be made on all-India level on the basis of regional comparison.

I will now take up in some detail the focal areas of research interest of Professor Bose.

On the Caste System

I have already mentioned that Bose's understanding of the operation of the caste system grew out of his creative experience as *khadi* constructive worker among the untouchable caste in a slum in Bolpur town. The question of how the system continued to elicit the loyalty of those very groups which were down-graded by it intrigued him. He rejected such simple ideological explanations as that the trick was made by the Brahmans through skilful perpetuation of a fatalistic myth of divine origin, reincarnation and notion of purity and pollution. In a series of brilliant articles– "The Hindu Method of Tribal Absorption" (1941), "Caste in India" (1951), "Some Aspects of Caste in Bengal" (1958)–Bose proposes that the root of persistence of the caste system is to be found in the economic and cultural security provided by the "non-competitive, hereditary, vocation-based productive organization" which operated in nearly isolated village communities and was guided by general norms of inter-ethnic cultural tolerance (see Bose, 1931, 1934a, 1936). Further, the institution of *sanyas* (asceticism) provided at least a limited avenue of freedom and prestige to the individuals who were otherwise bound to the rigid hierarchy of the system. Bose has been quick to point out that such an ideal pattern of caste-based rural society could thrive adequately only when there was adequate ecological and demographic space to set up new villages. A demographic base for the caste system was thus clearly hinted in his article, "Competing Producive Systems in India" (1968).

The above logic led Bose to propose that fundamental structural change and even breakdown of the caste system would be possible only when the economic base of the system was qualitatively transformed. It was this consideration that prompted him to initiate a series of research on change in traditional occupation in different regions of India, particularly West Bengal. His general proposition has been that caste as an economic system and as a regulator of social life is disintegrating at different rates in different regions of India. Bose was particularly curious about what has happened to the caste system in a city like Calcutta which has been exposed to nearly two hundred years of modern commercial, industrial and urban development. He sums up his findings based on a rapid survey during 1962-63 (Bose, 1965: 90-105) as follows:

> It can be said, therefore, that the diverse ethnic groups in the population of the city have come to bear the same relation to one another as do the castes in India as a whole.....Actually, the superstructure that coheres the castes under the old order seems instead to be re-establishing itself in a new form. Calcutta today is

> far from being a melting pot on the model of cities in the U.S...........In Calcutta the economy is an economy of scarcity. Because there are not enough jobs to go around, every one clings as closely as possible to the occupation with which his ethnic group is identified and relies for economic support on those who speak his language, on his coreligionists, on members of his own caste and on fellow immigrants from the village or district from which he has come. By a backwash, reliance on earlier modes of group identification reinforces and perpetuates differences between ethnic groups.

Bose has laid great emphasis on the conscious or ideal model of caste as a normative system while studying change. For example, the recent proliferation of politically competitive caste associations are not considered by him as indications of strengthening of the caste system. He feels that these recent developments rather indicate deviations from the non-competitive ascribed traditional system towards a competitive one. In other words, the old structures are being used in various new combinations, in new social meaning (Bose, 1958).

Although Bose has utilized traditional textual categories such as *sattva, raja, tamas* and *dharma, artha, kama* and *moksha* in the classification of cultures, he is very critical about simplistic extrapolation of textual notions in the study of Indian civilization without taking full note of the historical and social context. For example, he is critical of Weber for assuming that the Indian theory of *karma* carries only a social message of *status quo*. Bose finds that the notion of *karma* has been used as a doctrine of moral endeavour by Buddha at a certain turning point of history, whereas it was utilized by later day Brahmans and other upper castes for the perpetuation of *status quo*.

Apart from his persistent interest in the study of changes in the productive organization of caste, Bose feels that one of the major foci in the study of the transformation scene should be to find out how the castes continue to operate as self-regulating corporate groups guiding the social life of their members. A number of studies on the operation of 'caste associations' in different regions of India was initiated by him. In some of these the role of the local chieftains as well as temples and *muths* in the regulation of caste norms was also brought into focus (Bose, 1960).

Tribal Studies

Bose intended to begin his professional career with an intensive field research on the Juang of Orissa. But after a brief spell of field work in 1928 which resulted in the publication of three short papers (Bose, 1928, 1929a, 1930), he had to leave the State of Keonjhar under the orders of the police. After that Bose never got an opportunity to do prolonged intensive field research in a tribal community. The brief field study among the Juang, however, gave him the basic insight on how tribes following a relatively primitive productive technology (like swidden cultivation) were being absorbed into the agriculture and craft-based Hindu caste society.

In his various insightful papers on the tribal groups the emphases have been on the following problems : Where do the tribal economy stand *vis-à-vis* the caste mode of production (Bose, 1955a, 1968)? How are the tribes absorbed in the Hindu caste system (Bose, 1941, 1949a)? What are the roots of the tribal separatist movements (Bose, 1964a)? In his book, *Tribal Life in India* (1971), he makes the following observations in the introductory chapter: "Barring a very small fraction, there is little difference in economic life between them and their peasant-and-artisan communities. The difference between our rural folk and urban classes is undoubtedly greater than that between the former and the tribal communities so far as their occupations are concerned".

The Changing Structure of Indian Civilization: Unity and Diversities

Hindu Samajer Gadan

From Bose's writings it appears that as early as 1929 he had already decided that his subject matter was not "tribes" or local systems of caste in villages, but the total structure of Indian civilization. During 1942-45, as a political prisoner under the British Government, he gave a series of lectures on the structure of Hindu society to the fellow political prisoners. These lectures formed the basis of his Bengali book, *Hindu Samajer Gadan*, [*"Structure of Hindu Society"*] (1949a). This was written quite a few years before 'comparison of civilizations' became a proper subject of study of anthropologists under the leadership of Robert Redfield. The layout of the chapters of the book is indeed very imaginative and original. Starting with a prelude quoting *Chaitanya Charitamrit* at great length, the chapter headings are as follows:

First Chapter

Description of a few forest dwelling jatis: Juang *jati;* their rituals; their cultural pattern; their relationship with other *jatis.*

Second Chapter

History of the Munda jati: Cultural pattern of the Munda; the rise of kingship and Moslem rule; during the days of East India company, a new disturbance; the coming of the Christian Missionaries and later history; the course of cultural transformation.

Third Chapter

The spread of Brahmanism in Chotanagpur: A branch of Munda *jati* in Panch Pargana; Manda festival; social movement among the Oraon; Tana Bhagat movement; conclusion.

Fourth Chapter

The Kolu Oil Pressers.

Fifth Chapter

The structure of Aryan society : Ramayana and Mahabharata; what is the aim of *Varna-Dharma?* A review of *Sruti* and *Smriti* literature; concluding discussion on the *Sastras*

Sixth Chapter

The (composite) nature of Aryan culture: The Holi festival.

Seventh Chapter

An Image of India : the responsibilities of the king; production and distribution in the villages; fairs; pilgrim centres; cultural unity of India; some observations on economic ideas.

Eighth Chapter

Ancient History of the Varna order : Mohen-jo-daro; during the time of Buddha; India prospers in commerce and industries; ideals of urban life; another (dark) side of society.

Ninth Chapter

Medieval history: Changes among the educated section of the Hindus; a picture of Hindu culture during Moslem rule (in *Chaitanya Bhagabat*).

Tenth Chapter

Trends of Change during the British period: Raipur, the rise of Bolpur town and a few other villages; Jajigram.

Eleventh Chapter

The present state of the Varna order.

Twelfth Chapter

Social movements among various castes: Jogi jati; Namashudra; Caste discrimination among the Moslems.

It will be apparent that the broad sweep of Bose's presentation is essentially historical. Into this broad canvas of time he brings in many dimensions of Indian social structure and social processes: the tribal enclaves and their absorption, the dual themes of self-sufficiency of village communities and their broader links with kingship, fairs and pilgrim centres, norms of sacred and secular life in the ancient texts, social movements in the medieval period in response to Islam, the impact of British rule and the emerging economy of Indian society, particularly of the caste system. We learn from this book that an anthropological study of Indian civilization will involve a combination of many perspectives: analysis of classical and medieval texts, administrative records, particularly of land tenure, and studies of villages, individual caste associations and the wider social networks of the civilization in kingship, fairs, pilgrim centres, and so on.

The persistent focus of this survey, however, has been on a study of the fate of the *Varna-jati* system at different phases of Indian history. He ends the book (p. 156) as follows:

> The historical situation in which the classical *Varnajati* system of social order came into being will not be repeated in modern times. It will also not suit our times, for the population of India has increased manifold and land per capita has diminished considerably. Yet if we discover some values and social designs in the traditional system which has relevance for the modern times, it will be unwise not to

utilize them in solving our contemporary problems. *For, in the ultimate analysis, the human kind cannot be set apart by time and space.*

Culture Zones of India and the Pattern of Indian Unity

To the students of Indian society and history, the great cultural divide has always been the Aryan North *vis-à-vis* the Dravidian South. This has also been indicated by Iravati Karve's extensive study on kinship system (1953). As an acute observer of cultural facts and an indefatigable traveler (see his *Paribrajaker Diary*, "Diary of a Wanderer", 1940) Bose observed that the linguistic divide was overlain on a different set of cultural divide based on some important items of material culture–North West, continuous with West Central Asia and East continuous with Southern Asia (Bose, 1956a). This proposition was later on elaborately worked out on the basis of an extensive survey of the distribution of a set of material traits (Bose, 1961) and of forms and techniques of potters all over India (Saraswati and Behura, 1966). Apart from the intrinsic theoretical interest of unraveling archaic and persistent culture-historical processes through distribution studies, one of Bose's special interests in bringing the archaic links into relief was to indicate how regions or states of India, which are to-day separated by differences of language, share many elements of material culture in common.

In his introduction to *Peasant Life in India: A Study in Indian Unity and Diversity*, he proposes a pyramidal imagery of the unity of Indian civilization.

> If regionalization is in evidence to a certain extent in relation to the material arts of life, it is apparent already that the degree of differentiation is less in respect of the country's social organization. What is more reassuring is that... if one rises to higher reaches of life confined to ideals or faiths or art, the differences which one noticed at the material level of life gradually become feebler and feebler. They are eventually replaced by a unity of beliefs and aspirations which gives to Indian Civilization a character of its own.
>
> The structure of Indian unity can therefore be compared to a pyramid. There is more differentiation at the material base of life and progressively less as one mounts higher and higher (Bose, 1961 : Introduction).

In another article, "The Geographical Background of Indian Culture" (1950), Bose discusses how through the economic tradition of caste system a 'kind of uniformity grew up between geographically, or even ecologically, distinguishable regions of India.' He also writes about the various traditional cultural media which provided a mechanism through which the unifying thoughts and feelings of thinkers, artists and saints of India were brought to the door of the most distant communities and enabled them to share some common intellectual and emotional elements of the civilization.

In his Jagadish Bose Memorial Lecture of 1971, Professor Bose stated that in contrast to the civilization of Europe which is essentially based on repeated experiences of war leading to the spirit of nationalism, Indian civilization developed a pattern of cultural pluralism under relatively peaceful conditions sheltered by the geographical barriers along its frontiers:

Indian Civilization encouraged diversity of cultures, while in its economic organization, it tried to weave all communities into a network of interdependent, but distinct, entities (1971).

Civilization as A Phase of Confidence

Bose feels that the creative potentialities of the traditional structure of Indian Civilization cannot be properly assessed if the observations are only limited to the post-medieval and recent phase of recession of the civilization. The career of a civilization has also to be studied in a phase of expansion and confidence.

In a Bengali article, "The Temple of Konarak", Bose refers to the expansive and confidence phase of Indian civilization in a vivid manner:

> The temple of Konarak was built in a glorious period of Orissan history. King Narasinghadev of Ganga Dynasty had just defeated the Sultans of Gaura with his powerful army..........The state was prosperous and the people were infused with a passionate mood to enjoy life and to assert independence. The architects were brought up in this atmosphere and tried to give shape to this confident and lively mood in their work......The sculptures are full of life. The sculptors' minds were not laden with any false shame........Even today, partly buried under a debris of broken stone pieces, withstanding the ravages of time, the temple of Konarak preserves a vivid picture of a by gone confident past....... (Bose, 1949 : 250).

Bose has tried to capture the expressive modern thrust of Indian civilization through a number of critical character sketches of a few outstanding personalities. In the Bengali book *Nabin O Prachin* (New and Old), Bose writes about Gandhi's *satyagraha* and search for truth, Tagore's creative painting, Jamini Roy's views on art and Ramkinkar Baij's paintings (Bose 1949).

Although Bose has been a persistent student of Indian civilization, he has not made any conscious effort to distinguish the concept of 'civilization' from that of 'culture'. He has, however, thrown some interesting hints on the general characteristics of a civilization.

In the particular case of encounter of East and West in Bengal, Bose states that the civilization of Bengal cannot be merely defined in terms of spatial and temporal continuity of tradition:

> In this formidable adventure of cultural reorganization, Bengali culture has always been in the process of *becoming*, instead of merely being......... This tendency to *become* something is the characteristic of any civilization..........When there is a continuity between *aspirations* we regard the two as belonging to one civilization (Bose, 1968 : 278).

Thus, according to Bose, the study of civilization is essentially a study of the inner moods, that is, matters of the mind, responding to the changing life experiences of a people.

On Problems of National Integration and Modernization

In 1966, Professor Bose gave a series of lectures on "Problems of National Integration" at the Indian Institute of Advanced Study at Simla (Bose, 1967). The main theme developed in these lectures is that the post independence spurt of sub-nationalist movements has its roots in the fact that different parts of India, and different communities within the same state, have been subject to unequal forces of economic, social and political change. Under such a situation the rising middle class tended to create boundaries around narrow parochial lines in order to consolidate their sectarian advantage.

Professor Bose has taken a consistent stance against a communal basis for administrative categorization of backwardness. His suggestion has been that modern India should set her primary task as dispersal of political power to the toilers irrespective of castes and communities (Bose, 1952, 1954). As the Commissioner for Scheduled Castes and Scheduled Tribes during 1967-69, he emphasized the same point in his various reports.

The persistence of narrow parochial loyalties in post-independence era continued to disturb Bose. I have already mentioned how he undertook a social survey of Calcutta, with the specific aim of finding out to what extent new civic associations were coming up in this city.

Gandhism

Young Bose had a great deal of admiration for the spectacular heroism of the Bengali terrorists. But, as a rugged individualist and rationalist, he sought a more constructive and less romantic path to heroism and social transformation. Gandhi's call for *satyagraha* seemed to offer such an opportunity. Ever since responding to the Non-cooperation Movement in 1921, Bose has been an ardent student of Gandhi's ideas and activities. What particularly impressed Bose about Gandhi was that he carried on an experiment with endeavour for "truth" (morality) with ordinary people. Instead of depending on the middle class intelligentsia to spearhead political movements, Gandhi's main focus was on involving the common people to bring about institutional change.

Bose's intellectual involvement with Gandhism has passed through three phases. He first made an exceptionally thorough classification of the total range of Gandhi's ideas in terms of clusters of themes (Bose, 1934). Next he attempted a critical analysis of Gandhi's economic and political ideas and action programmes (Bose, 1940).

In an interview with Bose on 4 December 1945, Gandhiji suggested to him that if he watned to interpret his ideas truthfully he should actually observe him at work and not merely rely on his writings and speeches. Such an opportunity came when Bose accompanied Gandhiji as his personal secretary during his famours pilgrimage to Noakhali in 1946-47. Bose's critical observations on Gandhi came out in the form of a book, *My days with Gandhi* (1953), which has been extensively used by Erik Erikson in his book *Gandhi's Truth* (1969). Bose describes his book as "unfolding the story of the tragedy of a great soul, how it hungered for the company of men and kept itself tied to their common joys and sorrows........" (Bose, 1953 : 8).

In a chapter, "An Excursion in Psychology", Bose speculates that the enormous humaneness of Gandhiji had its base in his life-long aspiration to identify himself with 'woman', who is 'the incarnation of *ahimsa*'. Bose writes:

It follows from all this that, according to Gandhi, progress in Civilization consisted in the introduction into human life and social institutions of a larger measure of the law of love or self-suffering which woman represented best in her own person. This was a profoundly transformed projection on the broad canvas of social life of an attitude which had become into being in the privacy of his social life (*ibid* : 203).

Bose wrote a critical account of the various *satyagraha* movements which have occurred from time to time on the Indian soil. His main focus in this research was on finding out to what extent and by what processes leadership in these movements involved the common masses, the toilers.

Contributions in Prehistoric Archaeology

Professor Bose carried out pioneering field research in palaeolithic archaeology of Mayurbhanj in collaboration with Dharani Sen. The work was designed to establish stratigraphic sequence between different types of tools recovered by excavation. Hitherto different types of palaeolithic tools in Penninsular India have almost been used as index "fossils", without taking the stratigraphic context into consideration. Bose was completely against this practice and tried to establish, purely on the basis of stratigraphy and correlated techtonic movements, a regional scale which might later on be used for dating in nearby areas, instead of using the pluvial and glacial cycle sequences established in far away places like Narmada Valley and Soan Valley.

The other line of research which was pursued by workers associated with Bose was to correlate the findings of prehistory with contemporary ethnographic information on ancient crafts like pottery, casting of nonferrous metals, etc.

Contributions in Methodology

It has been mentioned before that the American Diffusionist School had a profound impact on Bose. This finds clear expression in his little book on *Cultural Anthropology* (1926). In his study of distribution of elements of temple architecture, he tried to evolve a method of dating temples by combining distributional techniques with epigraphical information. One of his major conclusions was that different elements of architecture traveled at different rates in space (Bose, 1949).

In the Anthropological Survey of India, he encouraged researchers to collect information on the distribution of selected material traits from all over India (Bose, 1961) and of some major ancient craft techniques (see Saraswati and Behura, 1966).

As a teacher of Human Geography in Calcutta University, Bose initiated his students to study the ethnic-based ecological niches and their land utilization patterns centering around rural weekly markets (Bose, 1949a, 1950, 1950a). He also initiated special studies on carrying capacity of land under hunting and gathering and shifting cultivation (Bose, 1968).

In caste studies, he initiated his students to two sets of enquiries: (a) drift from caste to non-caste occupations (Bose, 1949); and (b) studies on the organization of caste *panchayats* through records of disputes handled by those associations over a period of time (Bose, 1960).

I have already mentioned that in his Bengali book, *Hindu Samajer Gadan*, he has given several guide-lines for the study of Indian civilization. Taking a broad perspective of social history, he has utilized several techniques: ethnography, analysis of cultural element in festivals, use of classical texts for deriving the ideal model, use of medieval literature such as *Chaitanya Charitamrita* for the study of social movements, analysis of the nodal social roles of king, pilgrim centres, fairs and markets, analysis of land revenue records and, finally, study of economic history of a region (such as Bolpur Thana area during the British Period).

During 1962-63, Bose initated a brief sociological survey of the 80 wards of Calcutta with the help of 12 research scholars. Besides making general observations on the distribution of linguistic and religious groups and their occupational specializations in different wards, and a survey of voluntary associations, cartographic methods were used in preparing land use maps based on the assessment records of the Corporation of Calcutta. Another technique used in this rapid survey was the study of family histories of a number of old influential families in different wards (Bose, 1968).

As early as 1929 Bose considered it worthwhile to use relevant Indian textual categories for the analysis of social data. He indicates how categories like *artha, kama, moksha, dharma,* etc., may be used for the classification of cultures (1929 : 19-20). One of his students, Baidyanath Saraswati, has recently followed Bose's example, in extensive and yet judicious used of textual categories, in the study of Indian civilization (1970).

It will be evident from the above discussion that Bose has not approached his varied problems in terms of a limited rigid set of methodological tools and theoretical perspectives. His main approach has been that of a natural historian. He feels that the field anthropologist should first of all be a crafty explorer who will be ever prepared to devise tools appropriate in the field situation. In an yet unpublished manuscript he has written :

> My intention has been to demonstrate that very useful work can be done if an anthropologist begins, as in bird watching, with observation and more observation. And as he observes, questions arise in his mind, to which he tries to find an answer by the right design of fresh observations. As one thus proceeds through such effort and constant comparision in parallel fields, where some of the factors are common and others are not, and if one dares to walk alone, then he perhaps gains ability to add his little bit to the store of scientific knowledge.

This natural history approach is a matter of daily habit with him. Professor Bose keeps diary of his daily social encounters and observations which ultimately find a place in his periodic creative outpourings. He wrote a book *Paribrajaker Diary* (The Diary of a Wanderer) in 1940.

A Functional Definition of 'Culture'

In 1929 when Bose published his *Cultural Anthropology,* Malinowski (1922) and Radcliffe-Brown (1922) had already published their functional ethnographies. But a functional theory of culture had not yet been built into the text books in cultural and social anthropology. In Bose's book, however, one finds a clear expression of the 'adaptive functions of culture' and of the 'soul of culture':

> Beneath the outer framework of culture, there lies a body of beliefs and sentiments which are responsible for the particular manifestation of culture. Such a body of ideas and sentiments grow out of life's philosophy, and is consequently conditioned by the needs and aspirations of each particular age. Historical developments bring in their train a number of unresolved problems; and if the cultural

> heritage of an age does not serve those needs, it is sure to undergo modifications by those who inherit it.
>
> Culture is thus in a perpetually unstable equilibrium with the experiences of men (Bose, 1929 : Chapter II).

I have elsewhere mentioned that Bose has suggested that Hindu textual categories such as *sattva, raja* and *tama* should be used in the classification of cultures. Professor J. B. S. Haldane employed this scheme for the description of what he regarded as cultural behaviour among animals (Haldane, 1957). Bose has also suggested that four distinct categories of behaviour may be identified in any culture: (1) *Vastu* or material object, (2) *Kriya* or habitual action, (3) *Samhati* or social grouping, and (4) *Tattwa* or knowledge. The last again may be divided into two as the knowledge is *Vichramulaka*, i.e., based on experiments or criticism or *Viswasamulaka*, i.e., based on faith (Bose, 1929 : 42-45).

A Science Policy for India

I will end this meandering discourse on the many splendoured pioneering intellectual adventures of Professor Bose with an anecdoted on what he felt should be the 'science policty' in modern India. To an abrupt query from me about how he would have organized science in India if he was placed in charge of it, he immediately replied :

> Hypothetically speaking, my first task would be to orient the major endeavour of science towards our main social problem, that is poverty. What we first need is millions of properly trained technicians who can help the villagers grow better crops, breed better livestocks, improve sanitation, modernize the crafts and introduce new small-scale industries. Out of the requirements of these practical tasks, science courses will have to be devised in order to develop specialized research on agriculture, plant and animal genetics, engineering, etc., and also on relevant problems of social reconstruction. But, over and above these application based research, we must have a highly selective minority of outstanding scholars who would pursue science for its own sake as a pure intellectual endeavour. Unless the nation provides a secure and honoured shelter for these scholars the spiritual quality of the overall endeavour of science will be disturbed.

I am certain that in the social sciences too, Bose wants the bulk of our activirties to be oriented towards helping the society to overcome the threshold of poverty and to revitalize social life in villages and towns, while leaving a place for pure theoretical research only for a minority of dedicated scholars who genuinely belong to that order. Bose has no misgivings whatsoever that such scholars will not periodically seek inspiration from probing deeply into the roots of the malaise of the social world around them.

References

Boas, Franz (1911), *The Mind of the Primitive Man*. New York.

——(1940), *Race, Language and Culture*. New York.

Bose, Nirmal K. (1927), "The Spring Festival of India". *Man in India*, Vol. 7.

——(1928), "Marriage and Kinship among the Juangs". *Man in India*, Vol. 8.

——(1929), *Cultural Anthropology*. Calcutta.

——(1929(a)), "Juang Associations". *Man in India*, Vol. 9.

(1930), "Juang Associations", *Man in India*, Vol. 10.

——(1932), *Cannons of Orissan Architecture*. Calcutta.

——(1934), "Caste as a Social Phenomenon". *The Calcutta Review*, August, 1934.

——(1934a), *Selections from Gandhi*. Calcutta, (Later revised and reprinted in 1948 and 1952).

——(1935a), "The Contact of Cultures" (I). *The Calcutta Review*, January, 1935.

——(1935b), "The Contact of Cultures" (II). *The Calcutta Review*, February, 1935.

——(1935c), "The Contact of Cultures" (III). *The Calcutta Review*, March, 1935.

——(1936), "Hindu Social Organisation: A Speculative Essay". *The Visva-Bharati Quarterly*, February 1936.

——(1940), *Paribrajaker Diary*. Calcutta.

——(1940a), *Studies in Gandhism*. Calcutta. (Second and Third editions, published in 1959 & 1962).

——(1940), "The Hindu Method of Tribal Absorption". *Science and Culture*, Vol. 7, October, 1941.

(With D. Sen) (1948), *Excavations in Mayurbhanj*. Calcutta.

Bose, Nirmal K. (1949), *Nabin-O-Prachin*. Calcutta (First published in 1930).

——(1949a), *Hindu Samajer Gadan*, Calcutta.

——(1949b), "Suggestions for improvements in methods of dating Indian temples", Presidential Address, Anthropology and Archaeology Section, Indian Science Congress Association, 1949.

——(1949c), "The interview method in human geography". *Cal. Geog. Rev.*, March, 1949.

——(1949d), "Adaptation to environment". *Cal. Geog. Rev.*, June.

——(1950a), "Notes on Planning Field Investigation". *Cal. Geogr. Rev.*, Vol. XIII, No. 3, Sept. 1950.

——(1950b), "Geographical Background of Indian Culture", In *Cultural Heritage of India*, Ramkrishna Mission Institute of Culture, Vol. 1, 1950.

——(1951), "Caste in India". *Man in India*, Vol. 31, Nos. 3 & 4.

——(1952), "Democracy and social change in India". *The Modern Review*, April 1952.

——(1953), *My Days with Gandhi*. Calcutta.

——(1954), "Who are the backward classes?" *Man in India*, Vol. 34, No. 2.

——(1954a), "The return of the individual". *Man in India*, Vol. 34, No. 3.

——(1955), "The role of mental attitudes in Cultural contact", *Man in India*, Vol. 35, No. 2.

——(1955a), "Tribal Economy". *The Adivasis*, Publication Division, Govt. of India, New Delhi.

——(1956), "Some Observations on Nomadic Castes in India". *Man in India*, Vol. 36, No. 1.

——(1956a), "Cultural Zones in India". *Geog. Rev. Ind.*, Vol. 18, No. 4, Dec. 1956.

——(1958), "Some Aspects of Caste in Bengal". *Man in India*, Vol. 38, No. 2.

——(1958a), "East and West in Bengal". *Man in India*, Vol. 38, No. 3.

——(1959), "Comparative Study of Civilization". *Man in India*, Vol. 39, No. 3.

——(1959a), *Modern Bengal*. Calcutta.

——(1959b), "Hints for preliminary survey works in tribal areas". *Cal. Geog. Rev.*

——(1960), "The use of proceedings of caste panchayat". *Jour. Soc. Research*, Vol. 1, No. 1. July 1960.

——(1960a), "Conflict and its resolution in Hindu Civilization", *Jr. Deptt. Letters*, Calcutta University, 1960.

——(1961), "Introduction", *Peasent Life in India*, Anth. Surv. Ind., Memoir. 8.

——(1964), "Changes in tribal cultures before and after independence". *Man in India*, Vol. 44., No. 1.

——(1964a), "Integration of tribes in Andhra Pradesh", *Man in India*, Vol. 44, No. 2.

——(1965), "Class and Caste", *Man in India*, Vol. 45, No. 4.

——(1965a), "Calcutta: A premature metropolis", *Scientifc Americana*, Sept. 1965.

——(1966), "Indian villages and ancient towns", *Jr. Ind. Anth, Soc.*, Vol. 1, No. 1.

——(1967), *Problems of National Integration*, Simla.

——(1967a), "Some methods of studying social change". *Man in India*, Vol. 47, No. 3. 1967.

——(1967b), *Culture and Society in India*, Bombay, 1967.

——(1968), "Competing productive systems in India", *Man in India*, Vol. 48, No. 1.

——(1971), "An Anthropological View of Indian Civilization", Acharya jagadish Chandra Bose Memoral Lecture, 1971 (Mimeographed).

——(1971a), *Tribal Life in India*. Delhi.

——(1971b), *Lectures on Gandhism*. Ahmedabad.

Erikson, Erik (1969), *Gandhi's Truth*. New York.

Haldane J. B. S. (1956), "The argument from animals to men : an examination of its validity for anthropology", *JRAI*, Vol. 86. pt. II, July-December, 1956, pp. 1-14.

Karve, Iravati (1953), *Kinship Organisation in India*. Poona.

Kroeber, A. L. (1928), Review of "Cultural Anthropology" by Nirmal Kumar Bose, *American Anthropologist*, Vol. 31.

Kroeber, A. L. (1917), "The Superorganic", *American Anthropologist*, Vol. 19, pp. 162-213.

Kroeber, A. L. and Clyde Kluckhohn 1952 *Culture : A Critical Review of Concepts and Definitions*. Cambridge, Mass.

Malinowski, B. (1922), *Argonauts of the Western Pacific*. London.

Radcliffe-Brown, A. R. (1922), *The Andaman Islanders*, London.

Saraswati, B. N. (1970), *Contributions to the Understanding of Indian Civilization*. Karnatak University, Dharwar.

Saraswati, B. N. and N. K. Behura (1966), Pottery Techniques in Peasant India, *Anthropological Survey of India*, Memoir No. 13.

Sinha, Surajit (1969), *Urgent problems for research in social and cultural anthropology : Perspective and Suggestions*, Indian Institute of Advanced Study, Transactions, 10 : pp. 162-169.

Sinha, Surajit (1971), Is there an Indian Tradition in Social/Cultural Anthropology : Retrospect and Prospects, *Journ, Ind. Anthrop. Soc.*, 6 : 1-14.

10

RELEVANCE OF N. K. BOSE'S CIVILIZATIONAL APPROACH IN UNDERSTANDING TRIBAL SITUATION TODAY

Sukant K. Chaudhury

Nirmal Kumar Bose (1901-1972), probably, was one of the original thinkers and indigenous anthropologists, who questioned western approaches of understanding Indian society. Bose is one of the finest field-workers among the twentieth century anthropologists in India. He has been a wanderer, cutting across communities and regions in India. He has been truly termed as a field-scientist by André Béteille (1975). Though all of us know that he did not concentrate on working on a specific community or topic, yet he focused on various aspects of Indian civilization. It has later come to be known as civilizational approach to understand Indian society. He never emphatically pursued the civilizational approach, but his thinking and writings have definitely culminated into such an approach. His articles entitled "The Hindu Method of Tribal Absorption" (1941), "Some Aspects of Indian Civilization" (1971) and "An Anthropological View of Indian Civilization" (1972a) provided the base for the civilizational approach.

In a nutshell the approach is concerned with how the tribal communities in India are interacting with other societies, particularly caste communities. Further, he rejected the idea of complete isolation of the tribals from the wider society.

Bose started his academic career as an Assistant Lecturer in Pre-historic Archaeology in Calcutta University in 1937. Later on he became a Reader in Human Geography and continued in the same capacity till 1959. He was the Director of Anthropological Survey of India from 1959 to 1964. Later on he served as the Commissioner for Scheduled Castes and Scheduled Tribes from 1967 to 1970. He was the editor of *Man in India* for a long period of 14 years, i.e. 1958-1972.

Bose worked on a variety of topics in general and understanding tribes and their transformation in India in particular. Among the tribes he studied include Juang of Pal Lahara, Orissa, and Munda of Chotanagpur. Bose was deeply concerned with the tribal problems. During his stint as Commissioner for SC & ST from 1967 to 1970, he produced very informative and analytical reports and whose extracts have been published in his book *Anthropology and Some Indian Problems* (1972b). In the 1967-68 report, he had identified poverty, insanitation and lack of education as major problems of SCs and STs and had suggested, "if we decide to depend upon whatever resources we can command today, we should perhaps be better advised to try through education and organization to help all Scheduled Castes and Scheduled Tribes to modernize themselves largely through their own effort, although they must be assisted by official as well as non-official agencies working towards the same end. It is only then that they can take their due share in the transformed system of production which we are all trying to build up in our country. It is also by means of this positive approach towards self-development that we can get rid of the inequalities, which have been left over to us from the past" (Bose 1972:152-153). In the 1968-69 report, Bose wrote that malnutrition and unbalanced diet are serious problems in poverty stricken tribal areas. He wrote, "The production capacity of our agriculturist has to be increased, food diversified, and the people educated in the art of securing balanced food even in their restricted environments (Bose 1972b).

Bose suggested diversification of occupation for Scheduled Castes and Scheduled Tribes in terms of working in industries. He said that Scheduled Castes in particular should be taken away from caste based occupations which will loosen the ranking system. He also suggested that education must be given a priority for developing the SCs and STs for which school buildings should be constructed properly. They should be constructed on iron joist pillars with iron trusses and purlins and galvanized corrugated iron-sheets on the roof. The rest of the parts, i.e. walls, doors, flooring, etc., be done by the villagers either with *pucca* bricks or mud wall, etc. The structure will be suitable for at least 40 years. There will be no complaint regarding roof-leaking or annual repairs (Bose 1972b: 173).

He wrote a piece entitled "The Weakest Link" (1972b), where he said, "Even among the scheduled castes and scheduled tribes, there are poorer and still poorer sections, neglected and even more neglected sections. It is, therefore, the foremost duty of all concerned to ensure that these weaker sections, who, in fact, form the "weakest link" among the scheduled castes and scheduled tribes are located and given special attention for their development through specific programmes undertaken for their uplift, based on their felt needs." Bose also worked on leisure. In an article entitled "The Effect of Urbanization on Work and Leisure", Bose observed that the nature of leisure and entertainment varies from society that depends on farming and a society that relies on non-agricultural economic pursuits. He further observed that while work and leisure are more or less seasonally distributed among the farmers, these are not the same among the industrial urban working population rather different classes of industrial working people have different shades of leisure activities. Moreover leisure becomes more personalized and range of choices becomes wider among urban industrial working people. By leisure, Bose meant how one uses leisure time after a hard day's work. He expressed that amateur clubs or libraries punctuated their normal activity with social services of various kinds, thereby tending to give rise to a sense of social consciousness that has been attributed to one of the results of India's contact with the West. Bose asserted 'with an increasing urbanization of rural India we are perhaps on the threshold of an edge in which we are seeking to strive for new roots into culture of ancient times so that we shall be furnished with strength to face the problems and responsibilities of the present'(Bose 1957).

Delivering the sixth N. K. Bose Memorial Lecture in 2006, L. K. Mahapatra (2006) observed that Bose had been a nationalist to the core and had interrupted his studies several times to participate in the movements initiated by Mahatma Gandhi. He was very close to Gandhiji and for sometime, he served as his personal secretary. He wrote many books on Gandhi including *Selections from Gandhi* (1934), *Studies in Gandhism* (1940), *My Days with Gandhi* (1952), *Mahatma Gandhi and One World* (1986), *Lectures on Gandhism* (1979). He worked on Indian culture and said that both culture content and acculturation were vital processes in establishing a democratic way of life in India. On this aspect his books include: *Cultural Anthropology* (1929), *Culture and Society in India* (1967). Bose defines culture as the crystallized phase of man's activities; it includes certain materials and techniques with the aid of which man experiences supreme emotions of pleasure, which are, however, of unknown value. Baidyanath Saraswati (2002) says that the relation between culture and experience has been highlighted by N. K. Bose.

Further, Saraswati (2002) quotes Bose where he has explained the Indian intellectual tradition: "In the Hindu scriptures, the desires of mankind are classified into three categories; viz., those connected with (1) *Artha* or economic needs, (2) *Kama* or sexual desires, and (3) *Moksha* or the desire for peace through spiritual emancipation from the sorrows and sufferings of human existence. Now, all that we understand by culture goes to satisfy one or more of these impulses. It thus helps human beings to live happily through a satisfaction of their basic needs and desires. The observance of *Achara* or customary practices prevalent in a country or in a particular social group existing therein, is thus *Dharma*, which literally means that which sustains life. The observance of culture can thus be reduced to a threefold *Dharma*, viz. *Arthadharma*, *Kamadharma* and *Mokshadharma*."

Each of these *dharma* acts in four phases; viz (1) Vastu or material objects, (2) *Kriya* or habitual actions, (3) *Samhati* or social groupings and (4) *Tattwa* or knowledge. The fourth phase is again divisible into two, namely knowledge or *Visharamulaka*, i.e. based upon criticism, and *Viswasamulaka*, i.e. based upon faith. There are certain items of knowledge which are necessary to be improved by constant criticism. Knowledge regarding the workings of a machine or human society is of this order. A more correct acquaintance with the subject helps us to deal with those things in a more efficient fashion. But knowledge regarding the existence of

God is not of this order. The mere belief in the existence of God is enough for a religious man; a critical examination of its evidence is unnecessary, for it does not help a man to live a better life. This is the reason why we should distinguish clearly between two kinds of *Tattva*, namely that which becomes more useful through *Vichara* and that in which *Viswas* is the chief element; criticism being, to say the least, out of place."

"The three principal desires of mankind thus act in four main phases. But in each of these three *Dharma*, viz. *Artha*, *Kama* and *Moksha*, we recognize another tendency which is governed by man's eternal love for the beautiful or *sundara*. This love for the beautiful is not necessarily of sexual origin; it runs through all the other spheres of human activities as well. It is an important principle which brings into the divergent phases of man's cultural life a unity of purpose and movement, which may be more or less deep seated in operation" (Bose 1929).

In 1949, he wrote *Hindu Samajer Garen* in Bengali which was later translated into English with a long introduction by Béteille in 1975, entitled as *The Structure of Hindu Society*. It provided a bird's eye-view of Indian society and culture including the problem of integration. Béteille said that Bose emphasized a proper understanding of Hindu civilization by anthropologist, which would require a different approach than the ones usually applied to understand tribal community of North America, Melanesia or Australia. It was in this sense that Bose saw a kinship between his work and that of American anthropologist A. L. Kroeber (Béteille 1975: 1-2).

He wrote an ethnographic note on the oil-pressure caste entitled "The Kolus or Telis" (Bose 1975). It is a very interesting piece he begins with a discussion of protein, fat consumption in Germany, England and other countries and then proceeds to Indian oil-pressure caste. He studied those oil-pressures of Seraikela, Orissa, known as Telis. Bose said that the Telis do not have a single method of extracting oil, rather have many methods in the same region. Oil-pressure caste is regarded as low whose water is not acceptable by high castes; this is why others are reluctant to adopt their occupation for fear of losing caste or being degraded. However, he also said that during the course of time, "in India those who accept caste distinction, some new communal or social practices are introduced or when some change or improvement in craft practices takes place, this may be immediately followed by the emergence of a new branch whose members seek to confine the ties of marriage to their own small group" (Bose 1975).

Remarking upon Indian civilization, Bose (1971) said that "multiplicity of fractional views of truth was a dominant element in Hindu religious thought and it is of significance that it spread from one corner of India to another eventually even pervaded some forms of non Brahmincal thought in the country in later times. .....this also brought about uniformity in Indian civilization as much as the productive organization of caste and of property relationship had done in other spheres of life". Further he said, "when we view the whole of Indian civilization there is a greater diversity in the material aspect of life and multiplicity of caste, religion, faith and sect. In India each guilt was encouraged to follow its own *dharma*, which was guided by the advice of colleges of the Brahmin which were either located in centers of learning or of pilgrimages" (*ibid*). Béteille said that Bose, in fact, spoke about two models of Indian civilization – (a) Brahminical model; and (b) Tribal model.

The Brahmanical model may also be called the caste-model, which is based upon ranking and hierarchy. Probably, it is a superior model, not because of its political system or ideology but because of its superior technology. Such a technology produces enough to support and sustain a larger population. As we know, everything is ranked in Hindu Society, starting from food to clothing, to occupation and also bride-giver and bride-taker. But, it is not an undemocratic structure. It is democratic in the sense that all other communities were allowed to exist with their own practices. The tribes became caste, adapted their rituals, which Bose called the Hindu method of tribal absorption. He described it in the following manner–one person, two persons. one family, two families came into contact with their Hindu neighbours and in course of time became attached to the Hindu economic system, and then were absorbed partially within the social fold also. The tension between one section of the people and another was not intense because the gap between rich and poor was not much. Besides, while the tribals are attracted by the gods and goddesses of Hindus, the Hindus also quite often, adopted the gods and goddesses of the tribal people. Undoubtedly, the mode of absorption of Hindu rituals and other cultural traits by the tribals was slow.

Going back to the Brahmanical model, Bose said that it was a super-structure. He further said, "There was a superstructure guiding the religion and cultural life of the community as a whole. Each small component called a *jati* was left free to pursue its own rights and ceremonies, so long as it did not militate against the moral codes of Brahmincal society." Bose mostly took Indian civilization synonymous with Hindu civilization.

Further, he said that through ages, Hinduism has tried to promote ideas and spiritual exercise, designed to promote the growth of every individual soul in this direction. Individuals and communities have been encouraged to remain in their special worlds, with the result that, even if the economic and social organization of caste have suppressed individualism at one level Hindus have remained loyal to individualism of another kind and never allowed themselves to be fused into one uniform mass.

Comparing Indian civilization with that of the West, Bose says that the Indian social or economic condition is predominantly an organization of peace. It encourages the co-existence of many cultures, many separatenesses; but it does not make a large community strong enough to wage war. It is natural that an organization designed for peace will fail in the event of war. But, on the other hand, it may also be true that an organization of war may fail men when they have to live in peace with one another. And here, let us try to observe and understand the shape which European civilization has been taking during the last century or two.

Even in Europe, there have been protests all through the past two centuries against the present state of affairs. Some have sought spiritual refuge in poetry or science, human service or mysticism. As the control over nature's material resources has gone on increasing, as large sections of the population have been saturated in plenty, men's minds have wandered away from this in search of something which would give them solace and anchor in a world which is engrossed in a perpetually unsatisfied search for satiety.

When we see India in course of its long history of three thousand years or so, we notice certain broad points of strength and weakness. Ever since the Afghan, Tatar and Moghul invaders professing Islam came to the land, it had been proved again and again that the political structure of India was very weak in self-defence. In it, the defence of the State became the exclusive business of several castes and not of all the inhabitants of the State. Many cultures and religions existed side by side with one another; but the feeling of distinctness which was thus encouraged failed when there was need of combining the people into one 'nation' for purposes of defence.

Further, Bose writes, that educated Indians are today conscious of the element of weakness in our social system; and those who wish to see in India the rise of a mighty nation which can match its strength against that of any other nation, are impatient with every element in Indian civilization which tends to weaken it from the military point of view. Caste has been held largely responsible for the absence of a sense of national unity. But what is overlooked is that caste was designed for one purpose, nationalism in Europe for another. The multiplicity of faiths in India, her variegated ways of life, with different kinds of food and dress, her many languages, have also been equally blamed for our lack of the sense of national unity. The fact that the spiritual quest for a transcendental view of truth has, time and again, proved attractive to the highest individuals in the land, has proved distressing to those who want to 'secularize' and 'modernize' India–an India which should, according to them, become as powerful a nation as any other in the modern world.

Taking into account Kroeber's ideas of civilization, Bose said that tribals are a part and parcel of Indian civilization. The colonial approach for the tribals was of isolation. They called a tribe isolated or relatively isolated community, and it was an anthropological whole. Bose said that this could be the situation for African tribes and Australian aborigines, for tribes in North America and Melanesia. But the Indian situation is different where the tribes interacted with Indian society. He took the case of Juangs. The Juangs were shifting cultivators. The Britishers had put a ban on shifting cultivation. Then the Juangs looked for an alternative mode of occupation. They moved to nearby multi-caste villages and took up some occupation. They got involved in the *Jajmani* system, became a part of pure and impure hierarchy. They started performing *Lakshmi Pooja*, the concept of *paap*, *punya* and *dharma* were used but fowl sacrifice simultaneously went on. Similarly the Oraons continued fowl sacrifice on the day of *Diwali* while simultaneously lights are put-on. In this manner, the tribals are not found in isolation but were interacting with the larger civilization.

Undoubtedly, the scale of interaction differed–probably in middle and central India it was more compared to south Indian tribes. The impact of outside world is found more on the Oraon, the Munda and the Santhal. The land-tenure system among the Munda is more elaborate than the others. The technology of the Santhal is more advanced than others. In fact, Béteille calls Santhals peasants, not tribes. There has been no forceful imposition of any cultural traits on the tribes. It has only resulted out of a regular interaction.

Here I would speak about the Kondhs of Orissa, where I did field work. The Kondhs are good producer of tamarind, turmeric and tendu leaves. Today, the above three trades have reached the multinationals. Thus, indirectly the Kondhs have gone global without getting its fruits (Chaudhury 2008). British administrator, Captain Macpherson wrote that the Kondhs used to send cart loads of turmeric though middlemen, who used to be from neighbouring Oriya caste community. Even today, despite governments' best efforts through cooperatives and other marketing societies, middlemen are found (Chaudhury 2004). Thus, the point here is to focus on how tribals are interacting with the wider communities. They also took part in fairs and festivals of Hindu communities including that of the king's paraphernalia. Indian society has been a literate society and not a pre-literate one, thus, producing the civilization and we know wherever civilization is there will be script, there will be writings and history. The tribals are part of this history. In fact, Bose tried to reconstruct the structure of Indian civilization through the twin approaches of ethnology and indology.

Surajit Sinha, a student and close associate of Bose, furthered Bose's civilizational approach in his studies. He said that there cannot be one common approach to the study of primitive society of different countries because each community is a bounded unit having its own culture, notwithstanding the fact that cultural osmosis takes place between communities. The British construction of Indian society has been based on caste system. Indian society consists of many self-regulating villages, where various endogamous *jati* groups live, pursuing hereditary occupations. They were arranged in a rigid system of birth-ascribed status hierarchy. The early British administrators also spoke of certain human groups who lived in hills and forests, or in the planes near the forests. They lived in relative isolation from the caste based peasant villages as unstratified endogamous groups. They were doing multiple occupations including settled and shifting cultivation, hunting and gathering. They were pre-literate groups and were placed outside the Brahmanic civilization. They were called tribes in the analogy of similar groups in aboriginal America, Africa and Oceania. Then, tribes were categorized as a special category for the purpose of census and administration. After independence, Government of India accepted the category of Scheduled Tribes (Sinha 1980).

Broadly speaking, Sinha emphasized the fact that the tribal cultures of India are unique and are not necessarily universally shared by primitive tribes in other parts of the world. Besides, they shared many thing with Hindu peasantry (see Sinha 1957).

Sinha also studied the state formation among tribes (see Sinha 1962). About the Bhumji tribe of Barahabhum, he analysed in details the state formation and how they have created a myth of Rajput ancestry. There are several tribes in India who have become castes in their own manner, but they only adopted few cultural traits like worshiping Hindu pantheon and following a few rituals.

In this manner, Sinha mainly focused on tribe-caste continuum and tribe-peasantry continuum (see Sinha 1965) to explain his approach. He clearly mentioned that tribes in India are not living in isolation rather are always in some kind of contact with the wider caste and peasant communities. In general, there are many common points between Bose and Sinha in the sense that both of them spoke of tribes as a part of Indian civilization and Indian tribes do not share many features with tribes found in Africa, America or Oceania.

References

Béteille, André (1975), "Introduction", in N. K. Bose, *The Structure of Hindu Society*, New Delhi: Orient Longman.

Bhattacharya, R. K. and Jayanta Sarkar (2002), *Passage through Indian Civilization: N. K. Bose's Thoughts and Work*. Kolkata: Anthropological Survey of India.

Bose, N. K. (1929), *Cultural Anthropology*. Calcutta: Arya Sahitya Bhawan.

——(1934), *Selections from Gandhi*. Ahmedabad: Navjivan Trust.

——(1940), *Studies in Gandhism*. Calcutta: D. M. Libarary.

——(1941), "The Hindu Method of Tribal Absorption", *Science and Culture*, Vol. VII, No.4.

——(1952), *My Days with Gandhi*. Calcutta: Merit Publications.

——(1957), The effect of urbanization on work and leisure. *Man in India*, Vol. 37, Jan-March, pp. 1-9.

——(1966), *Mahtma Gandhi and One World*. New Delhi: Ministry of External Affairs, Govt. of India.

——(1967), *Culture and Society in India*. Calcutta: Asia Publishing House.

——(1971), "Some aspects of Indian civilization", *Man in India*, Vol.51, No. 1.

——(1972a), "An anthropological view of Indian civilization", *Man in India*, Vol. 52, No. 2.

——(1972b), *Anthropology and Some Indian Problems*. Calcutta: Institute of Applied Anthropology and Social Research.

——(1975), *The Structure of Hindu Society*. New Delhi: Orient Longman.

Chaudhury, S. K. (2004), *Tribal Identity*. Jaipur: Rawat Publications.

——(2008), "Anthropology of Tribal Development: The Kondh Case" in S. K. Chaudhury and S.M.Patnaik (eds.) *Indian Tribes and the Mainstream*. Jaipur: Rawat Publications.

Mahapatra, L. K. (2006), *6th Nirmal Kumar Bose Memorial Lecture 2006*. New Delhi: Indira Gandhi National Centre for the Arts.

Sarswati, Baidyanath (2002), "Professor Nirmal Kumar Bose: A Gandhian Anthropologist", in R. K. Bhattacharya and Jayanta Sarkar (eds.). *Passage through Indian Civilization: N.K. Bose's thoughts and work*. Kolkata: Anthropological Survey of India.

Sinha, Surajit Chandra (1957), "Tribal Cultures of Peninsular India as a Dimension of Little Tradition in the Study of Indian Civilization: A Preliminary Statement", *Man in India*, Vol. 37, No. 2.

——(1962), "State Formation and Rajput Myth in Tribal Central India", *Man in India*, Vol. 42, No. 1.

——(1965), "Tribe-Caste and Tribe-Peasant Continua in Central India", *Man in India*, Vol. 45, No. 1.

——(1980), "Tribes and Indian Civilization: A Perspective", *Man in India*, Vol. 60, No. 1 & 2.

11

VERRIER ELWIN'S ANTHROPOLOGY

Sachchidananda

Verrier Elwin was born on 29 August 1902 at Dover in England. He was the eldest of the three children of Edmund Elvin, an Anglican Bishop working in West Africa. His father died early when he was seven years of age. He was brought up by his mother. After school, he joined the Oxford University from where he graduated in English literature. He decided to stay on to study theology. On finishing his theology course, he was appointed the Vice-Principal of Wycliffe Hall. After staying there for a year, he resigned. Life in Oxford offered the search for truth, dignity and interest. Yet it did not satisfy him. At that time, he thought about India. His family had a long connection with the country. The Catholic religion lays great stress on spiritual ideal known as reparation. He had a strong desire to make reparation to the poor for the wrong done to them in India. He made his decision to give up his Oxford career and go to India. He was aware of the fact that he was leaving the life of scholarship and plunging into an unknown world. At that time he did not know much about India. A friend from Ceylon came into contact with him. He was a supporter of the Indian national movement. He introduced him to the writings of Tagore and Gandhi. He began to read books on Indian philosophy. He was particularly attracted to the personality of Gandhi. Hindu mysticism claimed his attention.

At about this time, he came to know about Father Jack Winslow, the founder of an *ashram* type mission organization called Christ Seva Sangh. He had been a missionary in western India for many years. But after some time, he broke away from the conventional ecclesiastical order to identify himself more closely with the poor and with Indian nationalism and culture. He had studied certain aspects of mysticism and knew a lot about *yoga* in theory and practice.

The Christ Seva Sangh was founded by him to explore the possibilities of orientalisation of Christianity. Two of his friends from Oxford and Cambridge were attracted to Winslow's plan and had decided to join him in his *ashram* in Poona. Elwin finally decided to join them. However, he had no money to pay for his passage to India. The Christ Seva Sangh undertook the responsibility to take him to India by rail across Eurpoe and then by a boat going to Colombo. Although the journey was uncomfortable, there was a lot of excitement in the group about the great work they were going to do.

After spending a few days in Ceylon, the group went to Malabar and then to Poona. In the *ashram* they slept on the floor, ate Indian food. They used to remove the sandals before entering a building and their dress was white *khadi*. In January 1928, they visited Gandiji's Sabarmati Ashram. Elwin was greatly impressed by Gandhi, the people around him, the discipline and austere living. The impact of these few days at Sabarmati was extraordinary. He remained in constant contact with Gandhiji for the next four years. It was there that he met Sardar Vallabh Bhai Patel who suggested that he should go to Madhya Pradesh and work among tribals.

This idea appealed to him and he approached the Biship of Nagpur in 1932 for his advice in this regard. The Bishop suggested that he should go to village Karanjia in Mandla district. This village was located on a hill slope in the midst of dense forest. Elwin thought that he could establish a small settlement there and propogate a way of life which was a mixture of Franciscan and Gandhian ideals. A small body of workers, which included Christians, Muslims, and Hindus and some local tribal people, were put on job. Each person had complete freedom to follow his own religion. The community organized itself into a small society which was called the Gond Seva Mandal. The life at the settlement followed the pattern of an *ashram*. A little mud chapel of St. Francis was built. There was a tree plantation programme. A guest house was built. A dispensary was also put up. A co-educational school was started. A leper home was also created.

However, there was deep conflict brewing in Elwin's mind. The mission administration was unhappy about his association with the national freedom struggle. Elwin did not see eye to eye with it on the question of conversion. Even Jack Winslow of the Christ Seva Sangh urged him to convert tribals and untouchables so that they could lead better lives. The result was that by 1936, Elwin was completely disillusioned and surrendered his priesthood. It was in that year that he moved to another village, twelve miles away and slowly began to devote his time exclusively to research. In these years he was helped by research grants from Merton College, Oxford, and from the Leverhulme Foundation. He was also occasionally helped by J.R.D. Tata who showed a great deal of interest in tribal matters. Later he moved to set up a home in Patangarh which was in the Maikal hills. This place was more delightful and more friendly than others. At Patangarh also, Elwin opened a dispensary, school, guest house and leper home. All through the Second World Was he largely remained in this village. It was from here that his major books were written and published. He did go out for long visits to Bastar and Orissa.

Verrier Elwin was not a conventional anthropologist. Anthropology is a vast subject, the science of man as a whole. As such we need different kinds of people to study it. We need scholars trained in pre-history, physical anthroplogy, social anthropology and linguistics. Elwin felt that scholars from a humanist background should also contribute to it. He divided anthropologists into two categories. He called the first variety 'technical anthroplogists'. These were trained in anthropological disciplines. The other category was called 'humanist anthropologists'. He was attracted by the practical application of anthropology for human development and took inspiration from Professor A. C. Haddon of Cambridge who held that service to humanity was to show that the proper study of mankind was to discover man as a human being.

For Elwin, anthropology did not mean spare time field work. He detested anthropologists visiting an area for two to three weeks, take hundreds of interviews and return to the universities writing pompous articles about 'what they have failed to observe'.

According to him it meant his whole life. His method was to settle down among the people, live with them, share their life as far as an outsider could. It took him seven years to produce the book on the Baiga. For the Agaria he took ten years. He spent ten years on the collection of folktales and folksongs of Chhattisgarh. All these studies were proceeding at the same time. This meant that he did not depend merely on asking questions and seeking interviews. The knowledge of the people gradually sank in and became part of him.

Long and extended field work gave a novel twist to the anthropologist's credo of participant observation. The best example of this is his rich description of his own first marriage in 1939 in his long essay entitled 'I married a Gond'. The tribal wedding was carried over in four days. He described all the rituals in detail. Some of his friends thought that he had married the Raj Gond girl, almost half his age, in the spirit of science.

He came to anthropology through poetry. When he went to tribal areas he found people talking poetry. An old woman spoke of fire as a flower blossoming on a dry tree and of an umbrella as a peacock. Children playing around the fire at night regaled themselves with riddles which were in poetic form.

Elwin's first book was on Baiga. He was fascinated by the story of their creation and by Nanga Baiga who was the founder of the tribe. The Baiga were shifting cultivators. They were pursued by the forest officers determined to make them stop their axe and hoe cultivation and take to the plough. The Baiga were practicing shifting cultivation for centuries as this was the only possible thing to do. But they were forced to take up plough cultivation. Many were reduced to poverty. They all suffered from psychological disturbance. According to their tradition it was a very wrong thing for them to lacerate the breats of the Mother Earth with the plough. They were also stopped from hunting. This escalated their anxiety as it affected their livelihood.

His next book was on Agaria, a small group of blacksmiths and iron smelters who were scattered all over Mandla and Bilaspur districts. In this study he concentrated mainly on the techniques of craftsmanship with the mythology that vitalized them.

The publication of the book on the Baiga attracted the attention of many anthropologically oriented administrators like W. G.

Archer and J. H. Hutton. Archer invited him to visit Chotanagpur where he met Sarat Chandra Roy who had written a whole series of books on Bihar tribes. After Roy's death in 1942, Elwin and Archer edited *Man in India*, the anthropological journal founded by Roy, for some years.

In May 1940 he got an official assignment as a Census Officer in Bastar. Later on he was designated as Honorary Ethnographer. For this he settled down in Patangarh. He traveled all over the area and collected lots of notes and photographs of the Hill Marias of Abujhmar. However his main interest was in two of the tribes – the Bison-horn Marias of the south and the Murias of the north. He wrote a book entitled *Maria Murder and Suicide* trying to discover why these simple people were led to homicide. The Maria were a tough and formidable tribe with very high incidence of homicide, six times that of the Central Provinces.

The administration was worried about this and Elwin offered to help. He interviewed a large number of Marias serving sentences of murder. He visited many villages, talked to the relatives of murderers and their victims, got the opinion of the village elders. An analysis of the reasons and motives for murders were revealing. Property disputes accounted for 15%, family quarrels for 16%, jealousy, infidelity and sex motives for 17%, 19% murders were committed under the influence of drink. Witchcraft accusations and motives of revenge accounted for the rest.

Elwin's most important work in Bastar was to study the *ghotul*, the unique youth dormitory of the Muria. The Muria live to the north of the Marias on a large wooded plateau in substantial villages. The *ghotul* was the central focus of Muria life coming down to modern times from Lingo, the heroic ancestor of the tribe who founded it. All the unmarried boys and girls of the tribe had to be members of the *ghotul*. Their membership was elaborately organized. After a period of probation, boys and girls were initiated and given special titles which carried with them graded ranks and social duties. Leaders were appointed to guide and control boys and girls. The boy's leader was called the *sardar* and the girl's leader was known as *belosa*. Boy members were known as *cheliks* and girl members were known as *motiaris*. Boys and girls were given important duties to perform on social occasions. The boys made beautiful little combs for the girls and tobacco boxes for themselves. The girls made necklaces, pendants and belts of beads and cowries.

What gave the *ghotul* its unique character was the approved and recognized relationship between boys and girls. They were two types of *ghotuls.* In the older type, each *chelik* was paired off with a *motiari.* He was formally married to her. Divorce was allowed though infidelity was punished. In the other type of *ghotul,* any kind of lasting attachment between *chelik* and *motiari* was forbidden.

The *ghotul* was literally a night club. The real life of the *ghotul* was in the fire light. After supper the boys and the girls gathered round the fire and they danced for an hour or two. After some time they prepared to sleep. The little boys and girls slept in long rows while those who had permanent or temporary partners lay down with their sleeping mates. They left the *ghotul* very early in the morning.

The Muria regarded the *ghotul* as their school. The children were given lessons in cleanliness, discipline and hardwork. They worked very hard for public good. They were available for the service of state officials or for labour on the roads. The were to work at a wedding or a funeral. Among the Muria, there was a strong sense of domestic morality and conjugal fidelity. Adultery was rare and when it occurred it invited supernatural punishment.

Elwin wrote a voluminous book of over 750 pages under the title *Muria and their Ghotul.* The book was translated into French. The book was well received in scholarly circles. The message of the *ghotul* was that youth must be served and freedom and happiness must be valued more than any material gain. It was hailed as 'kingdom of the young'.

Late in 1942 he was invited by the Administrator of the Eastern States Agency to tour the tribal areas in Orissa to enquire into the life and habits of the tribal people and make recommendations towards the solution of the problem of shifting cultivation. The terms of reference were social, religious, economic and physical conditions of the tribals. He was also to find out which elements of tribal life and culture should be preserved and which should be regarded as anti-social. He was to pay special attention to the health care and education of people. The report expected to provide a full picture of the problem against the background of which future policy could be framed.

It was in this context that Elwin began his studies in Orissa in December 1942. Although the report was submitted in a few months' time, Elwin's interest in studies in this region was aroused. The Orissa explorations resulted in the publications of four books, one each on the Juangs, Kuttia Khonds, Bondos and Saoras. He worked in Pal Lahar and Keonjhar among the Juangs. The Juangs had been reduced to abject poverty. They had been deprived of their normal means of livelihood which was shifting cultivation. They were given cattle and land in villages located on the foothills. They were unfamiliar with the plough and could not take care of the cattle as a result of which they died in a year or two. They became serfs of the peasants and made a miserable living by making baskets. Even worse than their economic decay was the complete collapse of their religious and cultural lives.

In his report Elwin recommended that the Juang demanded great sympathy. They lived in forests capable of yielding great wealth. Some portion of that wealth should be made available to them so that they could enjoy fuller and happier lives.

Soon after this he was appointed Honorary Anthropologist to the Orissa government. The Juang were covered in *Notes on the Juang*. The Bondo were dealt with in *Bondo Highlanders* and the Saoras were described in *The Religion of an Indian Tribe.* Besides these, long papers were written on Kuttia Khonds and Gadabas. The Kuttia Khonds were a section of a very large tribe of Khonds who were scattered all over Orissa. They were confined to the desolate hills and forests in the north western corner of Ganjam district. They were very poor and timid. They were tormented by Dom moneylenders and landlords. They were constantly shifting their villages which they built in such inaccessible places where there was no level ground. They were passionately devoted to shifting cultivation. Even in 1944 the desire for human sacrifice was fundamental to Khond psychology. Human sacrifice was abolished by the government in the middle of the nineteenth century. It was believed that human blood offered to the Mother Earth would make it more fertile. In almost every village the old implements of sacrifice (the knife, the chains, the blood bowl) were hidden away in the priest's house. The human sacrifice was replaced by the sacrifice of buffaloe. At the place of sacrifice an old human skull was brought out as a symbol of divinity.

In December 1943, Elwin made a study of the Bondo which was a very small tribe numbering less than three thousand. They are located in Koraput district. He selected two sets of villages, one representing their older settlement and the other in which they were influenced by contact with Gadaba. The book is a conventional ethnography, a description of social organization, rules of marriage, individual affiliation by clan and moiety, the tribal pantheon and ritual, etc. Bondo life was marked by courage, freedom, equality, independence and industry. The defects of these qualities were also evident. Courage became indifferent to human life. Freedom and independence degenerated into aggression. The Bondo drank too much. He was often lazy and not very clean. He wasted a lot of time to make any performance or ceremonial perfect. Elwin regarded him as 'a noble savage'.

Elwin's study of Saora extended over seven years. He concentrated on one section of this large tribe living in the districts of Ganjam and Koraput. The villages he covered in the hills above Gunupur, were at the time completely untouched by missionary or other external influences. He made friends with the villagers and the people made a two roomed hut for him to live. This was really an exception. By and large, the Saora did not want to have visitors. After an outsider left the village, they made special sacrifice to purify the place from possible magical defilement. In one area there was a fixed pattern. For a forest officer they sacrified a goat, for a sub-inspector of police, a fowl, and for an anthropologist, a large black pig.

The Hill Saoras lived in large villages. They erected 'menhirs' and sacrificed buffaloes for their dead. Their religious needs were served by male and female shamans. They engaged in both terraced and shifting cultivation. Their men put on a long brightly coloured loin cloth and women wore a hand woven brown bordered skirt and did not usually wear anything else. They had a characteristic tattoo mark down the middle of the forehead. They retained their own language and very few of them spoke any other. Saora women had an important role alike in festivity and funeral. Their voice mattered in tribal affairs. They could hold their own with their men. The institution of the shamanin (female priest) contributed to such a state of affairs. Saora houses were well built in long streets and some of their chieftains were comparatively wealthy. They were laborious but were victims of shocking expoitation to which they were subjected by their landlords and moneylenders.

The main subject of Elwin's study was Saora religion. The people did not resent his enquires. They insisted that he be present in all their festivals and religious ceremonies. They took him to their houses, made him sit close to the priest and explained it in great detail during the course of the ceremony. He was also invited to attend funerals.

Once when he was down with malaria, Saora priests and priestesses attempted to cure him by their own techniques. He learnt by personal experience a great deal about their medical ideas that he might have otherwise missed.

Saora life was completely dominanted by religion. Beyond and around this life and this visible world was an unseen realm of vital reality, peopled by a host of spirits whose activities impinged on normal existence at every turn. The ghosts lived in an underworld which was something like the world of the Saoras on this earth. It was the great desire of both male and female spirits to find partners among the living. They came to them in dreams and begged them to marry them. There was a special class of girls who at the age of puberty had dreams of these unearthy lovers and agreed to marry them. The marriage was an elaborate affair like an ordinary marriage. When it was over, the girl became *kuranboi,* a priestess who henceforth would be able to do the work of divination and healing with the aid of her unseen husband. But in spite of the realm of fantasy in which they lived, these women were devoted servants of their tribe. They were always ready to minister the sick and console the suffering. Men were also subject to these experiences and became the medicinemen of the tribe. The work of these simple doctors had great survival value. It made the patient believe that he was going to recover. The medicinemen took their profession seriously and worked very hard at it.

Elwin's study of the Saora is considered as the most detailed study of an Indian tribal religion. It covers an impressive range of topics: the apparatus and techniques of ritual, the causes and cures of disease, the rites of festivity, and the rites of the dead and various forms of invocation and prayer. The material cultural aspects have not been forgotten. The different types of alter, the instruments and the objects of sacrifice, the icons or pictographs through which religious sensibilities find expression have been ably described.

With his strong background of literature and love for poetry, Elwin was attracted to the study of folklore and myth of the tribes he worked with. He collected folktales of the tribals of Madhya Pradesh which he published in articles and books, His first book *Folktales of Mahakoshal* brought to light tales from Mandla, Balaghat, Bilaspur, Raipur, etc. These tales were collected over a period of ten years of living with Baiga, Agaria, Binjhwar, Maria, Muria and Pardhan. The folktales have been taken directly from eastern Hindi or Chhattisgarhi. Elwin translated them into English and saw to it that no extra words, no fresh images or alien ideas entered the translated text. In *ghotuls,* story telling had become a fine art. In Bastar folktales, he presents the story of the origin of the clan gods of Marias and Murias such as Anga, Lungopen, the cult hero of the Gond. The relationship between a man and his elder brother's wife is the central them of the Lingo legend.

Elwin's most outstanding work in the field of folklore is *The Myths of Middle India,* which is regarded as some sort of an aboriginal Purana. This book abounds in unusual stories, unreal names and far fetched analogies like in Purana. It reveals without embarrassment or self-consciousness, theories of the origin of life on earth and sexual functions. The myths in this book are collected from Madhya Pradesh, Chhattisgarh, Orissa, and some neighbouring areas. The tribes and castes covered in this book are the Agaria, the Bhuiya, the Bisonhorn Maria, the Bondo, the Gadaba, the Juang, Ahi, Lohra, Kamar and Saora. A comparative study of the folktales and the myths reveal that the tribes have borrowed from Puranic and epic traditions. There is a remarkable similarity in the myths and legands of different castes and tribes. Elwin classified the stories in the earlier and later traditions in terms of themes.

Elwin collected folk songs both in Madhya Pradesh and Orissa. He collected twelve Pradhan love songs from Maikal hills and Chhattisgarh. The songs are related to festivals, marriage, sex and other themes of tribal life. The songs are presented in English with an introductory note.

During his tours in the North East, Elwin collected folktales from several tribes and these were published under the title *Myths of North Eastern Frontier of India.*

Elwin was also interested in tribal art and aesthetics. He published a book on tribal art of Middle India in which he presented a superb collection of wood carvings from Santhal Paraganas. He also included in it the Jadu Patua scrolls 'tribal comic strips', which tell ancient stories of Santhals in pictures. This book reveled a good many unexpected treasures and stimulated designers elsewhere. Later he also published a book on tribal art of the North East. His Shillong home was a veritable museum of tribal tools, implements, artifacts and beautiful beads, trinkets and ornaments.

The term 'philanthropology' was coined by A. H. Quiggin, the biographer of A. C. Haddon of Cambridge University. It was used to describe Haddon's great concern for tribals. It means the service to humanity and to show that the proper study of mankind is to discover man as a human being. Once this knowledge is acquired and the real state of the tribal is known, steps can be taken to help them come out of their sad predicament. Elwin endorsed the entire concept and popularized the term.

When he worked among the Baiga, he was struck by their appalling poverty, disease, and destitution. He was haunted by intense suffering of these people. He expressed his views on the protection of tribes, which caused great flutter among academics, administrators and social workers. He was accused of wanting to keep them as they were, to hold up the development and to preserve them as museum pieces. It was a deliberate misrepresentation of his views. Elwin felt that the tribals should be allowed to develop with their own culture. He wanted to ensure that they did not lose their joy of living. He wanted to give them a breathing space to build up pride and become economically self-sufficient so that they would not be overwhelmed when the outside world came down upon them. In fact, he wanted them to make terms with their past and get used to cope up with the challenges of the present.

In his book on the Baiga (published in 1939), he advocated the creation of a national park under the direct control of a Tribal Commissioner. Inside this area, the administration was to allow the tribesmen to live their lives with happiness and freedom. Wide powers were to be given to their traditional panchayats and headmen. Outsiders settling in area would have to take permits. Missionaries of any kind would not operate in that area. Economic and educational development was to be speeded up. Fishing and hunding were to be freely permitted. The power of subordinate officials was to be severely curbed. In fact, the tribal groups were to be given three freedoms: freedom from fear, freedom from want, and freedom from undue interference. Oppressive landlords and moneylenders as well as corrupt and rapacious officials were to be banned. It was not a policy for the isolation of tribes. What he wanted was planned and controlled contact.

The entire concept was misunderstood not only at that time but for many years after. It was regarded as the approval of all anthropologists. It struck to them for a long time as a stigma. In another book entitled *The Loss of Nerve,* he referred to three kinds of tribal communities. The first was represented by the old Gond aristocracy, some tribal landlords and middlemen who have become the elite of tribal society by their enterprise and endeavor. They have fully adopted the Hindu way of life but would like to be known as tribal. The second category which is most numerous is a group of Gonds who have adopted the Hindu way of life but are suffering from the essence of frustration and loss of nerve. The third category comprises tribals living in isolated areas who continue to lead a vigorous and healthy tribal life. Elwin is largely concerned with the second category of Hinduised tribals who have suffered from moral depression and decay. The depression has been caused by loss of land, curtailment of their rights in the forest and their enability to face new challenges coming from the entry of outsiders in their areas. To meet this situation, Elwin advocated the policy of planned acculturation so that they regained their joy of life and overcame their loss of nerve.

By the early forties of the last century, Elwin gained full credibility by his writing not only in India but in the anthropological circles of the west. The Oxford University awarded him the D.Sc. degree on his publications. His papers came to be published in *Man,* the journal of the Royal Anthropological Institute. In 1946, when the Anthropological Survey of India was established, he was invited to join as its deputy director. He became a member of the Asiatic Society and later was elected as one of its fellows. He was also elected a fellow of the National Institute of Sciences of India. He was not happy in the Anthropological Survey as he did not like the administrative work and wanted to work on his own research projects. In April 1949, he resigned.

In 1952, he was invited by the Governor of Assam, Sir Jairamdas Daulatram. He had long talks with N. K. Rustamji, who was then the Advisor for tribal areas including what was then known as the North East Frontier Agency. At that time he toured extensively in Manipur. In December 1953 he was invited as an expert for interviewing candidates for the newly created cadre of the Indian Frontier Administrative Service. During this visit he was also invited by Pandit Jawaharlal Nehru, the then Prime Minister. He was approached to join the NEFA administration as a tribal advisor. It was at this time that he became an Indian citizen. The NEFA assignment changed the character of his research work. He had to survey the vast tract of mountainous country, stay in the interior for six to seven weeks, collect anthropological data, write reports on the general condition of the tribes and make suggestions to the administration. His main concern came to be Applied Anthroplogy. It was shortly after this that he wrote his book entitled *A Philosophy for NEFA*. In 1955 he was invited to deliver the Patel Memorial Lecture. The lectures were broadcast by the All India Radio. It was published as a book entitled *Philosophy of Love*. His basic ideas on this theme are as follows:

> Love illuminates knowledge. It gives meaning to beauty. It is the heart of virtue. Love's great artillery is more powerful than the weapons of hatred and properly directed, it can overcome them. Love gives dignity and stature to every man. It chastens the proud and redeems the sad, the guilty and the ashamed and gives to the poorest a meaning and reason for life. His personality is expanded to essence of unity with all things. Love brings him freedom from fear. It brings him peace and fills his soul with gentle power that will unite conflicting forces (1964 : 348).

In 1959 he was appointed the Chairman of the committee to study the working of the special multipurpose tribal blocks in the Community Development Programme. The Committee took about a year to complete its report. It was a long report running into 550 pages. It dealt with varied aspects of development. There were chapters on staffing problems and training, land, forest, agriculture and animal husbandry, health services, education and communication, women's programmes. The most important chapter was on the fundamentals of an approach to the tribes. Elwin bemoaned the absence of a tribal touch in the Community Development Programme. The term 'tribal touch' caused a certain amount of ridicule from uninformed and unsympathetic officials. Elwin emphasized that the administration has to ensure a square deal for the tribals, saving them from exploitation and ensure that they will be in a position to administer and develop their own areas in their own way. It does not mean a policy of mere preservation. It implies constant development and change, a change that will enrich their lives and bring them closer to Indian life and culture.

In April 1960, the Scheduled Tribes Commission was appointed. Shri U. N. Dhebar was its chairman and Elwin was one of its members. Elwin contributed substantially to the writing of its report. It insisted on getting a fair deal for tribal people, politically, economically and in the field of administration. It was a very lengthy report and Elwin was asked to abridge it. It was published under the title *A New Deal for Tribal India.*

With the advent of independence great schemes of development came into being. At this point of time, a two-fold policy was necessary for the tribals. One was to ensure that people were not culturally emasculated in a way that would rob them of their identity and character. India is like a rich and varied tapestry. Pandit Nehru had said that the tribes had to be encouraged to maintain their own culture. However, culture must be a living thing subject to change. Nehru's formula of developing the tribal people along the lines of their own tradition and genius seems to be the best policy. Elwin also emphasized that special care and protection given to the tribesmen must not cast any shadow on the unity of India. They must be educated to feel that they are full citizens of the republic with real rights and duties. Any tribal policy had to be based upon protection, development and social justice. There was no question of reviving the vanishing features of tribal life. It was more a problem of introducing change without being destructive of the best values of their life.

Elwin's first contribution to the philosophy of tribal change and development was contained in a report submitted to the Prime Minister, who wrote a long note giving a general support to his ideas. At the behest of the administration, Elwin wrote a book entitled *A Philosophy for NEFA.* This book was enlarged and republished in 1957 with a foreword by the Prime Minister in which he laid down his famous five points *(Panchsheel)* for the tribal people. The book dealt with tribal problems under the heading of material needs, psychological adaptation and social, religious and cultural problems. It emphasized that tribal rights in land and forest should be respected. A tribal leadership should be built up to take up the work of administration and development. Indigenous social and cultural institutions should be promoted. Tribal councils should be given wide powers. They should not be overwhelmed by a large number of development projects. In fact the idea was to hasten slowly so that the tribals adapt to the changes. The last recommendation was that development work should not be judged by the amount of money spent. The problem of indebtedness should be solved without delay partly by legislation and partly by availability of easy credit flow from the government. The problem of industrialization in tribal areas should take into consideration the rehabilitation of the dispossessed tribal people generously. It is necessary to fight the danger of pauperization and the perpetuation of backwardness. Unintelligent benevolence can be as great a danger as intelligent exploitation. Finally, we must try to ensure that people do not lose their freedom and zest for living.

Elwin's diagnosis of the tribal predicament was always contentious. A. V. Thakkar branded him as an isolationist, a politician who wanted to divide India and create an *aboriginalsthan,* a special protectorate to be ruled by an ethnographer. Elwin replied that he was only a protectionist. His most trenchant critic was G. S. Ghurye. The svat between them lasted for their whole life. The invectives used by both the scholars were no less than missiles in a real war. In his book entitled *Aboriginese. So Called and their Future* (1943), he charged Elwin as a no-changer and revivalist. In the same year, Elwin published a small book called *The Aboriginals* in which he defended strongly his stand on the tribals. His presidential address to the Anthropology Section of the Indian Science Congress in January 1944 was an exercise in self-justification. The title of his address was 'Truth in Anthropology'. He distanced himself from some British anthropologists who distinguished tribal religion from Hinduism.

In 1959, Ghurye published the second and enlarged edition of his earlier book under the title *The Scheduled Tribes.* Ghurye was incensed by the fact that his ideas did not carry any weight with the policy makers in the Government of India. In 1972, a volume on the tribals was published by the Vivekananda Kendra in Kanyakumari, describing Elwin as a noted anthropologist and a veteran son of India, who rendered life-long service to Indian tribes, perhaps as nobody else has done. In 1980, at the age of 87, Ghurye published a book entitled *The Burning Cauldron of North East India*, in which he charged Elwin as a British isolationist who exercised a malevolent influence on the elite of independent India, contributing to the Balkanisation of Bharat. Elwin was not there to rebut the arguments of Ghurye. But in one of his letters to Archer, he had referred to Professor Ghurye as an 'anthropological quisling'.

On his demise, S. C. Dube wrote the following: 'Elwin was not a dry-as-dust technician. He was a poet, artist and philosopher, who by his individual effort produced more and better work than many of the expensively staffed and large research organizations in the country.' Another eminent intellectual summed up the loss to literature and humanity in the following words : 'When the news came of Elwin's death, from secretariat to little mud huts, from NEFA to Madhya Pradesh, in urban artistic literary and journalistic circles as in remote villages, many thousands who had met or read of him knew that greatness had departed (Guha, 1999). W. G. Archer eulogized him as a pioneering ethnographer of the tribes of Central India.

The famous Africanist anthropologist, Victor Turner, acknowledged Elwin's vivid and elegant prose, while regretting the omission of a prior analysis of a social and political structure of the rules of property and inheritance as well as the rights and obligations of the different sections of the Saora community. In his book *The Craft of Social Anthropology* he complained that Elwin did not write as a social anthropologist but as eclectic ethnographer and in his interpretation used the language of the theologian. According to him, Elwin neglected the sociological analysis of the structural relationships within and between Saora villages. This would have helped a better understanding of Saora ritual. All that Elwin provided were bare morsels of sociological information interpolated in descriptions of religious customs.

Some of the tribes studied by Elwin were visited by professional anthropologists. The Muria, Ghotul, Baiga and the Bondo Highlanders have been restudied. In each case, the new scholars have been inspired by the depth of his fieldwork, his eye for detail and facile pen. In all these areas he is loved and vividly remembered as a defender of the tribal. The struggle between isolation and assimilation is continuing. The cultural battle is unresolved. In Independent India it is the pressure of economic development that has weighed heavily on the tribals. The forests have been denuded, their common property rights have almost been destroyed. The tribals have had to make way for factories and mines. In many areas, high dams have come up and they have become victims of development. The tribals effected by submergence bemoaned their loss of land and way of life. They refer to the timeless relation to the earth, the forest and the animals. There is concern for such groups among the intelligentsia. There is increased awareness of how isolated cultures have to pay an appalling price for development which they do not share.

In NEFA, Elwin established a Department of Research for writing monograph on the tribes of the region. A large number of monographs have been published covering most of the major tribes in Arunachal Pradesh.

The shadow of Elwin may be discerned in the report of the Bhuria Committee which was submitted to the Parliament to make Panchayati Raj real and effective in the Fifth Schedule areas. It was stressed that tribal societies have been practicing democracies inspired by egalitarian spirit. There is a harmonious relationship between man and nature. This would pave the way for sustainable development. However, with the incursion of outside populations, this state of affairs suffered serious blows. To meet these challenges, the tribal communities should be put in command of their economic resources. The Gram Sabhas and local settlements should be given the charge of land, forest and minerals. The traditional tribal conventions should govern them as far as possible.

In fact the tribal policy for which he worked and delineated as Nehru's *panchsheel* is the foundation of the tribal policy of the Government of India.

Elwin's Works

Elwin was a prolific writer. He wrote on Christ, St. Francis, Mahatma Gandhi's truth, *khadi* and on the philosophy of love. He was also a poet and authored novels and reports of various kinds.

The works listed below are those that are related to tribal studies, myths, folklore and art.

1. *Leaves from the Jungle: Diary of Life in a Gond Village,* 1936.
2. *The Baigas* London, John Murray 1939.
3. *Folktales of Chhattisgarh,* Calcutta, Oxford University Press, 1940.
4. *Loss of Nerve.* 1941
5. *The Agaria,* Calcutta, Oxford University Press, 1942.
6. *The Aboriginals,* Oxford University Press, Calcutta, 1943.
7. *Maria Murder and Suicide.* Calcutta, Oxford University Press, 1943.
8. Folktales of Mahakoshal, Calcutta, Oxford University Press 1944.
9. *Folktales of Maikal Hills* (with Shamlal Hivale) 1944.
10. *Muria and their Ghotul,* Oxfor University Press, Calcutta, 1947.
11. *Myths of Middle India,* Oxford University Press, Calcutta, 1949.
12. *Nagaland.* Adviser's Secretariat, Shillong, 1960.
13. *Tribal Art of Middle India.* Oxford University Press, Calcutta, 1951.
14. *Tribal Myths of Orissa.* Oxford University Press, Calcutta, 1954.
15. *Religions of an Indian Tribe.* Oxford University Press, Calcutta, 1955.
16. *A Philosophy for NEFA.* NEFA Administration, 1957.
17. *The Myths of the North Western Frontiers of India.* NEFA Administration 1958.
18. *The Art of North Eastern Frontier of India.* NEFA. Administration, 1959.
19. *India's Northeastern Frontier in the Nineteenth Century,* Oxford University Press, Calcutta, 1959.
20. *The Tribal World of Verrier Elwin.* Oxford University Press, Calcutta, 1964.
21. *Kingdom of the Young,* 1968.

12

S. C. DUBE: An Intellectual Portrait

Yogesh Atal

Twenty-fifth of July is the day of the birth of a man who never celebrated his birthday. On this day, in 1922, he was born in a small township of Seoni, in the then Central Provinces. His parents named him Shyama Charan. Born in a Brahmin caste, Dube was suffixed to his name. Shortened as S. C. Dube, his name was known the world over as one of India's most distinguished social scientists.

This great character in the history of Indian social sciences passed away on 4 February 1996 due to severe cardiac arrest. But he died a preferred death: "I should die with a pen in my hand and with an incomplete sentence on the paper". That is what happened. His three books were in press, and he had to contribute a paragraph, or two, on the phenomenon of "post-modernity" in one of his essays under print when suddenly he collapsed and had to be hospitalised. But he was conscious enough to insist on calling his publisher to his bed for final instructions. He promised to dictate those paragraphs to his wife as soon as he recovered. That time unfortunately never came. His plans to do a book with me in Hindi, upon my return to India after my retirement from UNESCO, also remain like an incomplete sentence. To be sure, he had several other projects in mind, but he yielded to destiny and left us deprived of his forthcoming contributions that would have further enriched Indian Social Science.

In his last correspondence to me, when I was stationed in Paris at UNESCO, he expressed the desire that I should come back to

India. "Now you should return"; this was the briefest letter I had received from his pen. Hidden in the handwritten text was perhaps the message that his end was near. I decided to pre-pone my home leave to meet him in January 1996. When I informed him of my decision, he asked me in his characteristic style to bring a good pipe and some fine tobacco. Knowing his deteriorating health, I was a bit hesitant to obey his command, but finally changed my mind and bought the stuff at the Charles de Gaulle airport while leaving for India.

Needless to say how keen was he to receive the gift. He immediately, and enthusiastically, filled the pipe and enjoyed the puff. Mrs. Dube stared at me, but she also had no courage to deny him this pleasure. It reminded me of an earlier occasion when he had to undergo an operation, and my surgeon brother had proscribed smoking. But he remained adamant and had his puff before going to bed the night before the surgery. I was told that managing him in the theatre posed problems for the anaesthetist[1] because of the complication caused by smoking, disregarding the instructions. My father went to see him the following day. He was greeted with full respect due to an elder. Taking advantage of this, my father politely mentioned to him that he should have followed the instructions of the doctor and refrained from smoking. To this, his reply was equally polite and yet firm: "how often do you heed to such advice?"

With all the ailments, Dube did not give up smoking. And he always smoked the pipe or, occasionally, the cigar. It was only in the aeroplanes that he switched to cigarettes, as pipe and cigar were not allowed. When my son designed the cover page for his book[2] that I had edited, he drew his pencil sketch but sans the pipe in the mouth. Professor Dube just patted him, acknowledging the message, but that was it.

After I met him upon my arrival from Paris in January 1996, I left Delhi to visit my relatives. During this time he suddenly fell ill and had to be hospitalised. I rushed to Delhi, but by then he was back home. We spent full two hours together, with my doctor brother in company. For the first time in my long association with him, Professor Dube rose from his bed to see me off and came right up to the lift. He let me go to my home town again and suggested that he would arrange a dinner upon my return when he would also invite some literary personalities commonly known to us. This gesture puzzled me. My brother interjected: "your visit this time has served as a tonic for him; he will recover soon, it seems". For me, it appeared demonstration of his strong will to fight the diseases –diabetes, heart, and....

I left for Udaipur in the hope that he will be back to normalcy and that we shall have some time together in the company of other common acquaintances. But that was not to be. The day I was preparing to return to Delhi from Udaipur, my brother phoned to tell me that he was no more. I regret my absence when he last breathed.

Over the years our relationship, which began in 1957 as that of a teacher-pupil, developed into fictive kinship of filial ties. While he treated me as his son, my children always addressed him as "uncle". When *Jan Satta*–the Hindi newspaper then edited by Shri Prabhash Joshi–devoted one full page to Professor Dube, I was also invited to contribute an article on him. The page carried a photograph of his nuclear family. When I met him during my sojourn in India soon after, he showed me the clipping and quibbled: "This photograph is incomplete. You are not there."

Some time later we spent a week together in Paris for a UNESCO meeting. There I fell ill and he took my full care. Oddly enough, there he once remarked: "I very much hope you would be there to give me *mukhagni*"[3]. That rendered me speechless. I feel lucky that I was at his cremation to pay my tearful obeisance; but the electronic crematorium did not allow performing the ritual of *mukhagni*. Of course, I was in the party which took his ashes for immersion into the river Ganga.

On his death, I felt orphaned once more.

II

At 74, he was alert, with a photographic memory, and an untiring urge to communicate his thoughts through his pen. In his later years, he switched over to Hindi in which he wrote numerous articles and made several speeches on topics ranging from hard core social sciences to contemporary concerns. He also served on the jury for the award of prizes in Hindi literature. He himself received the Moortidevi Award of the Bharatiya Jnanpeeth for 1993. Earlier he was awarded the S. C. Roy Gold Medal of the Asiatic

Society of West Bengal in 1976, and the Doctor of Letters by the Kashi Vidyapeeth in 1987. Even as a student of B.A. (Honours) he won the World Politics Essay Gold Medal in 1943.

Orphaned by his mother's death when he was barely seven, Dube was socialized by his father who was Manager of the Court of Wards in Chhattisgarh. His schooling started in poorly equipped village schools, and later in residential schools. From the Model School in Jabalpur he did his matriculation and then went to Nagpur for his further studies. Even while at school, Dube developed the habit of reading and writing. As a child, he began producing a hand-written magazine for his family audience. His first published articles were on films, and then on other social issues. These were published in prominent magazines of the time such as *Hans* and *Vishal Bharat*. After doing his B.A. Honours in political science, with a first class and first position, from Nagpur University, Dube began his career as a lecturer in political science at Hislop College, Nagpur. By this time, he had also published a collection of folk songs of Chhattisgarh in Hindi.

At Nagpur, he met Professor D.N. Majumdar of the Lucknow University–already a big name then in anthropology—who had come to deliver some lectures based on his field research amongst the tribals. Majumdar was impressed to see Dube's monograph on the folklore of Chhattisgarh and offered to publish its English version through the Ethnographic and Folk Culture Society that he had founded in Lucknow. With Majumdar, Dube also discussed his plans for doing a Ph. D. on the Kamars of Chhattisgarh. Dube also came in touch with Professor D. P. Mukerji, a pioneering sociologist teaching at Lucknow, through his sister-in-law (WiSi) –Mrs Sumati Mutatkar[4]—when he visited Nagpur. Herself a great musician, she knew Professor Mukerji because of his immense expertise in classical music.

It so happened that soon after this rendezvous, Dube was offered a lectureship at Lucknow University, in the department of political science. Dube's move to Lucknow brought him further closer to both Majumdar and Mukerji. Looking for a colleague to help him develop the newly created department of Anthropology[5], Majumdar invited Dube to teach anthropology classes in addition to his teaching assignment in political science. Dube, a political scientist by training, thus, formally entered the arena of anthropology and became one of the pioneers of Indian anthropology[6].

His popularity as a teacher and his work on the Kamar – his dissertation for the Ph.D. degree from the Nagpur University — drew the attention of Professor Christoph von Fürer-Haimendorf, who was then teaching at Osmania University in Hyderabad and was planning to return to England at the School of Oriental and African Studies, University of London. At his suggestion, the Osmania University appointed Dube to head the Department of Sociology. Thus Dube moved to Hyderabad and into the domain of sociology-anthropology. While teaching at Osmania, Dube undertook a project to study the village of Shamirpet. Although the book based on this study followed the technique of conventional ethnographic description, Dube made a significant departure in field research by deploying an interdisciplinary team of researchers, and studying a rural community rather than a tribal group. At this stage, the School of African and Oriental Studies (SOAS) of the London University invited him, in 1952, as a Visiting Lecturer in Indian Anthropology. During his sojourn in London he completed his manuscript on the Shamirpet and gave it to Routledge & Kegan Paul, who chose to publish it in their Series titled *International Library of Sociology and Social Reconstruction.*

Upon return from London, he joined the Cornell-India Research Team and supervised field work in the Rankhandi-Jhaberan area of Uttar Pradesh along with some noted American anthropologists[7]. This assignment earned him also the visiting Professorship at Cornell. Returning from there, he joined the Anthropological Survey of India as the Head of the newly created Nagpur Station. Only a few months later, in the summers of 1957, he was appointed to the Chair of Anthropology at the University of Saugar when he was still under thirty-five–the youngest person to be appointed to professorship in those days.

It may be mentioned that until 1957, the University of Saugar had the Department of Anthropogeography, which was split into two separate departments of anthropology and geography in that year. Dube was the first professor of the newly created department at Sagar. In 1960, he went on lien to join as Director of the Central Institute of Training and Research in Community Development at Mussoorie. The Institute later on was reconstituted as National

Institute of Community Development and was relocated at Hyderabad with Dube as the first Principal.

As academic administrator, Professor Dube also functioned as Director of the Indian Institute of Advanced Study, Shimla, Vice Chancellor of Jammu University, and Chairman of the University Grants Committee of Madhya Pradesh. Apart from his assignments at London School of Oriental and African Studies, and at Cornell, he did an 18-month consultancy at the United Nations Asia-Pacific Development Centre in Kuala Lumpur, Malaysia. He was also associated in various capacities with UNESCO, United Nations University, and the East-West Center, Hawaii.

III

Professor Dube had an enormous circle of friends, colleagues, and admirers in fields as diverse as academics, politics, the civil service, and the media. He was a great host who welcomed every visitor irrespective of his age or status, and he excelled in conversations on diverse topics that matched the interests of the visitors. Other than English and Hindi, in which he was proficient both as a writer and speaker, Dube conversed with ease in Marathi, Urdu, Bundelkhandi, Chhattisgarhi, and the dialects of Western Uttar Pradesh. Even to his juniors and to those who were his subordinates – the clerks and *chaprasis*, he spoke in a polished and courteous language. While riding a taxi driven by a Sikh chauffer he would never forget to seek his permission to smoke.

Dube was a perfect gentleman; a thoroughly cultured persona. He was an example of a queer mix of modernity with tradition; he displayed objectivity of a social scientist alongside the sensitivity of a litterateur; he occupied positions of power and yet he encouraged disagreement and dissent. Not the founder of any school, not a narrow specialist, but rather a wanderer in search of new pastures, Professor Dube was an investigator of the contemporary against the backdrop of history and against a vision of the future. He was a frontiersman, an itinerant explorer of new territories for research and reflection. To call him an anthropologist or a sociologist is to force him in a narrow cage. He transgressed disciplinary boundaries and encouraged others to do the same. It would be most appropriate to call him a social scientist. He did not pay any attention to his critics who questioned his credentials[8].

Delivering the First D. N. Majumdar Memorial Lecture in 1972, he foresaw the contours of a newly developing paradigm for social sciences. Let me quote his prophesy:

> By and large, academic anthropology in India continues to maintain a semblance of the classical "grand design" and keeps within its fold cultural and social anthropology, physical anthropology, and prehistory. It is becoming increasingly evident, however, that this federal character will not last. Ethno-linguistics could never become as effective a part of anthropology in India as it did in the United States. Now prehistory is discovering its natural affinity with archaeology and is slowly being absorbed into that discipline. Physical anthropology remains attached to cultural anthropology and is not making a determined bid to find a place for itself among the life sciences. This has contributed to its retardation. Anthropology and sociology have come closer in spite of the presence, in both these disciplines, of purists who make a deliberate attempt to avoid the pollution of their "own" subject by the other. Evidently, these purists are fighting a losing battle. With anthropologists seeking a new and larger unit of study the fusion of social anthropology and sociology is imminent. If we have to move from micro to macro studies this is both necessary and desirable. Nostalgia for the academic tradition and false pride in disciplinary labels are bound to be counter-productive. Those who care for understanding are increasingly rejecting the artificial disciplinary boundaries. Vested interests, rather than reason, appear to account for the continuing clash.[9]

Dube is mainly known for his books on *Indian Village* and *India's Changing Villages*–both published by Routledge & Kegan Paul in 1955 and 1958 respectively. Earlier he published *Folk Songs of Chhattisgarh* (1948) and *The Kamar* (1951)[10]. I remember to have also seen his tiny text book on anthropology, published from Hyderabad.[11] His other books include *Explanation and Management of Change, Contemporary India and its Modernization, On Crisis and Commitment in Social Sciences* (edited by Yogesh Atal), *Modernization and Development: The Search for Alternatives, Indian Society, Tradition and Development, Development Perspectives for the 1980s,* and *Understanding Change: Anthropological and Sociological Perspectives.* Besides this, he has authored eight books in Hindi. His book on *Indian Village* has been translated in several Indian languages, beginning with Hindi that I did in 1974. His book on Indian society, published by the National Book Trust has also been translated into several Indian languages. NCERT has also published his elementary textbook in sociology, which was available in both English and Hindi. *Manav aur Sanskriti* is a text book on anthropology in Hindi, first published in 1960; I helped him in that project, and jointly we did coin some terms – for example, *sambodh* for concept, *matuleya* for avunculate, *pitrashvsreya* for amitate, etc.

Quite individual and distinctive in style, Professor Dube was very versatile; he was a prolific writer and an eloquent speaker both in English and in Hindi. As a teacher, he enthralled his students and inspired them to work and to explore uncharted territories. As a frontiersman, he did not create a "school" of his own. His doors were open to all[12]; even those who were not his formal students felt at home with him. He showed his genuine enthusiasm over the achievements not only of his colleagues and students but even of those who may have been his opponents. Wherever he went, he spotted the sparks, and encouraged them to become torches. Ultramodern in his life style, dubbed as a "deluxe professor", Dube was a teacher in the true Indian tradition. A great intellectual, an inspiring teacher, a generous human being, and a secular Indian, Dube was distinctly different, and nobly national. To his students and fellow colleagues, neither did he discourage from exposure to the wider world, nor did he encourage insulation of disciplinary boundaries at the national level. He kept his ideological commitments away from serious objective analysis of Indian reality. He was all for a judicious mix of available approaches and techniques to maximise the realistic understanding of the social phenomena.

Professor Dube's intellectual journey coincides with the journey of Indian sociology and anthropology. He played an influential role in shaping these twin disciplines. Having a degree in political science, and having taught the subject at Hislop College, Nagpur and at Lucknow, he was increasingly drawn to anthropology. As a researcher, he chose to be an ethnographer, studying for his Ph.D. the Kamar of Chhattisgarh, and then moved on to produce the first full-length monograph on an Indian village that became a classic, and made a publishing history with several editions and translations in various vernaculars of this country[13]. This book did not only mark a departure from tribal studies by an anthropologist, it also ushered in an era of team research. His next publication related to the study of India's Community Development Programme that was launched by the Government of independent India to bring about planned change in rural India. This book again made a radical departure. As the title itself suggests, it focussed on *India's Changing Villages* and analysed the "human factor" in Community Development. It is interesting that in the first book on Kamar, there was very little reference to change; the second book concluded with a chapter on change; and the third book was fully devoted to the changing scene. While in the preparation of the second book, Professor Dube involved a multidisciplinary team from his own University; the third book resulted as part of an international team, called the Cornell-India Project. And from there on, Professor Dube chose to write on broader issues related to development, bureaucracy, communication, leadership, modernization and tradition. I must, however, put it on record that he undertook two research projects for the Planning Commission on "Rural Health and Hygiene", and on "Leadership and Communication" while in Sagar[14], in which he was joined by his wife, Dr Leela Dube, who supervised the entire field work. While both the projects were completed and their reports submitted to the sponsors, they never saw the light of the day. I had seen the manuscripts ready for the press. But it is not known why did he not publish them.

Professor Dube set the trend way back in the 1950s for village studies and for the study of change. His was the first full-length monograph on an Indian village; and it has become a classic reference. Again, on India's Community Development, he came out with the very first monograph in 1958. Both these publications made him a pioneer in village studies in India.[15] He was concerned about the gaps in the ethnographic map of India, and the need for monographs on tribes and villages. He also wanted sociologists to document the changes that were occurring. He encouraged his students to work on topics such as the changing frontiers of caste, unity and extensions of an Indian village, cross-cultural comparative studies, multi-village studies on health and hygiene, on leadership and communication, and on minority groups such as the Anglo-Indians. His own field work took him to tribal Chhattisgarh, Andhra Pradesh, Uttar Pradesh, and Madhya Pradesh.

Dube was, in the real sense, a frontiersman. Rather than harping on the same theme and concentrating on a narrow specialty, he chose the challenging task of exploring new territories and extending the frontiers of knowledge to make Indian sociology more relevant to the cause of national development. He was an ardent advocate of interdisciplinary orientation and a promoter of research interests on a wide range of topics of contemporary significance. He did not believe in creating a "school" of his own and building a cadre of faithful followers. He encouraged his students to participate in the adventure of ideas, and to try fresh initiatives rather than walk on trodden paths. He did not allow his class of students to become an insulated endogamous group; he encouraged his colleagues and students to have wide ranging affairs with different intellectual traditions. That is the reason that he is regarded as pioneer in several branches of sociology and social anthropology in India: political sociology, sociology of mass communication, economic development, and rural development, sociology of education, modernization and development. In each of these fields, he made seminal contributions by raising issues of theoretical and national relevance. His writings led many scholars to focus on different issues and carry out field investigations.

Dube wrote in simple language without unduly burdening the text with abstract and abstruse concepts. That does not mean that he wrote as a journalist. While reviewing his *Indian Village,* James Silverberg asked the reader to read in between the lines for theory. The descriptive accounts were couched in structural-functional terms, and the analysis of change invariably focused on the repercussions of an event of change in all aspects of the system – both cultural and social.

IV

We may briefly summarise Dube's conceptual contributions to the understanding of Indian society.

The Concept of an Indian Village

In his paper on "Social Structure and Change in Indian Peasant Communities", presented at the Third World Congress of Sociology, held in France in 1956, Dube elaborated the framework that he had suggested in his *Indian Village.* "While it is true", Dube wrote in his book, "that many problems are common to the entire countryside, this practice tends to give one an impression that the village as a social and cultural unit possesses a basically uniform organization and structure of values all over the Indian subcontinent...For a proper understanding of their social structure as well as their problems, it is necessary to classify them into clearly distinguishable types. For such classification several criteria could be employed, including, among others, the following :

(i) Size, population and land area.
(ii) Ethnic composition and caste-constitution.
(iii) Pattern of land ownership.
(iv) Structure of authority and power hierarchy.
(v) Degree of isolation.
(vi) Local traditions." (Dube, 1955: 3)

Dube cautioned his readers that in ..."view of the operation of factors delineated above, it is difficult to regard any one village as typical or representative of rural India as a whole. In fact, I would go a step further to say that such a village could hardly be regarded as representative even of its culture-area, except in a very general way" (Ibid: 6). In view of this, he recommended a "series of studies of village communities from different parts of the country covering the many divergent patterns of organization and ethos. Until this is done our picture of social systems in rural India will remain vague and inadequate" (Ibid: 6-7).

While hinting at the need for village studies in different parts of the country, Dube did provide elements of the definition of an Indian village. He mentioned three features that seem to be common (Dube, 1955: 7-8):

1. "As a territorial, as well as social, economic and ritual unit, the village is a separate and distinct entity".
2. "These settlements have a composite population comprising a number of groups belonging to different Hindu castes, and in some cases to tribes as well as to other religious groups. As far as the Hindu section of the population goes, these diverse groups are inter-dependent and integrated in the social, economic, ritual and administrative organization of the community. No caste alone is self-sufficient, for it requires the services of several

other occupational castes which hold the monopoly of certain crafts and professions. This system of co-operative labour, based on a pattern of inter-caste relations approved by tradition, is not confined only to economic activities but also extends to ceremonial and ritual life. The hierarchical organization of castes within the community is so fixed that the structural patterns of rural India that the tribal as well as the non-Hindu ...segments of the population come to be regarded as other castes in the village."

3. "The members of this local group are bound together by ties of mutual and reciprocal obligations."

Advancing further his conception of the village in India, Dube said "we have to view the village both as a distinct isolable entity and as a link in the chain of a wider inter-village organization. An individual village derives some of the characteristic features of its organization from the great national tradition of India, while the traditions of the region or the culture area in which it is located also contribute substantially toward shaping its value-orientation, ethos, and general pattern of life" (Dube, 1955: 259). He felt that the Indian village is "sufficiently isolable, but it is not an isolate, and has therefore to be viewed as a community within a larger community" (*Ibid*).

Establishing links of the village community with the wider society, Dube suggested that the village community is to be seen as organised both in terms of kin and caste and also in terms of territorial affinities. Thus, an individual is linked to the wider community, on the one hand, through his family, group of near kin, lineage, affinal kin, sub-caste, caste, and Varna; and on the other, through family, village, inter-village organization, region and nation. These two sets of groupings constitute the social structure of a village as a subsystem of the national society. This is shown in the following diagram: [16]

"The village as a unit of social structure cuts across the boundaries of kin and caste and unites a number of unrelated families within an integrated multicaste community". Dube classified Indian village communities in terms of their structure into three main groups: (i) single settlement village; (ii) nucleated village; and (iii) dispersed village. According to him, the "first two have a number of common features. They are stable populations generally, with a common past and a number of shared values. They recognize and emphasize their individual identity, and in certain situations act as a unit. Their economy is built largely around agriculture; economically and socially the agricultural castes are the most important, while the non-agricultural occupations are subsidiary to agriculture. Land is greatly loved and valued, and the community as a whole shares some common problems and acculturative influences. Being largely caste-structured, the community finds itself integrated in terms of traditional patterns that define the interactions between the different segments of the community in the fields of economy, socio-religious life, and village administration" (Dube, 1990: 112). He offers the general outline of the social structure of Indian peasant communities as a "structural model". In suggesting this, Dube said that "while few village communities will present exactly the same picture, a large number of them will be found to possess the major characteristics and features delineated above".

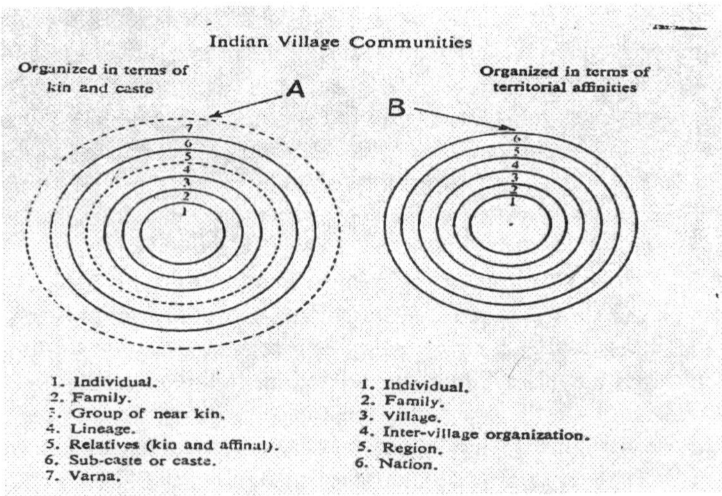

Paradigm for Analysing Change in India

Dube suggested that changes should be located in the various units of the social structure. In doing so, various forces and factors operating in the society must be identified and the outcome of the interplay of these should be studied to gauge the trends of change. Indian social structure is exposed to a number of influences. Here are some of the prominent ones:

(i) Western Impact: resulted in the introduction of the new administrative pattern resulting in the evolution of a set of executive, judicial and legislative institutions;

(ii) Modern systems of transport and communication, and industrialization have given greater national cohesion to the land;

(iii) Western-type education also has been influential in bringing about change;

(iv) Nationalist revival set in motion a series of important changes; and

(v) Nation-building activities of the government in the British days and community development activities after independence served as powerful influences.

As a consequence of these forces and factors, many changes were noticeable in the structure and organization of Indian village communities. Some of these listed by him are:

(i) Shift from an ascribed status system to an achieved status system. "The society being largely caste-structured, the ascribed or caste status of a person still contributes materially toward determining his status, but there are unmistakable signs that a rival system is growing, which takes sufficient account of an individual's distinctive qualities and attainments in ranking him".

(ii) "While there is a general loosening of caste structure at one end, there are signs that it is consolidating at the other end in some rather unexpected directions".

(iii) There is the "general weakening, and even breakdown of the formal authority structure of individual castes".

(iv) "In recent years, there has undoubtedly been a change from a kin-oriented outlook to an interest-oriented outlook, and a gradual breaking up of large effective kin groups has been in evidence".

(v) "While higher levels of the community take to modernization, the lower levels take to Sanskritization".

Writing in the 1950s, Dube did not subscribe to the view that the village community was disintegrating. While recognising the trends of change that were affecting the traditional social structure,

Dube was of the view that because "the primary groups of kin and caste have continued to be effective units of social control even in semi-urbanized areas, there is no immediate threat to their position in the village communities, and consequently the latter are likely to continue to be organized on their basis. Even with the growth of rural towns, these structural features are not likely to change beyond recognition" (*Ibid*: 114-115).

Phenomenon of Directed Cultural Change

Dube's involvement in the study of the Community Development project in a district in Uttar Pradesh led him to focus on the "human factor" in a programme of planned culture change. While his formulations about social and cultural change in India as a whole took note of the general trends initiated by the processes of Westernization and Modernization that became prominent during the British rule, his intensive study of a project area helped him understand the actual dynamics of change that resulted in either acceptance or rejection of innovations introduced by external change agents. His book, *India's Changing Villages*, offers insights through carefully prepared case studies into the dynamics of change. The personality factor – both of the change agent and the recipient, social status of the recipient, administrative rigmarole, and cultural-traditional factors including faction-politics and group-dynamics within the village were identified as key variables affecting the prospects of any innovation.

In his later writings, Dube built upon his field experiences and readings of sociological and anthropological theory to reflect upon India's development. All his essays and books, published after *India's Changing Villages* are devoted to theoretical explications of the concepts of "Tradition" and "Development". They provide good guides to new researchers and policy makers as they clarify the concepts and suggest directions for interpreting change and developing blueprints for development. They can well be called paradigmatic essays.

Perspective on Tradition

Dube drew attention to the fact that early thinking on development not only neglected culture, but also regarded tradition as an obstruction to modernity. "The basic flaw in a great deal of thinking

Dube was, however, not an advocate of an insulated social science for India. In fact, he took issues with those adumbrationists who assigned all virtue to sacred texts and derived explanations for the existing reality from the prescriptive commentaries of ancient sages. He was equally concerned about the emergence of radical criticism of the structure of Indian society and of those scholars who had rediscovered Marx. He was of the view that such critics function only as a demolition squad and rarely produce dependable Marxist analyses.

Dube was disturbed about the lack of relevance in social science research, and was concerned about the blind pursuit of the trivia. "Why the response of Indian sociology to the travail and trauma of independence was so feeble and why its efforts to deal with the ferment and convulsions characterizing the post-independence decade were so half-hearted? Why have we not produced a relevant and meaningful sociology – a science imbued with social concerns, a discipline with a human meaning and purpose?" Commenting on the kind of research that was carried out and reported, he wrote: "Through a series of logical acrobatics, tortuous statistical procedures, and mystifying model building we appear to arrive at convoluted generalizations that often turn out to be statements of the obvious, their pseudo-profound terminology notwithstanding". In his address to a Plenary session at the time of the Tenth International Congress of Anthropological and Ethnological Sciences, held in December 1978 in New Delhi, he said that the Third World anthropologists have not played "a more decisive role" to "enrich the discipline with the articulation of a grass roots consciousness...Some of the self-proclaimed leaders of the profession in these countries have not been able to decolonise their minds either in respect of theory and method, or in the choice of themes for research and analytical treatment....Their intellectual styles continue to be imitative." Without hiding his anger at such development, he boldly remarked: "A curious aspect of international social science is that some operators of little academic worth, who are subject of endless private jokes and a favourite theme of discussion at cocktail parties, can get catapulted to dizzy heights. This recognition of chicanery and willingness to serve any patron confuses the honest social scientists."[17]

Advocacy for Commitment

Dube was of the view that Indian sociology is suffering from a certain crisis of commitment. Although he did not specifically define his concept of commitment, one can decipher some of its indicators from his writings. He expected a committed social scientist to carry out 'relevant' research, focussing on national needs and key problems of vital concern to society. He also preferred the role of a social critic for the social scientist. Regarding the distinction between 'pure' and 'applied' research as artificial and futile, he wanted a committed social scientist to carry out "purposive research on vital and live issues of the day". Dube made a fine distinction between *objectivity* and *ethical neutrality*. "*Objectivity* involves also questioning and evaluating the assumptions implicit in theoretical formulations and research programmes. *Ethical neutrality* can induce one into playing it safe and even turning away from controversial issues; objectivity makes more exacting demands. Balanced appraisals are a better help to thought than prescriptive arguments. Objectivity does not rule out deep human concerns; it should not."

In my Introduction to the book of his essays, I took a somewhat different stand. While he disagreed with what I had to say, he did not protest and let it remain. Let me quote what I had to say:

> "To me, this appears to be too fine a distinction, and one on which many may not agree. The question of commitment is not easy to resolve. Commitment to what? To whom? Who shall decide whether one is committed or not? Can there be consensus on commitment – even on relevance, national needs and priorities, or on solutions to problems? A social critic opposed to the establishment may be viewed as non-committed. Similarly, someone taking sides of the establishment –and thus regarded as committed – may be decried as a sycophant or, worse, an opportunist. Furthermore, where does one draw a line between journalism and social science? ...I feel that ethical neutrality is one of the elements of objectivity. While I agree that in the selection of a topic for research, or fixing priorities, there is no need to be ethically neutral–to that extent commitment to national goals in whatever they are defined is possible – but the treatment of the problem will have to follow the principles and procedures of science. The danger that a "committed" scholar would manipulate facts cannot be ruled out. Professor Dube himself makes reference to Project Camelot and Project Agile. As long as the two roles – that of a social scientist and of a committed citizen – are separately defined

> and performed distinctly, there is no problem, but if the two are allowed to be merged, they create a crisis of identity. We must accept that everything a social scientist writes is not social science. His being a social scientist is his public status–his description in terms of his major preoccupation, but like any other individual, he occupies various other statuses and changes many caps. When an economist or a sociologist becomes a minister, he may have occasions to use his economics or sociology in that role, but he is certainly not doing economics or sociology most of the time that he plays the role of a minister."[18]

But he was firm on his position. In his reflective essay, published in the *Festschrift* that I edited in his honour, he said : "I will continue to plead for commitment even if some of my own students, including very dear ones[19], misunderstand". Elaborating his view, he further said :

> "At no stage have I had a commitment to a person, a party, or an ideology, but at all times I did think of our commitment to the people we most often study. Do they have a voice in the decisions concerning their lives? Do they have choices and options in respect of what are known as development aims? In the name of 'national' development must they suffer the erosion of their cultural autonomy and the loss of their self-esteem? Must they accept goals formulated and foisted upon them by the elite? Is it their inexorable fate to gradually lose control over their resources, accept servitude, and submit to frequent uprooting for a kind of development that benefits them only minimally? The ambit of individual commitment, in my view, included such questions of public policy. Anthropology and sociology, in addition to their scholarly function, should also seek to give voice to the voiceless. I detest populist rhetoric. Anthropology and sociology should resist the temptation to coin catchy slogans. But their analytical insights and cultural criticism should certainly bring to light the degenerative and destructive aspects of well-intentioned policies."[20]

Concern for Proper Growth of the Social Sciences in India

As was said earlier, Dube was worried about the deterioration in standards in Indian social science. He expressed this worry in several of his essays. His book *On Crisis and Commitment in Social Sciences* represents this concern. To quote him:

> "The major weaknesses of Indian social science are all too well known. Both in teaching as well as research we place excessive reliance on foreign models. The so-called international styles of scholarship,

rather than contemporary national relevance, determine the content of our university curricula as well as the themes and models of our research. In general we fail to ask the right questions, and all too willingly accept the tyranny of established concepts. Our efforts reflect the absence of conceptual innovativeness and methodological rigour. In order to equal or excel our counterparts abroad in technical virtuosity we willingly undergo the torture of techniques and often end up murdering by methodology, both research problems and their insightful analyses. ..Our theoretical constructs are largely vacuous and we are timid in responding to the challenges of the day."[21]

He drew our attention to the following weaknesses in Indian sociology and anthropology:

1. The discipline appears to have become prisoner of a pattern. There is need for a different perspective: "In the world of today the *problems* to be investigated matter much more than the disciplinary labels under which research is conducted. These problems are best investigated through interdisciplinary perspectives and research procedures....but this needs most careful thought and adequate intellectual preparation. Runaway enthusiasm for a newly discovered interest can be self-defeating" (51).
2. "Our attachment to foreign conceptual models and research tools has been pathetic" (51).
3. "One of our basic weaknesses is that we are not asking the right questions" (52).
4. We have been overly concerned with segmental perfection to the exclusion of valid macro generalizations."
5. "We appear to have emphasized the autonomy of academic pursuits so much that they have been largely divested of social concerns".
6. "There is a regrettable absence of *meaningful* social criticism" (53).
7. "While a proliferation of institutions of social science research has occurred, little attention appears to have been given to the problem of institution-building" (54)[22].

Dube was very cautious about theory. He admitted that "we need sound theory. But how do we go about it? Shall we start running from nowhere in hot pursuit of theory? Such a blind race would yield perhaps only vacuous and spurious theory. The emphasis on theory building should not imply the undervaluation of data gathering...It is not being suggested that social sciences can rest with assembling a great mass of data". However, he cautioned that "we should not fail to be cognizant of the tyranny of established concepts. Without wide-awake awareness they can set invisible limits to thinking and data gathering." In his own writings, he never displayed over-enthusiasm for theory with the result that his reviewers talked of his "lucid style"[23], implying thereby that there was absence of theory in his work. To such a comment his retort was: "To be readable is not necessarily to be un-scholarly; and a social science book may have functions beyond the mere cultivation of scholarship". He discouraged "narcissistic intellection and the feverish search for theory" for, he felt that, such "theory, often phoney, distracts attention from larger issues of public policy...Theory is important, but the search for theory at the cost of human concerns is very disconcerting... And why do we shy away from hard and sustained field work? I am all too aware of the limitations of empiricism, but I am more distrustful of theorizing without a solid data base."[24] Prefacing this statement, Dube said that his "concerns are more serious...Why the loss of interest in tribal studies, especially at a juncture when the emergence of new forces is creating unprecedented turbulence in several tribal areas."[25]

Utilization of Social Sciences

In making critical remarks about the growth of Indian sociology and anthropology, nay the entire gamut of social sciences, Dube showed his concern for the utilization of social sciences for public policy. In his Paper presented at the National Seminar on *Social Sciences and Social Realities,* held at the Indian Institute of Advanced Study, Simla, in 1973, Dube listed six major possibilities of the utilization of social science research towards national development. I reproduce them below:

1. "Social science research throws up valuable background data from which the planner can make his own assessment of the prevailing situation, especially of the magnitude, complexity, and ramifications of the problems he has to handle.

2. Carefully designed analytical studies can illuminate critical areas of policy. The overt and covert dimensions of a given problem emerging in such studies provide the planner with a measure of foresight to deal with them effectively and efficiently.
3. These studies open up the possibility of testing the validity of the assumptions that must, of necessity, be made by the planner in setting his proximate and ultimate objectives.
4. They enable the planner to estimate the possible consequences and costs of the different choices available to him in determining the path for the attainment of his goals.
5. Diagnostic studies suggest *where* and *why* particular projects go wrong. Their unintended consequences are also brought to light.
6. Wide dissemination of social science research findings increases general awareness in respect of the situation to be met as well as the policy designed for this purpose. This may enhance credibility of particular policies and prepare the people for them. It may also help towards building up popular pressures for the reformulation of certain policies or for weeding them out altogether."[26]

The message that we get from Professor Dube is significant. As social scientists, we must not shut our eyes from issues of public policy, and we must not give up our strength that lies in empirical fieldwork. We must resist the temptation to be theoretical without firm grip over the data, and we must not offer unsolicited prescriptions for the problems that we hardly understand.

While he frankly admitted that "Social science research, let there be no illusion, is not a substitute for national development", he emphasised the explanatory power of the social sciences. As he grew in stature, Professor Dube was increasingly drawn towards policy making and planning. He continued to encourage young scholars to do rigorous field work, but he devoted his energies to engage in dialogue with policy makers and in popularising social sciences through his writings and lectures. His books were essential readings for the new initiates in administration. He also used popular weeklies, such as *Dharmayug* and *Saptahik Hindustan* – the most widely read Hindi magazines – to popularise social science orientation. Both within administration and in the reading public, S.C. Dube gained popularity, and succeeded in popularising social sciences. He was one of the few who could write and speak with the same ease and facility in both Hindi and in English. He also encouraged me to do the same.

V

In his contribution to the *Festschrift* that I edited in his honour in 1993, he looked back at the path he had travelled in an essay that was aptly titled "The Journey So Far". He remarked: "Indian sociology and social anthropology represent a significant intellectual quest. Now their edifice is solid; ideas-wise they matter...The younger generation has taken over with élan and vigour new themes and made some significant innovations...These developments are taking place in an environment of free dialogue and discussion – a fact that augurs well for the health and future of the disciplines".[27]

He began his end piece with the words:

> "I am coming to the end of my story, but it is not quite the end...A working retirement can be a glorious experience. Free from the constraints and pressures of office one can do just what one likes. I am in this happy position."[28]

He knew, however, that he was going. But he did not accept the defeat. In his letter of 8 August 1995, he wrote to me: "...my health is deteriorating and work seems to be the best remedy."

Like a sage, Professor Dube died in harness.

But did he die? Could he?

Notes

1. My own sister-in-law, wife of the surgeon.
2. *On Crisis and Commitment in Social Sciences*, New Delhi, Abhinav Publications, 1983.
3. It is the Hindu custom that the son of the dead performs the rituals at the cremation ground, and he is the one who lights the funeral pyre by pouring *ghee* in the mouth of the dead and putting embers into it. This is called *mukhagni.*
4. She retired as Professor of Music from Delhi University. She gave several performances at the All India Radio. She died recently in 2007.
5. It is interesting to note that Anthropology was introduced at Lucknow in the Department of Economics, along with Sociology. Professor D.N.

Majumdar was recruited in this Department as a Lecturer in Primitive Economics–the pioneers thus engineered infiltration of growing disciplines in conventional courses to overcome needless bureaucratic hurdles. After a few years, Majumdar succeeded in convincing University authorities for the establishment of a separate department of Anthropology. This is the reason that many senior Anthropologists and Sociologists who had graduated from Lucknow in those years had their formal degrees in Economics. And they pursued an interdisciplinary approach.

6. However, some later day puritans questioned his credentials and uncharitably referred to him as "self-selected anthropologist".
7. The American Team was also interdisciplinary, but headed by anthropologist Morris E. Opler, who had also written Foreword to Dube's book on *Indian Village*, based on Shamirpet village.
8. Concluding his essay , "Journey so far", in the *Festschrift* I edited in his honour, he wrote: "About evaluations of my work I am not much bothered...Let time and the wide world judge... A popular Sanskrit saying portrays the intellectual scene pithily: 'Opinions differ from head to head, the expression differs from mouth to mouth.' Let heads think with reason and mouths speak without malice."
9. S. C. Dube, *Social Sciences in Changing Society: D. N. Majumdar Memorial Lectures 1972*. Ethnographic and Folk Culture Society, Lucknow, 1973, p. 49.
10. *The Kamar* has been republished by Oxford University Press in 2003.
11. Since it does not figure in any of his bibliographies, I take it that he disowned that publication.
12. Concluding his piece titled "The Journey so far" in the *Festschrift* that I edited for him, he wrote: "Our house is open to young colleagues who seek to discuss their ideas and projects, and many of them receive our warm welcome". See *Understanding Indian Society* (ed. Yogesh Atal), p. 42.
13. It may be noted that in 1955 four books on Indian villages came out, but Dube's was the only full-length monograph; others were collections of essays, reporting the progress of field work.
14. I worked as a research investigator in one of them.
15. Both S. C. Dube and M. N. Srinivas are known for their pioneering work on village India, and both inspired several young researchers to undertake village studies. But Srinivas gained popularity because of his concepts of *Sanskritization* (published in *The Far Eastern Quarterly*, Vol. XV, No.4, August 1956), and of *Dominant Caste* (published in *American Anthropologist*, Vol.6, No. 1, 1959). His book on Rampura that threw up these concepts was published much later in 1976 as *The Remembered Village* (Oxford University Press), based on his

memory as his field notes were destroyed by arson at Stanford where he had gone to do the book after so many years of his field work. Fame came to Srinivas earlier than his first full-length monograph on Rampura; Dube earned a name and fame through his *Indian Village* way back in 1955 when no other village ethnography was published; and it remains the most quoted reference.

16. Taken from his essay presented at the Third world Congress of Sociology in 1956, and reproduced in his book, *Tradition and Development*, Vikas Publishing House, New Delhi, 1990, p. 108.
17. See Atal (ed.) *S. C. Dube On Crisis and Commitment in Social Sciences*, 1983, p. 61.
18. See Yogesh Atal, *S. C. Dube On Crisis and Commitment in Social Sciences*, Abhinav Publications, New Delhi. 1983. "Introduction" page 11.
19. This was a reference to me on my above comment.
20. See Yogesh Atal (ed.) *Understanding Indian Society: Festschrift in honour of Professor S. C. Dube*, New Delhi, Har Anand Publications, 1993, page 23.
21. From his essay on "The Social Sciences: Crisis and Commitment", in *On Crisis and Commitment in Social Sciences* (Atal ed.), 1983: p. 15.
22. From his *Social Sciences in Changing Society: D.N. Majumdar Memorial Lectures 1972* (pub in 1973) pages 51-54.
23. In his reflective essay in the *Festschrift* issued in his honour, he responded to this criticism in the following manner: "I suspect that at least a few of these observations are intended as left-hand compliments. This raises two important and interconnected issues– of the audience of the social scientist and of style. Are we always and necessarily addressing our professional peers alone? Or do we also have to carry our findings to the general reader? If an interventionist role is envisioned for the social sciences, should we not make our research results intelligible to the policy maker? I believe that social sciences have a conscientization function and a policy dimension. Recognizing them we have to adopt an appropriate idiom and style. Tortuous, abstruse, and convoluted writing may give the illusion of profundity, at least to the uninitiated." "The Journey So Far" in *Understanding Indian Society* (ed. Yogesh Atal); New Delhi, Har Anand Publications. 1993. p. 34.
24. *Ibid.*, 40.
25. *Ibid.*
26. *On Crisis and Commitment in the Social Sciences*, p. 29-30.
27. From "The Journey So Far" p. 40-41.
28. *Ibid.*

Books on S. C. Dube

Atal, Yogesh (ed.) 1993, *Understanding Indian Society: Festschrift in Honour of Professor S.C.Dube*. New Delhi, Har Anand Publications.

Dube, Leela and Sudheesh Pachauri (ed.) 1997, *Seemanto Ke Anveshak* (Hindi). Delhi, Vaani Prakashan.

This bibliography is not complete. It does not include Professor Dube's extensive writings in Hindi periodicals from 1980 onwards nor does it list his frequent contributions to English and Hindi newspapers and magazines. In his early career, he wrote articles for *Vishal Bharat*, *Hans*, etc., and later he wrote quite frequently in *Dharmayug* and *Saptahik Hindustan*–both of which had a wide readership and thus became instruments for the diffusion of social science culture through the writings of social scientists such as Professor S.C. Dube. It has not been possible to list his many broadcasts, most of which were published in journals and annual anthologies of All India Radio. His Forewords to books and the book reviews done by him do not find a place here. The most glaring omission is the non-inclusion of the translations of his books and papers in several Indian and foreign languages.

Books [in English] authored by S.C. Dube

Folk Songs of Chhattisgarh. Lucknow: Universal Publishers, 1948.

The Kamar, Lucknow: Universal Publishers, 1951. (Second Edition in 2003 by Oxford University Press, New Delhi).

Indian Village, London : Routledge & Kegan Paul, 1955.

India's Changing Villages, London : Routledge & Kegan Paul, 1958.

Explanation and Management of Change, Bombay : Tata-McGraw Hill, 1971.

India Since Independence: A Social Report 1947-72 (ed.). Delhi: Vikas Publishing House, 1972.

Social Science in Changing Society, Lucknow : Ethnographic and Folk Culture Society, 1973.

Contemporary India and Its Modernization, Delhi : Vikas Publishing House, 1974.

Man, Society and Education: Some Questions Concerning a Preferred Future, New Delhi, NIE Series, NCERT, 1977.

Tribal Heritage of India: Ethnicity, Identity and Interaction Vol.I, (ed.). New Delhi, Vikas Publishing House, 1977.

Public Services and Social Responsibility (ed.). New Delhi, Vikas Publishing House, 1979.

On Crisis and Commitment in Social Sciences (ed. By Yogesh Atal). New Delhi, Abhinav Publications, 1983.

Development Perspectives for the 1980s. New Delhi, Abhinav Publications, 1983.

Secularization in Multi-religious Societies: Indo-Soviet Perspective (edited with V.N. Basilov). New Delhi, Concept Publishing, 1983.

Modernization and Development: The Search for Alternative Paradigm. Published for the United Nations University by Zed Books, London, 1988.

Tradition and Development. New Delhi, Vikas Publishing House, 1990.

Indian Society. New Delhi, National Book Trust of India. 1990.

Understanding Change: Anthropological and Sociological Perspectives. New Delhi, Vikas Publishing House, 1992.

Research Papers and Articles

"Myths, Religion and Ritual of the Kamars", *The Eastern Anthropologist*. Vol. 1, No.1, 1947.

"Jungle Folk of Chhattisgarh", *India*. March 14, 1948.

"The Social Organization of the Kamar", *Nagpur University Journal*. No. 12, 1948.

"Dreams in Two Primitive Tribes", *Man in India*, Vol. 29, No.1, 1949.

"Inter-Tribal Relations, A Study", *Man in India*, Vol. 30, Nos. 2 & 3, 1950.

"Token Pre-Puberty Marriage in Middle India", *Man*, 53 (25), 1953.

"A Deccan Village", *The Economic Weekly*. May 8, 1954. later published in *India's Villages*, ed., M.N. Srinivas, Bombay, Media Promoters & Publishers, Pvt. Ltd. 1955.

"Ranking of Castes in Telangana Villages", *The Eastern Anthropologist*, Vol. VIII, No. 3 & 4, 1955.

"The Urgent Tasks of Anthropology in India Today", *Actes du IV Congress International des Sciences Anthropologiques et ethnologiques*, Vienne, 1956.

"Social Structure and Change in Indian Peasant Communities", *Transactions of the Third World Congress of Sociology*, Vol. 11, Presented at *World Congress of Sociology*. Evian, France, 1956.

"Some Problems of Communication in Rural Community Development", *Economic Development and Cultural Change*, Vol. V, No. 2, 1957.

"The Study of Indian Village Communities", *Presidential Address, Social Anthropology Section, Indian Sociological Conference*, Agra, 1958.

"Approaches to the Tribal Problem in India", *Journal of Social Research*, Vol. III, No. 2, 1960.

"The Human Element in Indian Development," *Kurukshetra*, Oct. 2, 1961.

"Social Anthropology in India", in *Indian Anthropology*, ed., T. N. Madan and Gopala Sarana, Bombay, Asia Publishing House, 1962.

"Men's and Women's Roles in India: A Sociological Review", *Women in the New Asia*, ed. Barbara E. Ward, Pans, UNESCO, 1963.

"Cultural Problems in the Economic Development of India", Paper presented in a Conference on *Cultural Motivations to Progress in South and South-east Asia*, Manila, 1963.

"A Framework for the study of Rural Leadership in Transitional Societies", UNESCO-NICD International Round Table Conference on the *Emerging Patterns of Rural Leaderships*, Southern Asia, Mussoorie, India, 1963.

"Bureaucracy and Nation Building", presented at the UNESCO Expert Working Group on *Social Pre-requisites of Economic Growth*, Cyprus, 1963.

"Social and Political Structures: Their impact on Agricultural Development", presented at the Conference on *Comprehensive Planning of Agriculture*, Rehovoth, Israel, 1963.

"A Framework for the Study of Rural Leadership in Transitional Societies", *Emerging Patterns of Rural Leadership in Southern Asia*, Hyderabad, National Institute of Community Development, 1965.

"The Study of "Complex Cultures", in *Towards* a *Sociology of Culture in India*, eds., T.K.N. Unnithan, Indra Deva and Yogendra Singh, New Delhi, Prentice-Hall of India, 1965.

"Bureaucracy and Economic Development", *Indian Journal of Public Administration*, Vol. XII, No. 3, pp. 343-351, 1966.

"Human Problems of Economic Development", *The Eastern Anthropologist*, Vol. XX, No. 1, 1967.

"Modernization and its Adaptive Demands in Indian Society", in *Papers in the Sociology of Education in India*, eds. M. S. Gore, I. P. Desai, and Suma Chitnis, Delhi, NCERT, 1967.

"A Note of Communication in Economic Development", *Communication and Change in Developing Countries*, eds. Daniel Lerner and Wilbur Schramm, Honolulu, East-West Centre Press, 1967.

"Communication, Innovation and Planned Change in India", *Communication and Change in Developing Countries*, eds. Daniel Lerner and Wilbur Schramm; Honolulu, East-West Centre Press, 1967.

"Strategies of Influencing Change", *The Anthropologist*, Special Volume II, 1968.

"Caste Dominance and Factionalism", *Contributions to Indian Sociology*, NS II, 58-81, 1968.

"Five Research Proposals", *Urgent Research in Social Anthropology*, Simla, IIAS, Vol. 10, 1969.

"Anthropology: Unity and Diversity", Lecture at the Association of Physical Anthropologists, Chandigarh, 1970.

"Modernization and Education", *Essays on Modernization of Underdeveloped Societies,* Vol. II, ed. A.R. Desai, Bombay, Thackersy & Co. Ltd. 1971.

"The Restive Students", *Psycho-Lingua,* Vol. 1, No. 2, 1971.

"Inaugural Address", Seminar on *Anthropological Fields Research on the Peoples of India,* Calcutta, 1972.

"The Changing Village", *The Eastern Anthropologist,* Silver Jubilee Number, 1972.

"Inaugural Address", *The Tribal Situation in India,* ed. K Suresh Singh, Simla, Indian Institute of Advanced Study, 1972.

"Social Development: A Value Perspective", presented in a Seminar on *India and Indo-German Relations,* at Bonn. Published as an occasional paper, Simla, IIAS, 1973.

"Images of Man and Society in Nehru's thought", Paper presented at the Seminar on *Jawaharlal Nehru and Social Change,* Punjabi University, Patiala. Published as Occasional Paper of Simla IIAS, 1973.

"Sociology of Economic Development", in *A Survey of Research in Sociology and Social Anthropology,* Vol. II. Bombay, Popular Prakashan, 1974.

"Keynote Address", *Higher Education, Social Change and National Development,* ed. J. N. Kaul, Simla, IIAS, 1975.

"The Summing Up", *Higher Education, Social Change and National Development,* ed. J. N. Kaul, Simla, IIAS, 1975.

"Social Sciences in India: The Tasks Ahead", *Culture and Society,* ed. Balakrishnan N. Nair, Delhi, Thomson Press, 1975.

"Religion in a Secular Society", Paper presented at the *Twenty-Fourth Congress of the International Institute of Sociology,* Algiers, 1975.

"Development Change and Communication in India", in *Communication and Change,* ed. Wilbur Schramm and Daniel Lerner, Honolulu, The University Press of Hawaii, 1976.

"Social and Cultural Factors in Development", *Asian Rethinking of Development,* eds. Yogesh Atal and Ralph Pieris, New Delhi, Abhinav, 1976.

"Theories and Goals of Education: A Third World Perspective", *Prospects,* Vol. VI, No. 3, 1976. Also presented at the UNESCO Conference on *Goals and Philosophies of Education,* Geneva, Switzerland, 1975.

"Oral Traditions and Cultural Development", in *East Asian Cultural Studies,* vol. XVI, nos. 1-4, 1976, Also presented at the UNESCO Conference on *Oral Traditions and Cultural Development,* Tokyo, Japan 1976.

"Changing Norms in the Hindu Joint Family", in *Concept of Duty in South Asia,* eds., Doniger O'Flaherty and J. Duncan M. Derrett, New Delhi, Vikas Publishing House, 1978.

"The Changeless Village is Changing", *The Times of India Annual, 1978.*

"Management of Rapid Change", in *Dynamics of Development: An International Perspective,* vol. I ed. Sudesh Kumar Sharma, Delhi, Concept, 1978.

"Harmonizing Dimension in Hindu Civilization Processes", Paper presented in *Indo-Soviet Symposium* on *Problems of Secularization in Multi-Religious Societies,* Tashkent (USSR), 1978.

"Anthropology and the Challenge of Development", Tenth International Congress of *Anthropological and Ethnological Sciences,* New Delhi, 1978.

"Mass Education and Social Development", UNESCO Seminar on *Development Change,* Lima, Peru, 1978.

"Inter-Personal Communication and the Mass Media", presented in Indo-US Seminar on *Communication and Development,* Poona, 1978.

"Communication and Nation Building", in *Dynamics of Nation Building* (ed. Yogesh Atal). Bangkok, UNESCO Regional Office for Social and Human Sciences in Asia and the Pacific, 1979.

"Indigenization of the Social Sciences", *Sri Lanka Journal of Social Sciences,* Vol. 3, No. 1, Third Conference of the Association of Asian Social Science Research Councils (AASSREC), Manila, The Philippines, 1980.

"Images from Space: Sociological and Socio-Psychological Aspects of TV Cultural Programmes", UNESCO *Communications Division,* Paris, 1980.

"Unrealised Utopias and Widening Disparities: Rural Development in India", presented at the *International Union of Anthropological and Ethnological Sciences,* Inter-Congress, Amsterdam, 1980.

"Inaugural Address", Seminar on *Gandhian Studies,* Kurukshetra, 1980.

"A Hundred Years of Indian Sociology", Seminar on *Hundred Years of Indian History, Sociology and Arts,* organized by *Illustrated Weekly of India,* 1980.

"Mass Education and Social, Development", in *Non-formal Education and NAEP,* eds. A.B. Shah and Sushila Bhan; Delhi, Oxford. University Press, 1980.

"Traditional Views of Change and Development", Paper presented in the *Ninth International Conference* on *the Unity of the Sciences,* Miami Beach (USA), 1980.

"Social Responsibility of the Broadcast Media", Keynote Address, *Asia and Pacific Mass Communication Institute Training Seminar,* Delhi, 1980.

"Environment and the Challenge of Educational Management", *Journal of Higher Education,* Vol. 6, No. 1-3, 1981.

"Tribal Development: Illusion and Reality," Bhopal, M. P. Tribal Research and Development Institute, 1980.

"Inaugural Address", Seminar on *Management of Change,* Jaipur, 1981.

"Inaugural Address", Seminar on *Socio-Economic Change in North India,* Kurukshetra, 1981.

"Crisis and Commitment in Social Sciences: Challenges to Intellectual Craftsmanship", RIHED /UNESCO *Training Programme on Research Methodology,* Singapore, published in ICSSR Newsletter, vol. XIII (l), 1982.

"Understanding Poverty", Lecture at the *United Nations Asian and Pacific Development Centre,* Kuala Lumpur, Malaysia, 1982.

"Understanding Indian Culture", presented at the *Third World Centre,* Mexico City, 1982.

"Social Sciences for the 1980s: From Rhetoric to Reality", *International Social Science Journal,* Vol. XXXIV, No. 3, 1982.

"Harmonizing Dimension in Hindu Civilizational Processes", in *Secularization in Multi-Religious Societies: Indo-Soviet Perspective,* eds. S. C. Dube, and V. N. Basilov, New Delhi, Concept Publishing Company, 1983.

"Dilemmas of the Third World", *Education for Development: Challenges and Dilemmas,* Bangkok, UNESCO, 1985.

"Social Sciences and Social Policy", *Relevant Sociology,* vol. 11, no. 2, 1985. Keynote Address to the Sixth General Conference of the International Federation of Social Science Organizations, Colombo, Sri Lanka, 1984.

"Indian Sociology at the Turning Point", in *Indian Sociology: Reflections and Introspections,* eds. T. K. Oommen and Partha N. Mukherji, Bombay, Popular Prakashan, 1986.

"Welfare of the Scheduled Tribes", in *Encyclopedia in Social Work in India,* Vol. III, Delhi, Ministry of Welfare, Govt. of India, 1987.

"Social and psychological implications of development", in *The Other Side of Development,* ed. K. S. Shukla, New Delhi, Sage Publications, 1987.

"Higher Education and Social Change", in *Higher Education in India: The Social Context,* eds. Amrik Singh and G. D. Sharma, Delhi, Konark Publishers Pvt. Ltd., 1988.

"Cultural Dimensions of Development", *International Social Science Journal,* No. 118, 1988.

"Professional Values", in *Higher Education in India: The Institutional context,* eds. Amrik Singh and G. D. Sharma, Delhi, Konark Publishers, 1989.

"Reflections on Rural Transformation: The Indian Context", *Silver Jubilee Lecture,* Jodhpur, University of Jodhpur, 1989.

"Changing Contexts of Anthropology", *The Indian Journal of Social Science*, Vol. 2, No. 4, 1989.

"Development Theory: From Present Impasse to a Fresh Orientation", in *Development, Politics and Social Theory*, ed. Iqbal Narain, New Delhi, Sterling Publishers, 1989.

"Yet another Chapter", in *The Vice-Chancellors Remember*, eds. M. V. Mathur and Romesh K. Arora, New Delhi, Associated Publishing House, 1992.

Books [in Hindi] authored by S.C. Dube

Manav Aur Sanskriti, New Delhi, Raj Kamal, 1960.

Shiksha Aur Samaj, New Delhi, Saatvahan, 1983.

Parampara, Itihas Bodh aur Sanskriti, New Delhi, Radha Krishna, 1991.

Shiksha, Samaj, Aur Bhavishya, New Delhi, Radha Krishna, 1994.

Sankraman Ki Peeda, New Delhi, Vaani Prakashan, 1994.

Parampara aur Parivartan,, New Delhi, Bharatiya Gyanpeeth, 2001 (posthumous).

Samay aur Sanskriti,New Delhi, Vaani Prakashan, 1996 (posthumous).

Vikas ka Samajshastra, New Delhi, Vaani Prakashan, 1996 (posthumous).

INDEX